Maureen O'Hara

MAUREEN O'HARA

~

THE BIOGRAPHY

AUBREY MALONE

UNIVERSITY PRESS OF KENTUCKY

Scholarly publisher for the Commonwealth,
serving Bellarmine University, Berea College, Centre College of Kentucky,
Eastern Kentucky University, The Filson Historical Society, Georgetown
College, Kentucky Historical Society, Kentucky State University, Morehead
State University, Murray State University, Northern Kentucky University,
Transylvania University, University of Kentucky, University of Louisville,
and Western Kentucky University.

Editorial and Sales Offices: The University Press of Kentucky
663 South Limestone Street, Lexington, Kentucky 40508-4008
www.kentuckypress.com

17 16 15 14 13   5 4 3 2 1

Library of Congress Cataloging-in-Publication Data

Dillon-Malone, A. (Aubrey)
  Maureen O'Hara : the biography / Aubrey Malone.
    pages cm
  Includes bibliographical references and index.
  ISBN 978-0-8131-4238-8 (hardcover : alk. paper) —
  ISBN 978-0-8131-4239-5 (epub) — ISBN 978-0-8131-4240-1 (pdf)
  1. O'Hara, Maureen, 1920- 2. Motion picture actors and actresses—
United States—Biography. I. Title.
  PN2287.O33M35 2013
  791.4302'8092—dc23
  [B]   2013022751

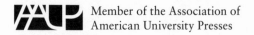

Member of the Association of
American University Presses

Contents

Illustrations follow page 138

Introduction

They've built a statue to her in Kells. Her website receives 250,000 hits a day. Every Christmas Day somebody in the world is watching *Miracle on 34th Street*, and every St. Patrick's Day somebody is watching *The Quiet Man*.

Maureen O'Hara (née FitzSimons) occupies an unusual place in the film pantheon, in that she was never nominated for an Oscar, yet she's the only Irish actress to have a star on the Hollywood Walk of Fame. She also worked with all the greats, both in front of the camera (Charles Laughton, Tyrone Power, Henry Fonda, James Stewart, among others) and behind it (Alfred Hitchcock, John Ford, Jean Renoir, Nicholas Ray, Sam Peckinpah). She always said that working with top-flight stars helped her to get the best out of herself.

O'Hara's belle époque was the 1940s and 1950s, when she occupied the front ranks of female action roles. The films she appeared in had an old-world simplicity, but that made them no less entertaining. She cantered across burning sands in a yashmak as a harem heroine and clambered up a ship's rigging in hoopskirts as a love goddess–cum–pirate queen. "There was always a fight in them between me and someone else," the rapier-slashing star told Joe Hyams in a 1959 *Los Angeles Times* interview, "usually another girl. That made up for the bad script." In all these roles she leavened the exotic superstructures with a large dose of Irish common sense. "Black is black and white is white," she declared, "I never stand on middle ground."[1]

She was good at taking her punishment in such ventures. She endured so many on-set injuries during her career that her colleagues joked she should have been awarded a Purple Heart. The payoff was that she was rarely out of work. "I've never been without a contract," was a frequent boast during her prime, "not for a split second. It's better that way because

I've always hated being in competition with other actresses for roles." She also hated being idle, so she often settled for material that was unworthy of her. "Show me the actress who didn't," she challenged.[2]

Was O'Hara willing to diversify to secure better roles? Grace Kelly was another Irish ice queen from Hollywood's golden age, but she forsook makeup to render herself suitably dowdy for *The Country Girl* and won an Oscar for her performance. Would O'Hara have been willing to do likewise? (Her famous hair remained a radiant red, even into her nineties.) Her critics accused her of having a limited range, but O'Hara begged to disagree. She seemed to struggle in comedic roles but proved her mettle in films that called on her to take charge of situations or find courage in the face of adversity. An indomitable coper with an iron will and an innate sense of the polarities of whatever conundrum she found herself in, she comforted the afflicted and afflicted the comfortable.

The Quiet Man became the insignia of her career, but she appeared in many other noteworthy roles, especially in the early years. Films such as *Jamaica Inn*, *The Hunchback of Notre Dame*, and *How Green Was My Valley* established her credentials and her captivating beauty. Other early highlights included the profound dramas *The Fallen Sparrow* and *This Land Is Mine* and, in the 1950s, two other John Ford offerings, *The Long Gray Line* and *Wings of Eagles*. She writes in her autobiography, "One critic, the bloody bastard, [said] that it took the likes of John Ford to drag a good performance out of me."[3] Although O'Hara worked well with other directors, the only Oscar-nominated films she appeared in were by Ford. In the 1960s and 1970s she expanded her range to play "mature" women and also appeared in acclaimed TV films such as *Mrs. Miniver* and *The Red Pony*, when the dreaded "black box" ate into cinema profits and threatened to torpedo the genre.

Versatility was one of her proudest traits. "I played every kind of role," she declared. "I was never petite or cute so there was never anything about me that would go out of style." But she never laid claim to genius. "I worked hard and always knew my lines." She had no time for Method acting, which she dismissed as so much "tommyrot."[4] Acting should be acting, in her view, not "becoming" the role. She placed a high value on punctuality and was always perfectly coiffed and made up before the cameras rolled.

She was loved for her naturalness, her lack of a diva quality. She didn't make an entrance, like Marlene Dietrich or Joan Crawford; she simply entered. Acting was the shy woman's revenge for her. In Cong in 1951 people chatted to her as if she were one of the extras on *The Quiet Man*, instead of its female lead. She mixed with kings but never lost the common touch.

Another accusation was that she "made nice" with the studio bosses to gain better parts and more money. This she also hotly disputed, claiming it was never the FitzSimons way to be meek or sweet and that money was never a priority for her. Nonetheless, Darryl F. Zanuck liked to advertise the fact that O'Hara was the highest paid actress on his lot, at $5,000 a week. If she was friendly with Zanuck and Harry Cohn and others, it was because of her naturally cordial disposition rather than any ulterior motive. She always told the executives what she thought of them, she insisted, but what she thought was usually complimentary.

Despite the aforementioned temper, she was blessed with a balanced personality. "I've never walked off a set," she boasted. "I've never had a temperamental fit in my life. I think I cooperate too much."[5] In fact, she did vacate the set on one occasion—while making *Ten Gentlemen from West Point* with the lascivious George Montgomery—but she wasn't being a diva. Montgomery had made a pass at her, and she was righteously indignant.

O'Hara was always more heroine than rebel. If you scratched the firebrand, you found the conformist. This was probably the result of her upbringing; domestic stability was the keynote, and an ideal evening was one spent singing and listening to classical airs. Religion was also a huge element in her life. She rarely missed Mass and was a God-fearing woman. On film sets, though, a different personality emerged. "I enjoyed tough directors," she claimed, "who didn't waste time with politeness and that sort of nonsense. We got right down to work."[6] When they did, she gave as good as she got, parlaying her natural vim and vinegar into innumerable set pieces.

As she made clear in her most talismanic role, "I'm not a woman to be honked at and come running. . . . We Danahers are a fightin' family." She objected to the clichéd depiction of redheaded women as spitfires, despite the fact that she was one herself. She liked opinionated people, even those with a tinge of nastiness and temper—all the things women aren't supposed to be. As regards her bossy image, she admitted it was true but claimed she didn't always get her way.

Her ambition wasn't to change the world; she wanted career stability and a boatload of kids. Like most ambitions, O'Hara's were realized only in part. She had one child and a stop-and-go career characterized by identikit action films and some thought-provoking dramas. Ruth Barton wrote that O'Hara's career could be understood only against the background of a controlling studio system that "fetishized" the strong female while simultaneously working to undermine her.[7]

She shunned the party lifestyle of Hollywood. Neither a drinker nor a smoker, she felt uneasy in the company of either. (A strong cup of tea was her preferred beverage, and her friends constantly complained about the lack of ashtrays in her house.) "If Clara Bow is the 'It' Girl," she giggled, "I'm the 'Don't' Girl."[8] She wore low-cut gowns in many of her movies but didn't see them as being in any way risqué. "They were lusty and bawdy," she said by way of qualification, "but healthy rather than suggestive."[9] How did she square being a sex symbol with having such a strong religious sense? She didn't have a problem being a sex symbol, as long as she wasn't promiscuous. Her attitude was that if God made a woman beautiful, there was nothing wrong with advertising the fact. Pursued by sex pests, she either turned a blind eye to them or yawned at their adolescent antics. "Beauty is a curse," became a familiar complaint.

She kept her figure without fads or fanaticism; her tips on beauty and skin care were equally unfussy. Conducting her career in an era before personal trainers and silicone implants, O'Hara expended little effort in this regard.

A pronounced sense of loneliness after being set adrift in a strange country was another matter. Because she didn't relish socializing, a stable home life became a priority. She didn't choose actors as husbands, so there was always a pecking order in her marriages: she would be the top money earner and the more visible presence. She would also be significantly busier than her spouse. Many marriages collapse under this imbalance, particularly when the woman is the dominant partner; hence the disaster with Will Price. When O'Hara finally did find happiness with aviator Charles Blair, she was nearing the end of her career. This probably helped the marriage prosper.

She always had the common sense to change direction when things weren't going her way. For instance, she reinvented herself in the 1960s, at a time when many of her colleagues were heading for the long grass. She believed she could be just as attractive at forty as other stars who were barely out of their teens. Many actresses felt "past it" at forty, due in part to the sexism rampant in movies then (and even now), but she refused to accept she didn't have something to offer modern audiences, and box-office receipts proved her right.

She retired at the beginning of the 1970s to forge a new identity as Blair's wife, but she was never going to be a stay-at-home one. And that didn't change when he died. She became the first female president of an airline—another in her long list of firsts.

The 1980s brought health scares and a hurricane, but she still refused to slow down. And then, just when we thought we'd seen the last of her onscreen, she emerged phoenix-like from the ashes to take charge of a family situation once again, playing a reconstructed Mary Kate Danaher (albeit a more waspish one) in Christopher Columbus's *Only the Lonely*.

At ninety she could have passed for a woman in her seventies or even younger. All that sword fighting with Errol Flynn and company obviously stood her in good stead. Maybe those fencing sessions were her aerobics. The next generation of actresses, who used stunt doubles for insurance reasons, would have to go to the local gym for the same advantage.

O'Hara's life would have made a great movie. Hers is the story of an era, of a flame-haired siren who jousted with the best and maintained her perch at or near the top of the Hollywood tree, despite being shunted into a raft of movies of dubious merit: that's a special talent in itself. In her movies, even in the duds, she always gave her all. Nobody ever accused Maureen O'Hara of not caring.

When she wasn't allowed to act, she sang, and when she wasn't allowed to sing, she fought. John Wayne called her "the greatest guy I ever met" and meant it as a compliment. She outlived Wayne, John Ford, Henry Fonda, James Stewart, and all the rest, finally retiring to the green fields of Erin like a salmon swimming upriver to die in the stream where it was spawned. She was "Queen" Maureen there—a legend, but an accessible one—and she grew old gracefully, never becoming the cane-thumping harridan she had once threatened.

She made her final career bow at the end of the last millennium because it seemed like the right time to take stock. Then she put her life down on paper in a well-received autobiography, letting the world know what life had really been like for the pale-skinned beauty from Beechwood Avenue who took her first public steps on the Abbey stage and went on to become Ireland's prime export to Hollywood.

If we look at the mosaic of her life as it's been presented to us, it all seems obvious. But was there another Maureen O'Hara behind the scenes? Was there someone whose inner thoughts belied the bromides she delivered so commodiously to the hordes of reporters who beat a path to her door? Was she a victim or a survivor of the men who used and abused her and of an industry that saw her as little more than a dollar sign in sequins? What was she really like as a person?

Being Ireland's first Hollywood superstar, she paved the way for a future generation of actresses seeking their own voice. She put the country on the movie map and was an ambassador for the Celtic Tiger long before that term was coined. She was something of a tiger herself, albeit one that purred as much as it roared. O'Hara was chilled champagne mixed with fire—a rare mélange. She ruled land and sea with a fierce passion in cinema's golden age, pitting herself against any protagonist in all manner of adventure sagas, a *dishabillé* love goddess with a huge sense of self and a debatable amount of estrogen, spitting out bile and devotion in almost equal measure. There was always a great thump of indignation in her; in certain moods, she became almost like a force of nature itself.

In the celluloid firmament there have been many shooting stars, but O'Hara has endured as an iconic figure. "There isn't a mortal man," wrote Gladys Hall, "who wouldn't rip the moon out of a stormy sky for Maureen. There isn't a woman who wouldn't step aside for her if she knew what was good for her."[10] With her mahogany hair, her hoydenish ways, and her whip-smart delivery of lines, she created a character prototype that seemed to define her country of origin as much as Ireland defined her.

1

Young Girl in a Hurry

Dublin, 1920—a city caught between insurrection and civil war. On the cusp of independence from the yoke of British tyranny, Ireland was divided within itself as it sought to come to terms with the death of its martyrs and the birth of its new identity. In a few years, brother would fight brother over the shape that new identity would take.

Such thoughts weren't foremost in the minds of Marguerita Lilburn and Charles Stewart Parnell FitzSimons as they cradled their second child in the fashionable suburb of Ranelagh on August 17, 1920. An argument broke out about what the child should be called. (Even this early, she was causing drama.) Her father liked the name Kate. A priest who was a family friend suggested Mary, since she'd been born just two days after the Feast of the Assumption. Her mother—a formidable woman—ruled this out, and they finally settled on Maureen.[1]

Marguerita Lilburn, a former operatic contralto, was widely considered to be one of the most beautiful women in Ireland. The young Maureen regarded her as "gorgeous," with her long red tresses. "When she left the house," she remembered, "you'd see all the men leaving their houses as well just so they could walk down the street beside her."[2] Charles FitzSimons, one of thirteen children, hailed from farming stock and was a retail hatter by trade.

Maureen, who earned the moniker "Baby Elephant" because of her early pudginess, had an interest in acting from as far back as she could remember. Her first dramatic outburst supposedly occurred when her mother tried to change her diaper. When she was five she started dancing with her own shadow. Theater was her priority then. Maureen and her brothers and sisters—younger siblings Florence, Charles, Margot, and Jimmy and older sister Peggy—acted out scenarios from dramas they made up themselves. "We were an Irish Von Trapp family," was the way she put it.[3] Peggy, a soprano, was the best singer. She was invited to perform all over Ireland at state and diplomatic functions and was even offered a scholarship at the prestigious La Scala College in Milan. She turned it down to become a nun, joining the Sisters of Charity.

Maureen taught her younger brothers how to walk and talk. Her main motivation was that she wanted them to participate in the backyard dramas she put on for the *spalpeens* of the neighborhood (*spalpeen* is a Gaelic word meaning "rascal"). The amount of attention young Charles received from their mother caused Maureen no small degree of concern: "My little brother Charlie was my mother's darling. I suffered such black jealousy of him, so bad that I'd often say, 'I'm going to have all girls when I grow up and get married. If I have a boy I'll make him scrub the floors!'"[4]

The FitzSimons world was hermetically sealed. "From my earliest childhood," Maureen confided, "my brothers and sister [*sic*] and I were so close we didn't need outside friends. I never quite outgrew that."[5] "My earliest memory," she recalled, "is of all of us sitting round the fire while Daddy and Mammy would entertain. Daddy was an actor and singer. Mother was a vain, magnificent woman with big black eyes and dark red hair. They both had a great interest in theater so that's where my love of performing comes from."[6] Her grandfather was different. He regarded the stage as the devil's stomping ground.

Maureen had grand ambitions: "When I was six or seven my sister Peg and I would sit in the back garden on a cement pathway where the sun always shone. I would say, 'I am going to be the most famous actress in the world, and when the world falls down on its feet and accepts me, I'll then retire in all my glory.'"[7] The rest of the family shared her grandiose ideas. "We thought we were going to stop the world. We believed it and thought it and spoke it. But we weren't smart ass."[8] Neither were they mollycoddled. "Everything Mother assigned to us had to be done exactly as she told us. If any of us made a mistake or deliberately bungled the job, my father, though kindly and possessing a fine sense of humor, did not spare the rod."[9]

Maureen and Peggy were inseparable as children. "If you threatened to spank one," her mother remembered, "tears would spring from the eyes of the other." Such togetherness became almost xenophobic in time. "As soon as they were old enough to get around, they took upon themselves the task of defending the house from invaders. Their weapons were gooseberries, which they stripped from their father's bushes and threw at passersby." There were other amusing moments in their near twin-like relationship: "When I took them to the seaside for their first visit and they stuck their toes into the cold water, the same idea struck both of them at once. 'Mommy,' they screamed, 'Please fetch the kettle of hot water and warm the sea!'"[10]

Maureen had an exploring mind. One day her mother discovered she'd ripped open a toy she had, a stuffed pony. Asked why she did this, she replied, "I just wanted to know if it's the same as me inside." When her mother inquired what that might be, she pronounced, "Oh . . . Lots of pipes and things!"[11]

When she was five, a gypsy predicted Maureen would be rich and famous but that this fame and fortune would slip through her fingers. She also predicted the young girl would leave Ireland one day. At six she had her first taste of the greasepaint when she read a poem onstage between two acts of a concert at school. She felt at home before an audience: it would be the pattern of her future.

She enrolled in the Ena Burke School of Elocution and Drama to improve her enunciation. She took singing and dancing lessons there. At ten she joined the Rathmines Theater Company, becoming an "official" actress at this tender age. She also started fencing, something that stood her in good stead for the swordplay that would become part and parcel of her career in years to come. She was doggedly unfeminine then, more at home hurling than playing with dolls. The idea of dating boys was light-years away. At ten she played Robin Hood in a Christmas pantomime.

"I was a blunt child," Maureen admitted, "blunt almost to the point of rudeness. I told the truth and shamed all the devils. I didn't take discipline very well. I would never be slapped in school. If a teacher had slapped me I would have bitten her. I guess I was a bold, bad child, but it was exciting. When I went to the Dominican College later on I did not have *beaux* as the other girls did. There was one lad who followed me around for two years. He told me at last that he never once dared to speak to me because I looked as though I would bite his head off if he did."[12] She also liked to knock at people's doors and then run away before they opened them.

But that wasn't the whole story. "There were two sides to me. The other side loved moonlight and quietness and music and fairies and no one speaking and beautiful paintings and dark green trees. My mother used to give what she called her Musical Evenings. I loved these more than I ever found a way to say. We children would be put to bed but I would not sleep. I would creep down the stairs and sit on a prickly mat outside the door, listening to my mother sing."[13] Marguerita sang in different languages; the music ranged from opera to folk.

If music was Maureen's first love, theater was her second. Films came way down the list: "I had never even thought of being in the movies. I seldom went to the movies and never thought they compared in any way to the theater."[14]

The FitzSimons family moved from Ranelagh to Milltown, as the city bled farther and farther out to the suburbs. On Sundays Maureen walked the Twisty Turny Lane, a narrow pathway close to her home that stretched for miles. She fished for minnows and sticklebacks in the river Dodder and bought gumdrops for a penny in the Dropping Well bar. She rode horses and swam and romped like her brothers. She started writing a book but tore it up when it refused to go in the direction she wanted.

She also pleaded with her father to form a soccer team for women. He was one of the first directors of Shamrock Rovers, a popular Dublin soccer club. He'd played Gaelic football in his native County Meath during his youth but fell out with authorities in the Gaelic Athletic Association (GAA) because of his preference for soccer. At the time, soccer was primarily a British game, and Gaelic footballers were banned from playing it or even attending matches. Charles left the GAA in protest and became more involved with Rovers. His eager daughter shared this new passion of his, "assuming her seat on match days in the director's box. A self-confessed tomboy in her youth, Maureen never missed a game."[15] Her two brothers played for the team as well.

"I was mad about Rovers," an excited O'Hara informed Eoghan Rice, who wrote a history of the club. "When I was young, all I wanted to do was play for them." In her teens she became more familiar with the team: "I idolized players like Sacky Glen and Paddy Moore. Sacky was great at getting balls into the box whereas Paddy Moore would just throw his head at them and score. It was very exciting to watch." In later years she was devastated to learn that Glenmalure Park in Milltown, where she'd first watched these players, had been knocked down to make way for a housing estate. "Glenmalure Park was like a second home to me. Every weekend the crowds used to flood past our house on the way to Milltown for the big game. I couldn't believe it when they knocked it down. I still haven't gone back to Milltown. I don't know if I could bear to look at it."[16] There was one distinct advantage to her father's ownership of 25 percent of the club: "Boys were all nice to me because they got into the soccer games free."[17]

Her growing beauty was downplayed at the time. Maureen's parents seemed to be unaware of it. Maybe they feared making her bigheaded or narcissistic. Her father playfully taunted her for having "skin like an elephant's hide and hair like hay," while her mother chastised her for "walking around with your head scrooched into your shoulders, and eating like a horse at meals." The reason for her stooped posture was an awkwardness about her height. Before she was twelve she was five feet six inches tall. Because Charles was six feet four, Marguerita started to worry about their daughter being "the tallest girl in Ireland."[18] She was relieved when Maureen grew only two more inches.

She won nearly every acting competition she entered. Radio Eireann, Ireland's only radio station at the time, asked her to perform in some plays it was airing. She jumped at the chance, receiving the princely sum of £1 for each of them.

Maureen joined the Abbey Theater at age fourteen, performing menial chores such as sweeping floors and painting sets to establish herself. Her mentor was playwright Lennox Robinson, a leading light in the Irish literary renaissance of the 1930s. Despite this, she would later complain that she "never got the chance to do anything worthwhile at the Abbey."[19] That wasn't the Abbey's fault—or hers. It was simply a question of timing. If she hadn't been pitchforked to stardom, she likely would have been a stalwart of the famous theater for decades to come: she was on the verge of landing a leading role when fame struck. (Her mother had appeared at the Abbey before she married, and her brothers would feature in some of its plays as well.)

She won the Dublin Feis Award in 1934, playing Portia in *The Merchant of Venice*. Two years later she became the youngest pupil to graduate from the Guildhall School of Music and Drama. In 1937 she was the inaugural winner of the Dawn Beauty Competition, which put a different perspective on the direction of her career. She pocketed £50 for her troubles.[20]

Like many actresses, a painful self-consciousness accompanied her need to perform. "One night when I was sixteen, father crept into the back row of the theater and I sensed that there was someone out front watching me, perhaps critically. My arms became like lead. I gave a rotten show that night. I grew up with the terrible feeling that I was being laughed at."[21] Despite her thespian success, her father insisted she develop bookkeeping and secretarial skills so she would have a more traditional career to lean on should La Scala not come calling.[22]

At age seventeen Maureen was offered her first major role in the Abbey, but before rehearsals began she met actor-singer Harry Richman, who pointed her in a different direction. She was having lunch with her parents in the Gresham Hotel when the manager introduced her to Richman.[23] They exchanged a few words, and that was that as far as she was concerned. She thought nothing of the meeting because Richman had been tipsy, but a few days later the Abbey rang, telling her mother that Elstree Studios wanted to see Maureen for a screen test, on Richman's recommendation.

Maureen's first impulse was to say no, but a friend reminded her that she could always come back to the Abbey if things didn't work out, whereas the offer of a movie screen test was a one-off opportunity. A few days later she went to London with her mother. They stopped at Elstree Studios to thank Richman, who was filming a comedy called *Kicking the Moon Around*. The film's director, Walter Forde, asked Maureen if she'd say a line in it, and she did. She was billed as Maureen FitzSimons for the first and only time in her career. This was the classic "blink and you miss her" cameo that most stars have somewhere in their back catalogs. The film itself was negligible, a musical comedy that acted as a showcase for Richman's limited talent. Using O'Hara's name, it was released in the United States as *The Playboy* and later as *Millionaire Merry-Go-Round*. (Years later, O'Hara spotted Richman on a Hollywood street and stopped to thank him for giving her her big break. Amazingly, he had no recollection of even meeting her, let alone making her a star.)[24]

Then came her first screen test. The stagehands rigged her up in an outfit that made her look like a hooker, which angered her: "They put me in this gold *lamé* gown with huge accordion pleats dangling from my arms and they covered me with Mata Hari makeup. The whole test was to walk to the phone, pick it up and hang it up again. I thought: My God, get me back to the Abbey."[25]

Afterward, though, she was invited to a talent agency run by Connie Chapman and Vere Barker. Barker introduced her to Charles Laughton, already a movie legend. Also in the room was Erich Pommer, Laughton's partner in their company Mayflower Films.[26] He was the ex-head of the major German studio UFA and had produced Erich von Sternberg's first big success, *The Blue Angel*. Pommer had arrived in England penniless after Hitler deposed him as the head of UFA. He believed that Mayflower would enable him to rise, phoenix-like, from the ashes of his old glory. Pommer wasn't overly friendly to O'Hara in the way Laughton was, having something of a stentorian manner. He offered her a job as his secretary if her film career didn't take off.

O'Hara wasn't nervous about meeting Laughton. "I have never been nervous in my life," she pronounced, "not of anyone or anything. I do not have any nerves, I suppose, and I do not have any fears." She added, "I did not get the swollen head either because so great an actor had sent for me. You can't get a swollen head when you are brought up in a family of six."[27]

Laughton wanted to hear what her voice sounded like, so he presented her with a book and said, "Please read from this." She replied, "I am very sorry but absolutely no." She would be happy to take the book and test for him the following day, she told him, but refused to do so unprepared.[28] Laughton was apparently impressed by her arrogance. He asked Barker if there was any existing film on her, and Barker mentioned the test she'd just done, so Laughton decided to take a look at it.

He was of two minds after viewing her screen test, as they'd daubed her with makeup and poured her seventeen-year-old body into gold lamé. Pommer rose to her defense: "Is it her fault if they made her up to look like a gargoyle? Let's send for that kid."[29] Laughton was still undecided after a second viewing, but he couldn't get the image of her "haunting" eyes out of his mind.[30] Irish journalist Valerie Shanley thought it went deeper than that. "Gentlemen may prefer blondes," she ventured, "but Hollywood is partial to a redhead. A cascade of pre-Raphaelite curls is what most likely mesmerised Charles Laughton when he first saw a screen test of Maureen FitzSimons."[31]

Maureen left not knowing whether Mayflower was interested or not. Nor was she perturbed about this. She didn't think about the screen test because, she said, "I didn't care very much. I was not filmstruck."[32] When she got home, though, she found a seven-year film contract from Laughton waiting for her. She was overwhelmed: "You could have knocked the whole family over with a shamrock." Her parents were dubious because she was so young. They mulled over the situation overnight, and the following morning they said yes. This was the matter-of-fact way O'Hara remembered the occasion: "I signed it, my local parish priest came up on his bicycle to 13, Churchtown Road to co-sign it and I was on my way."[33]

She decided to tour Ireland to celebrate. She packed "an old pair of slacks" and went trudging around the country for a break. She didn't even bring shoes with her, going barefoot because "I like the feel of it."[34]

Maureen then moved to London, and Laughton immediately put her in a movie that was being made on the quick. He wanted her to get accustomed to the way the camera worked, to see how she'd accommodate to it. The film was called *My Irish Molly*. Like *Kicking the Moon Around*, this title changed when it was released in the United States, where it became *Little Miss Molly*.

One could argue that O'Hara never looked as enticing as she does in *Little Miss Molly*, even if she isn't "Maureen O'Hara" quite yet. She wears no makeup, and there's no Hollywood glamour, but despite (or because of?) that, she is rapturously beautiful. Her accent is thick, which is perhaps why she didn't mention the film much. It also looks as if it were made in the 1920s rather than the 1930s, so primitive are the sets and the characters. Think Sean O'Casey meets Lady Gregory, and you'll have some inkling of what to expect.

The plot is ham-fisted. Child star Binkie Stuart displays Shirley Temple curls and a Shirley Temple voice (although she speaks so slowly at times it's almost as if she's been anesthetized). She's the eponymous orphan who comes to Ireland from Britain to stay with an aunt who is intent on cheating her out of an inheritance. Local lad Danny (Tom Burke) has his heart set on Molly's cousin (O'Hara), but she prefers American emigrant Bob (Philip Reed). Reed makes no attempt whatsoever at an American accent, sounding like Ray Milland throughout. It's a quaint film that O'Hara scholars should view if only to see early evidence of her natural instinct for dramatic timing and scene interpretation. (Was it this footage that Charles Laughton showed to Alfred Hitchcock to entice him to cast her in *Jamaica Inn*? Quite possibly.)

Laughton appropriated her like a cause after shooting ended. "He'd always wanted a daughter," she speculated, "and that's how he treated me."[35] He primed her in the mechanics of film, emphasizing the primordial importance of the camera in picking up nuances of expression that would most likely go unnoticed in the performance of a play. The devil was in the detail, he stressed. She had to fight her instinct to emote, or verbalize.

Laughton offered her a part in the gothic melodrama *Jamaica Inn*, based on a Daphne du Maurier novel. It was being directed by Alfred Hitchcock. One of the reasons Pommer and Laughton were interested in *Jamaica Inn* was that du Maurier's *Rebecca* had just been published to solid media attention, and they were hoping to jump on that bandwagon. Hitchcock was also hoping to direct the film version of *Rebecca* in Hollywood. He accepted the directing deal before reading the script for *Jamaica Inn* and would live to regret it: he was horrified by its amateurishness.

Meanwhile, Laughton thought Maureen's surname would hurt her career. "We don't think it would look good on the marquee," he exhorted, "we want to change it." "I'm proud of it," she protested. "It's a wonderful, old, old name."[36] But the die had been cast. "He didn't *suggest* I change my name," she sighed, "he just changed it. He gave me the choice of O'Hara or O'Meara. I said, 'Neither' and he said, 'Okay, you're Maureen O'Hara now.' That was it."[37] His choice was probably prompted by the fact that *Gone with the Wind* had just come out, and the name Scarlett O'Hara was in people's minds.

It's ironic that the film that made her name was also the one that eliminated it from the public eye.[38] She may have been Maureen O'Hara to the world, but "I have never ceased to be Maureen FitzSimons and I never will cease to be her. I am Maureen FitzSimons from Beechwood Avenue."[39] Perhaps, but as far as the moviegoing public was concerned, Maureen FitzSimons was—to coin a phrase—gone with the wind.

In *Jamaica Inn* she played Mary Yellen, an orphan who comes to live with her aunt and uncle at their eighteenth-century Cornish tavern. She then discovers that it's the headquarters for a ruthless band of brigands who wreck ships for a living so they can rob the contents. Their leader is Sir Humphrey Pangallan (Laughton). He takes a shine to Mary but eventually has to use her as a hostage to escape when his true exploits are discovered by undercover lawman Robert Newton. Mary is caught between loyalty to her family and love for Newton.

In the book, the main shipwreck occurs on Christmas morning, result-ing in Mary's loss of faith. This obviously wouldn't do in the film version, for a number of reasons (including O'Hara's strong faith), so it was excised, as was Mary's "atheistic" decision to offer "no prayers to God this Christ-mas."[40]

Laughton was disgusted that the villain had been changed from a par-son (in the novel) to a squire and threatened to walk off the picture if his character's occupation didn't revert to the original, but he was fighting a losing battle on that score. The austere public of 1939 wouldn't have coun-tenanced the idea of a clerical ne'er-do-well, not to mention the censors. Hitchcock initially had a problem with Laughton playing Sir Humphrey because of his history of villainous roles. Since the revelation that Hum-phrey is the leader of the brigands is the film's main surprise, he thought this would be hijacked by Laughton's presence. A war developed between Hitchcock and Laughton, with Laughton blithely indifferent to the direc-tor's indignation at being unable to control the actor or the production. Hitchcock would later exclaim, "I always say that the most difficult things to photograph are dogs, babies, motorboats, Charles Laughton and Method actors."[41] He found his main star unmanageable. "A Laughton picture is one long battle from start to finish," he snorted, "Laughton versus Laugh-ton."[42] Hitchcock said of the scene in which Laughton ties O'Hara up, "I am primarily interested in the Jekyll and Hyde mentality of the squire."[43] But even here, Laughton tries to thwart the director, using a silk scarf in-stead of a rope to bind O'Hara in what is a rare touch of sensitivity from the merciless psychopath.

The film begins atmospherically, with a pounding musical score coun-terpointing the crashing of the waves as a raid takes place. After the music stops, we get nothing but the continuous jabber of dialogue, which dilutes the drama of the piece enormously. Laughton is more a comic character than a fearful one, yet he holds the film together, as most of the other actors descend into a different type of melodrama. But O'Hara doesn't make this mistake, delivering her lines with a self-belief unusual in one so young—though her posh British accent seems out of place. She was caught in a dilemma for most of the film, however. Her challenge was to negotiate a middle ground between the Scylla of overacting and the Charybdis of being so outgunned by Laughton that her performance became invisible.

She achieved this simply by getting the material to speak for her and letting her impossibly beautiful features do the rest.

When *Jamaica Inn* was released, to Hitchcock's dismay, du Maurier insisted that her name be removed from the opening credits.[44] It was hard to blame her: she barely recognized her book. The film was poorly received by the critics. The *New York Herald Tribune* found it "singularly dull and uninspired, a mannered and highly lackadaisical melodrama." *Film Weekly* carped, "The makers of this film seem less at pains to make our hair stand on end than to prove to us that they can fake a shipwreck as well as Hollywood."[45] Frank Nugent's words touched a nerve: "It will not be remembered as a Hitchcock picture but as a Charles Laughton picture."[46] It couldn't seem to make up its mind whether it was high drama or farce.

There were some positive reviews. One critic wrote that, while the movie sacrificed subtlety to spectacle, "the newcomer, Maureen O'Hara is charming to look at and shows distinct promise as an actress."[47] In many ways, she was the real discovery of the film: "eighteen years old, fresh from Dublin and luxuriating in her colleen loveliness, hair a-tumble, eyes a-sparkle, lips a-pout."[48]

She invited her parents to London for the premiere, and her haughtiness was evident in her recollection of the event: "We were never impressed by the trappings of stardom and fame. Besides, my family was very prominent throughout Dublin, and we were theater and opera people."[49] Her odd attitude continued when she arrived at the cinema and surveyed the crowds: "They didn't make a fuss over me. Why should they? I wasn't a star yet."[50] But she seemed to *expect* a fuss. The "yet" is interesting. It hints at an expectation of glory.

After the premiere she had her first real taste of fame when she was besieged by fans. As her cab pulled away from the theater, she watched the crowd in hot pursuit. Three blocks later, there were still two "panting, persistent autograph fiends" following her.[51] She asked the driver to stop, then she got out and gave them her autograph.

The premiere changed everything for her: "I was a tomboy growing up. I was always jealous of the freedom boys had. I thought it was terribly unfair that they could do things like rob an orchard and not get into trouble. They call it 'box the fox' in Ireland—stealing apples. But after I saw myself on the screen in *Jamaica Inn* I realized the girl up there was beautiful. I didn't want to box the fox any more." No matter how many times she saw herself onscreen afterward, she couldn't replicate the excitement of that night. "The first one is always the sweetest," she said.[52]

She returned to Ireland for a brief vacation after the hype died down. While there, she had a disturbing experience with a group of women who seemed to resent her success. It happened one night when she accompanied Patrick Brock to a party at the house of a playwright he knew. In the car on the way to the party, there were a number of actresses who, according to Brock, "rebuffed every effort she made to be friendly." He concluded that they "stupidly thought that because of her blossoming film career she was arrogant. It was very sad. She was puzzled and hurt."[53] Maybe this was the night O'Hara realized she could never get her simple past back again.

Jamaica Inn fared better in the United States than in Britain, which was fine by Hitchcock: he knew America was where his future lay. Laughton thought Mayflower's days were numbered, so when RKO offered him a Hollywood contract, he jumped at it. He told O'Hara he would bring her with him: she would play Esmeralda in his new film, *The Hunchback of Notre Dame*. Laughton had another reason to snap up RKO's offer: a condition of his five-picture deal was that RKO would pay off Mayflower's avalanche of debts. Traveling from Europe to America meant that he could wipe the slate clean in more ways than one.

Things weren't so simple for O'Hara. Unfortunately, she'd just signed a seven-year lease on a house in Hyde Park and had lived in it for only six weeks.[54] That was now money down the drain. She'd also gotten herself entangled in a messy relationship during the making of the movie. On the way to the set, she would sometimes say hello to a production assistant named George Brown. One day a friend of Brown's told her George wanted to go on a date with her. She was flabbergasted, as they had exchanged only a few polite words up to this point. Brown took her horseback riding, and she fell off the horse, providing a convenient excuse to cut the date short. A few days later he asked her to dinner, and she agreed to go. Again, she had little to say to him. They danced for a while and then she excused herself, claiming she had an early start the next day. He started to plague her with phone messages, which she reluctantly took, shocked at his persistence. He then insisted that she meet him at a certain address before she sailed for the United States, and she grudgingly agreed. When she arrived at the house in question, her heart almost missed a beat. There she found preparations for a wedding ceremony. Brown told the official that O'Hara was twenty-one and therefore free to wed without parental consent. Before she knew what was happening, the ceremony was under way. She wanted to run from the room, but something stopped her. It was like an out-of-body experience, a surreal movie where nobody said "Cut" and her next line was "I do." It wasn't that her heart ruled her head, because she had no feelings for Brown. Nothing could explain it. Reader, she married him.

When the ceremony was over she ran from the building, hyperventilating, in the middle of a panic attack. What had come over her? In the words of one writer, she "accidentally" married Brown in the seedy ceremony.[55] Another attributed it to her being "in a limbo between girlhood and womanhood," or perhaps it was simply "an ill-considered act of rebellion."[56] When O'Hara got home, her mother knew something was wrong, but she wouldn't say what it was. She was too distraught to divulge anything.

O'Hara boarded the *Queen Mary*, the ship taking her to her new life in Hollywood, with her mother and Laughton. Her mother continued to ask her what was wrong, and she continued to sidestep her interrogations. She pulled off her wedding band and hid it in her purse, but her mother found it and confronted her. Eventually she broke down and confessed. Her mother was aghast and kept asking her daughter why she had done this insane thing, but there was no answer; it was as inexplicable to her as it was to everyone else. "It was not a marriage," she protested years later, "because it was never consummated."[57]

Meanwhile, Laughton had left his wife, Elsa Lanchester, behind in London. Lanchester and O'Hara didn't get along. Lanchester thought O'Hara wasn't as sweet as she appeared, remarking, "Butter wouldn't melt in her mouth, or anywhere else," an oft-quoted barb. This belief was fortified when she heard about O'Hara's secret marriage to Brown. Lanchester always thought O'Hara sublimated her guilt over this marriage and turned it into endless bursts of work throughout her career. Lanchester was understandably aggrieved by Laughton's attentions to O'Hara, who virtually became his surrogate daughter. Laughton and Lanchester had no children of their own, so this might have been expected. Lanchester said she refused to have children with Laughton after she discovered he was gay, but

O'Hara believed Lanchester had had a number of abortions and couldn't conceive as a result.

Though O'Hara had married Brown in June, it was July before the media got hold of the story. A report in the *Irish Times* stated: "The ceremony took place by special licence at St. Paul's Church, Station Road, Harrow, Middlesex on June 13. Mr. Brown remained behind to work in the new Paul Robeson picture *David and Goliath*. Mrs. O'Hara will not see him again until she returns to England in October next, a leading lady to Charles Laughton in *The Admirable Crichton*."[58]

An interview with Brown appeared in another newspaper the same day, suggesting that he believed O'Hara was married to him for keeps. He didn't sound like a man who had just cajoled a woman to the altar. "I am very pleased indeed to have an Irish association of some kind," he beamed, citing a connection to Eugenie Houghton. (O'Hara herself was a descendant of Richard Houghton, who had been Lord Mayor of Dublin twice, in 1651 and 1655.) "We kept our marriage an absolute secret," Brown continued. "It was our intention not to tell anyone about it until my wife came back in October. We intend to have another marriage ceremony in a Catholic church as soon as Maureen returns."[59]

Brown didn't work on *David and Goliath*. O'Hara didn't return for a Catholic wedding. She headed for greener pastures, and the undistinguished production assistant was left with only memories of what might have been. He would never see his runaway bride again.

2

Maiden Voyage

When O'Hara arrived in New York with Laughton in June 1939, the brave new world of the USA was a culture shock to her. She was suffering from what would later come to be called the Irish diaspora. As they passed the Statue of Liberty, Laughton nudged at her capacity for wonder: "Look, Maureen, how magnificent!" But she couldn't take it in. "I was 17 and so terribly homesick. I just wanted to go home."[1] That was impossible. There was already a media frenzy surrounding her, and she had to fight her way through a blizzard of photographers. The American press saw her as a "lovely 14-year-old colleen from Ireland." This was surprising. She may not have looked nineteen, her real age, but she certainly looked older than fourteen. Bosley Crowther described her in the *New York Times* as "the emerald shower that succeeds the initial explosion of a skyrocket."[2]

For moviemaking, O'Hara arrived at just the right time. There were more theaters in the country than banks by now, in excess of 15,000. More than 50 million Americans went to the movies every week. About 400 films were churned out every year. Box-office receipts totaled $673 million that year. Films were the nation's fourteenth biggest business in terms of volume and the eleventh biggest in terms of assets.

She would also be the beneficiary of new technology. Before the 1930s, audiovisual procedures were rudimentary and distracting to the action. Microphones were often positioned in the most awkward places. Rolling cameras had to be wrapped in soundproof cases to prevent their movement from being picked up on the sound track. This wasn't a concern anymore. The star system was riding high too, and television wasn't yet threatening the cinema's monopoly of audience attention. The advent of Technicolor was also a huge plus and guaranteed to showcase O'Hara's beauty.

RKO was looking for a new face at this time, having recently lost stars such as Katharine Hepburn and Constance Bennett. Ginger Rogers was the only big female name the studio had. Subsidiary performers Joan Fontaine and *farceuse* Lucille Ball brought up the rear, with Carole Lombard and Irene Dunne occasionally being loaned out from other studios.

Lew Wasserman, O'Hara's agent, negotiated a nearly 1,000 percent pay hike for her—from $80 a week to $700. This was phenomenal. She saw Esmeralda, the character she would be playing in *Hunchback*, as her ticket to the big time. "I didn't *go* to Hollywood," she propounded years later, "I was taken. I didn't go cold looking for a job. Charles Laughton signed me. He said, 'She plays Esmeralda.' They didn't dare say 'No, Mr. Laughton.'"³ It was happenstance, serendipity.

Her euphoria was mitigated by the fact that she didn't believe she deserved the adulation she was receiving as Laughton's protégée: "I realized suddenly that I was having all this attention really because I was a novelty. People were making a fuss over me because of something I hadn't yet done, something they just thought I *might* do." If her films flopped, she knew, her fall would be greater for all the hoopla and the buildup. She made a decision to discipline her vanity "before other people started doing it for me."⁴

O'Hara may have set her sights on Shakespeare as an Abbey debutante, but for now, the movies would do. She was breaking bread with Hollywood's elite, and she was already commanding a salary that the people back home could only dream about. She relished life at RKO. There was an intimate atmosphere there. Although it was one of Hollywood's "Big Five," along with Paramount, Fox, MGM, and Warner Brothers, RKO had neither the money nor the contractual clout of the other studios. Laraine Day summed up the cozy atmosphere: "The fact that they didn't have the tremendous star system like MGM made it a warm family. You knew everybody."⁵

Making *Hunchback* was a tremendous experience for O'Hara. Director William Dieterle was an eccentric who wore "white shirts, white pants, a beautiful white Panama hat and white gloves."⁶ Various explanations were adduced for his unique style: some people speculated that he had a skin disease, others that he had a germ phobia; or perhaps he was simply "a complete snob."⁷ The first time Dieterle saw O'Hara he thought she was too tall. Also, her hair had been fuzzed up to look like a golliwog. "Stick her under the shower!" he snapped at his hairdresser. O'Hara thought, "There goes the part."⁸ But her fears were unfounded; she had actually been cast from England.

The guts of Victor Hugo's 1831 book had already been filmed three times—as *Esmeralda* in 1905 and 1922 and under its own name in the 1923 silent classic featuring Lon Chaney. Dieterle, a German émigré, intended his film to highlight the evils of authoritarianism. To this end, the expressionist elements in Van Nest Polglase's sets and Joseph H. August's cinematography were "consciously designed to evoke the dark psychology of German cinema in the immediate pre-Nazi era."[9]

The character Quasimodo protects Esmeralda, just as Laughton, in real life, took a paternal interest in O'Hara. Laughton relished the role for many reasons, not least because he didn't have to diet or wear a corset.[10] The cost of turning him into Quasimodo was $10,000—an exorbitant sum at the time. O'Hara barely recognized him when he was fully made up. Because Quasimodo was deaf, Laughton put wax in his ears to block out sound, but he had to remove it when he was being directed by Dieterle. Laughton gave as much care to his makeup as he did to his performance. Some people viewed this as excessive, but it was very much part and parcel of Laughton, who apparently loathed his appearance—his obesity was caused by a glandular condition—and sought to change it whenever possible. Sponge rubber twisted the left side of his face and pulled his eye down. The hump weighed four pounds and made him sweat profusely. During the scene in which he's lashed on a wheel, Laughton reportedly asked one of his assistants to twist his foot roughly so his pain would be real.[11] Dieterle sometimes thought Laughton was overacting. Laughton started the part "with a theatrical idea," the director remarked, "which he carried around inside him as a pregnant woman does her baby."[12] Laughton cared too much about the film. In fact, he wasn't able to perform on the first day of the shoot because he was suffering from excessive tension. Dieterle was sympathetic and told him to go home. He came back the next day and was exemplary.

Not long after filming began, Hitler invaded Poland. With that news, a sepulchral quiet descended on the cast. O'Hara had never known such shocked calm. It was finally broken when Laughton, still in Quasimodo garb, positioned himself between the pillars of Notre Dame Cathedral and recited the whole Gettysburg Address from memory. For O'Hara, it was the best piece of acting she'd ever seen. When he finished speaking he went back to his chair as if nothing had happened. O'Hara sat looking at him, stunned by his conviction. She appreciated how much the idealism of the words suited the bell ringer's pained vulnerability.

Two days later England declared war on Germany. Laughton showed how moved he was by this development during the scene in which Quasimodo rings the bells for Esmeralda as an indication of his love for her. But he didn't just ring them; he practically pulled them down. Once again, everybody looked on in stunned silence as Laughton tugged on the ropes until his hands almost fell off. Dieterle was astounded. It was supposed to be a love scene, but, as he said, "It developed into something so powerful that everybody, including myself, forgot we were shooting a film. Something super-dimensional happened at that moment [and] I forgot to call 'Cut' as the scene ended." Laughton kept ringing, more feverishly by the minute. He eventually collapsed from exhaustion as the cast and crew watched in disbelief. Later in his dressing room, the overwrought actor poured his heart out to O'Hara: "I couldn't think about Esmeralda in that scene at all. I could only think of the poor people out there going to fight that bloody, bloody war."[13]

O'Hara had her moments of intensity too. A couple of scenes she performed herself really should have been done by a stunt double (Laughton's were). In one of them, as she waits for the hangman to put the noose around her neck, Quasimodo scoops her away on a rope, holding her aloft in his arms as he swings her to safety. No safety nets were used, so any false move by Laughton's double or herself could have meant instant death.

Quasimodo bonds with Esmeralda because he sees in her a mirror image of his own lostness. When she's wrongly accused of murder, their mutual victimhood is highlighted. At this point the film becomes more *King Kong* than *Beauty and the Beast* as he sacrifices himself to prevent her from being hanged.

Hunchback opened at the same time as *Gone with the Wind*. Although some of its thunder was stolen by that film, it still managed to earn more than $3 million at the box office (its original budget was $1.8 million). Reviews for O'Hara's performance in *Hunchback* were generally positive, with an occasional exception. One critic cynically opined, "Esmeralda could be as vibrant as Hayworth's Gilda but is almost wholly eclipsed by Laughton's dominant discourse of fleshing out Quasimodo beyond the rubber mask ambitions of Chaney into a fusion of his own personal anxieties and obsessions."[14] Another reviewer gushed, "The contrast between Laughton as the pathetic hunchback and O'Hara as the fresh-faced, tenderly solicitous gypsy girl is Hollywood teaming at its most inspired." Laughton himself thought O'Hara was, "in truth, a character actress."[15]

Asked years later about her abiding memories of making the movie, O'Hara said, "The magnificent sets, and running around barefoot and getting terrible blisters on the soles of my feet, and crowds of extras who came from all parts of the world. I love to talk to people and chitchat to them about their country. Laughton was also a joy to work with, especially because his mother was from County Cork."[16] (One of O'Hara's special talents was finding an element of Irishness somewhere in most of her costars' backgrounds.)

After the film was released, Laughton informed O'Hara that she couldn't go back to Europe because of the war. He also dropped another zinger: he'd sold her to RKO. This was in the days before an actress's "star power" prevented others from making decisions without her consent. She accepted the news philosophically. Laughton told her that Mayflower Productions was history, and if she stayed on its books, her contract wouldn't be worth the paper it was written on.

O'Hara emerged from Laughton's shadow to make *A Bill of Divorcement*, a remake of the Katharine Hepburn–John Barrymore drama about a man who returns home from a mental institution on the day his wife divorces him and tries to build a relationship with his daughter Sydney (O'Hara). Sydney, who fears that mental illness runs in the family and dreads having children herself, devotes herself to her father's care and breaks off her engagement. The film was directed by John Farrow and starred Adolphe Menjou in the Barrymore role, with Fay Bainter as the wife who puts her divorce on hold out of pity.

The original *A Bill of Divorcement* had made a star of Hepburn. RKO was hoping the remake would do the same for O'Hara, but things didn't pan out that way. The film had moments of quality but failed to thread them into any kind of steady narrative. What should have been a cathartic finale came across as wooden and downbeat. The *New York Sun* wrote that O'Hara's performance lacked "the intensity and desperation it must have; nor does she seem to have a sparkle of humor."[17] She might have argued that the material hardly called for humor. But because one is only as good as one's last movie, *A Bill of Divorcement* left a black mark on O'Hara's CV. They say a sequel never equals. A remake rarely does either, as proved here.

O'Hara's discomfiture was increased by the fact that Farrow had developed a crush on her before shooting began. He had an eye for Irish girls called Maureen, being married to Maureen O'Sullivan, who played Jane in the Tarzan movies. O'Hara was often confused with O'Sullivan throughout her career, and it always annoyed her. Farrow made suggestive comments to her on the set and even showed up at her house with food. O'Hara's mother warned her daughter about these unscheduled visitations. On some nights, O'Hara drove her car around the block innumerable times until Farrow's car disappeared from her driveway.[18] When he realized he'd been rejected, he turned on her, bullying her on the set. One day she had had enough and ended up socking him on the jaw.[19] The blow had the desired effect.

Her next film, *Dance, Girl, Dance*, was also fraught with problems. The original director, Roy Del Ruth, shot some scenes but left after creative differences with producer Erich Pommer—that man again. In later years the film was annexed by feminist critics, largely because Del Ruth was replaced by a woman, Dorothy Arzner. Arzner was the first female director to join the Directors Guild of America, which signaled her intention to do serious work.[20] She had a huge self-belief and an iron will, and she refused to make blancmange movies. Del Ruth had intended to make a standard "love triangle" story, but the new director played fast and loose with this substructure, morphing it into an analysis of male-female perspectives in general. She never openly admitted to being a lesbian, but most people presumed she was, including author Judith Mayne, who held that Arzner "adopted a persona that can best be described as butch: she wore tailored, 'masculine' clothing; her short hair was slicked back; she wore no make-up; and she struck poses of confidence and authority."[21]

O'Hara (Judy) and Lucille Ball (Bubbles) play members of a dance band run by Madame Basilova (Maria Ouspenskaya). Bubbles is the more brassy of the two; Judy, a ballet student, has more class. When Bubbles leaves the band, Judy stays on to advance her ballet skills under Basilova, but work is hard to come by. The dance troupe folds, and Judy is forced to take a job as a "filler" for Bubbles, who has managed to get a job in a burlesque theater.

Judy's job is to warm up the audience while Bubbles takes a break before providing more cheap thrills in act 2. The rest of the movie is standard enough. Judy and Bubbles vie for the affections of vacuous playboy Jimmy Harris (Louis Hayward), who imagines he has fallen out of love with his wife (Virginia Field). The audience doesn't buy it, even after he marries Bubbles. When Jimmy goes back to his wife, ballet producer Steve Adams (Ralph Bellamy) makes a play for Judy.

At first Arzner was discommoded by the floundering mess left by Del Ruth. "No one seemed to know what the script was all about," she complained. To "clarify" things, she decided the film should be about the tension between "the art spirit" as personified by O'Hara and the "go-getter" epitomized by Ball.[22] The film was notable for the fact that Arzner, a female in a primarily male industry, "reworked the familiar backstage story of feuding actresses into a musical that threw the spotlight on women for a change."[23]

Ruth Barton debunks O'Hara in her book *Acting Irish in Hollywood*, charging that "being Irish is one thing, classy another." Only when Judy comes down off her high horse to deliver an impassioned speech to the men ogling Bubbles in the finale does she find her true self, in Barton's view. Losing her temper in this scene, Barton argues, liberates Judy and allows her to express herself. "By accessing a more earthy and temperamental Irishness, she is no longer encumbered by being classy."[24]

"I know you want me to tear my clothes off," Judy fumes at the audience, "so you can look your fifty cents worth. Fifty cents for the privilege of staring at a girl your wives won't let you." These sentiments were close to O'Hara's heart in more ways than one. Her first directive to studio bosses was "no leg art." By this she meant she wouldn't do the kind of "bubble bath" shots that were becoming de rigueur for pneumatic actresses of the 1940s. "I come from a very strict family," she declared, "and I can't do some of the things other actresses can because my folks in Dublin would think I turned out all bad."[25] Was her modesty due to artistic integrity or vanity? She hinted at the latter motive in a 1948 interview when, asked why she didn't pose in bathing suits, O'Hara disclosed, "Because I don't think I look like Lana Turner in a bathing suit, frankly."[26] One has to commend her honesty.

Author Molly Haskell doesn't see *Dance, Girl, Dance* as a feminist parable. Ball may have been more vulgar, but O'Hara was "a little out of her depth in a vaudeville house, not exactly the temple of high art." She also found "something healthy" in Ball's vulgarity.[27] Whether unified or not, the two female characters are living in a male-dominated society, which, in the view of one writer, makes the "happy ending" ironic, merely underlining the power structure within which male-female relationships exist—that is, patriarchy.[28]

3

The Old Son of a Bitch

Now established in Hollywood—albeit tentatively—O'Hara threw herself into the social scene. After sampling the dubious delights of Romanoff's and Chasen's, she decided to take up badminton to avoid the grinding boredom that assailed most stars between movies.

Between games she began shooting *They Met in Argentina*, a musical in which she plays Lolita O'Shea, a Latin heiress caught between two men: an engineer and a sportsman. She looks more colleen than senorita in this conflation of song and dance routines. Lolita plays hard to get while selling a racehorse to hard-boiled Texan James Ellison, but she eventually gives herself to him. This became a pattern in O'Hara's movies, and it annoyed many of her fans. She described the film as "a stinker, but a stinker that made a lot of money. They all did in those days."[1]

They Met in Argentina was little more than a public relations exercise, Hollywood being anxious to expand into the hitherto neglected "bright spot" of the Latin American market.[2] This ambition didn't always go according to plan, however. Another film made the previous year, *Argentina Nights*, met with robust demonstrations when it was screened in Buenos Aires and ended up being banned. George B. Seitz's western *Kit Carson* was banned in Mexico the same year for its allegedly "offensive" portrayal of Mexicans.[3]

Despite her Cinderella-like rise to prominence, O'Hara was now frustrated, unhappy with the way her career was going—or not going. In the view of Ida Zeitlin, she "reached a pitch of despair where she was about ready to throw in the towel, to break her contract, to collapse against the stone wall of indifference and howl like a baby wolf."[4] This was a melodramatic way of saying the actress needed to wash away the memory of films like *They Met in Argentina* as soon as she could.

Wasserman was sympathetic to her plight but advised her to be patient, reminding her that bad films often paved the way for good ones. She told him she craved a part in John Ford's upcoming movie *How Green Was My Valley*, which had been the subject of cocktail party gossip for some time. "If it's just a line," she pleaded with her agent, "if it's only to carry a spear, get me a part in that picture or die." Her part-humorous, part-desperate imprecation was totally at odds with the young woman who had once been so cavalier about stardom. It was as if her confidence had toppled. "Nothing good's ever going to happen to me again," she predicted. "I'll never get a part. If I do, I'll break a leg the day they start shooting."[5]

Not long after *They Met in Argentina* finished shooting, she received a call from the studio telling her to go to a party at Ford's house. She was aware of the fact that, like herself, he had Irish blood, but she wasn't holding her breath that anything would come of it. When she met Ford at the party, he announced that he was both an Irish rebel and a freedom fighter—an example of Ford the unconscionable mythmaker. A few days later Wasserman told her Ford wanted to see her at Twentieth Century–Fox studios with a view to casting her in the movie. Wasserman was beside himself with excitement.

When she arrived at the studio she found herself in a room full of executives. Ford introduced her to them by saying, "Gentlemen, this is Maureen O'Hara, the young lady who insulted me. Called all my relatives a bunch of shawlees" (a *shawlee* being a poor peasant who couldn't afford a coat). O'Hara was outraged and denied making the accusation, but in an interview she did with Roddy McDowall, she admitted she had apparently said something to that effect about one of Ford's aunts.[6] Ford asked her if she could do a Welsh accent, and she answered him in (what else?) a Welsh accent (the lilt wasn't too different from an Irish one). He grunted when she finished and thanked her for coming, so she didn't know whether she'd impressed him or not. The next morning, however, Wasserman called her and said, "You've got it. He wants you for Angharad. Without a test." She was in shock. She hugged her cook, her secretary, and her part-time maid. Then she called everyone she knew to share her glad tidings.

Ford, who was affectionately called "The Old Son of a Bitch" by some members of his repertory company, had been born Sean Aloysius O'Feeney (the original family name, O'Fearna, had been anglicized). His parents hailed from Galway. He started calling himself Jack Ford when he came to

Hollywood, and he wore a patch over his left eye, claiming it was sensitive to light after a cataract operation. Alternatively, he told John Wayne he had injured his eye in a freak accident during a hunting trip, but it's also possible he wore the patch for effect, the way a rock star might don black shades to look "cool." O'Hara believed the latter. She often socialized with "Pappy," as she called Ford, during this time, visiting his house and becoming friendly with his wife, Mary, and his children, Barbara and Pat. He persuaded her to sing old Irish songs at these soirées and spent a lot of time engaging in one of his favorite hobbies: spinning tall tales about the "old sod."

O'Hara first met John Wayne at one of these evenings. It was St. Patrick's Day 1940. She was touched by his shyness and tried to draw him out. She never liked the way Ford chewed Wayne out, both on the set and off. Ford boasted that he'd taken Wayne out of nickel-and-dime singing cowboy movies to the big time. This was true, but who's to say Wayne wouldn't have made it anyway? Ford enjoyed making the actor feel small. "He kept calling me a clumsy bastard," Wayne laughed, "and kept telling me I moved like an ox." He didn't cave in at the slights, though; rather, he retaliated in kind. Ford expected and enjoyed that. He brought the mischief out in Wayne, and they often traded friendly insults. In time, Wayne would become O'Hara's favorite actor, her favorite costar, and her best friend. But they never became lovers. It was almost like a brother-sister relationship. He referred to her as "Aunt Maureen." If he was the Duke, she was the Duchess.

After Ford expressed an interest in giving O'Hara a part in his film, Fox refused to hire her unless the studio owned a piece of the actress. As a result, Fox bought one O'Hara picture a year from RKO. (In later years, Fox would farm her out to Universal, Columbia, and Warner Brothers.)

Before shooting began, O'Hara's mother returned to Ireland, and the actress became more independent. Her mother had enforced a curfew on her social engagements—she had to be home by nine on workdays and midnight on the weekends. O'Hara also took control of what she wore and how she looked. The first thing she did was buy a mink coat. Then she accepted an invitation to dine with President Franklin D. Roosevelt at his Birthday Ball in Washington. Even "Mommy" would have approved of that, but the event wasn't without incident. As Roosevelt sat down to eat, he said testily to O'Hara, "Don't you know Ireland is a communist country?" He was obviously pulling her leg, but she didn't realize it. She rounded on the most important man in the world and said, "I've never heard such rubbish in my life." This anecdote highlights O'Hara's naiveté (she refused to accept that Roosevelt was being mischievous, even in her old age), but more significantly, it reveals that she was brazen enough to tell the president of the United States he was talking nonsense.

Other outings followed. She missed her mother but enjoyed her new-found freedom. "I have been bossing myself through sheer necessity," she announced. She stayed on in the house she had been renting with her mother, refusing to move to Beverly Hills like a blasé bachelorette or call in a swank Sunset Strip decorator. As for entertaining, she refused to behave like one of her future screen characters, "gowned in slinky gold lamé, jeweled and coiffed to the painful point, with silverware agleam in the candlelight and honeyed phrases dripping from my lips."[7] That was for more showy types, as was shopping in high-class stores. She found Dresden china at thrift auctions and went to a tiny awning shop on Sunset Boulevard for her patio furniture. She was generous with her money and sent much of her earnings to her family, fearful that the war would impinge on Ireland.

How Green Was My Valley chronicles the fate of an indigent Welsh coal-mining family. It is narrated by a child, Huw, played by Roddy Mc-Dowall. Darryl F. Zanuck had bought the rights to Richard Llewellyn's highly acclaimed novel in 1940. Irish writer Liam O'Flaherty was initially assigned the task of converting it into a screenplay, but his focus was too political for Zanuck, as was that of Ernest Pascal. Zanuck's final choice was Philip Dunne. He advised Dunne to emphasize the human element of the story rather than trying to make it into "an English *Grapes of Wrath*."[8] Dunne had enormous respect for Ford, despite his crusty demeanor. He felt a kinship with the director based on their mutual Irish heritage, and the first time they met, Ford bantered with him playfully. Dunne recalled in his memoirs that Ford "convinced me he liked my script by referring to it as 'this crap.'"[9]

William Wyler had originally been chosen to direct *How Green Was My Valley*, but the "money men" at Fox dropped him because of his reputation for extravagance and also because some of the pro-labor scenes he had in mind could have been politically problematic. Zanuck suggested Ford as a replacement. The pair of them had just collaborated on *The Grapes of Wrath*, for which Ford had won his second Oscar. He was greatly looking forward to his latest undertaking, exclaiming to O'Hara at one point, "Remember, the Welsh are really Irishmen, only Protestants."[10] This was the excuse he gave to an aghast Dunne when he had the miners sing Irish songs instead of Welsh ones in the wedding scene.

Wyler had selected a bunch of "name" actors for the lead roles—Laurence Olivier and Tyrone Power were slated to play the parts Ford gave to Walter Pidgeon and Roddy McDowall, while Katharine Hepburn had been selected to play Angharad, the role that eventually went to O'Hara. (Zanuck wanted Gene Tierney for the part, so O'Hara was really the third choice.) Scottish actor Donald Crisp was cast as the father of the house, a role that would win him an Oscar. Abbey actress Sara Allgood was the mother, and Anna Lee was cast as Bronwen, Angharad's sister.

O'Hara and Lee clicked immediately, O'Hara warming to the "jolly hockeysticks" personality of her British counterpart. Every day in makeup they talked the hind legs off each other, as the Irish expression goes. But this particular activity didn't take much time. "No makeup for Maureen or Anna!" Ford would bark. One day Lee thought she looked too pale and put a little rouge on her cheeks. Ford came along and rubbed his thumb on her face. "Take off that stuff," he roared. "You're playing a Welsh virgin, not a Hollywood hooker."[11]

Walter Pidgeon plays the minister who falls in love with O'Hara's character. He wanted the part so much that when a cameraman told him he was shooting tests for the movie, Pidgeon advised him, "Make them all bad," hoping he might get a call. When he did, he had to wonder if the cameraman in question had actually done him this favor.[12] Dunne thought Pidgeon was the "one really phony actor" in the film.[13] He didn't make any attempt at a Welsh accent, sounding pointedly American at all times.

The war prevented shooting in Wales's Rhondda Valley, as originally planned, so California's San Fernando Valley was used instead. It took 150 builders six months to create the set, at a staggering cost of $1.25 million. RKO boasted that an all-time high of 3,500 extras were used for the crowd scenes. Tunnels were made of real coal, but because of the war, additional coal couldn't be found for the surrounding hillsides. Instead, they were painted black, requiring 20,000 gallons of paint to create this effect. O'Hara was resigned to the fact that Hollywood would be doubling for Llewellyn's native land, and she praised the elaborate set. It was so authentic she imagined it was really Wales. A lot of the actors and crew were Celts, so she had a sense of being reconnected to her roots.

She also enjoyed her interchanges with Pidgeon. "You are king of the chapel," she tells his character at one point, "but I will be queen in my own kitchen." To which he replies, "You will be queen wherever you walk." The script has this quiet dignity throughout, and O'Hara enhances it with a radiant performance. She has little dialogue in the film, which means she has to act with her eyes and with movement, a much tougher challenge. Sometimes her accent seems more Irish than Welsh, and she is perhaps too glamorous for a miner's daughter, but her presence in the film is very effective.

Ford's fine visual effects add to her onscreen presence. When she comes down the steps of the church after marrying Marten Lamont on the rebound from Pidgeon's character (she has to forsake him for fear of a scandal), a gust of wind billows the wedding veil behind her, creating a powerful image. Some viewers might have thought this was a coincidence, but O'Hara revealed that Ford had placed three wind machines behind her, "and I had to walk up and down those steps many times while he worked out that the wind would do exactly that."[14]

Ford didn't officially "direct" O'Hara. He wasn't interested in finessing her movements or gestures. He told her where to stand in a scene; after that, it was basically up to her. The positive side of this approach was that it conveyed an implicit trust in O'Hara, a belief that she knew what she was doing. Ford's intuition did the rest. He was like a portrait painter with light, framing the mood with deft nuances. "He didn't tell you to blow your nose or raise your finger or any of those things," O'Hara recalled. "All he'd say was 'Cut' and you'd ask if he wanted you to do more or less of what you were doing. I think that's why he employed the same people year after year in his stock company. He knew they knew what he wanted. He liked to work with people he was accustomed to. And, more importantly, people who were accustomed to him."[15] She also liked the way he improvised. "He wouldn't allow actors to stop in the middle of a scene if they made a mistake," she remembered. "We all knew that no matter what happened we had to use the accident and continue going. Very often in the finished movie you saw all those impromptu scenes and they were marvellous."[16] The years Ford had spent making low-budget movies in a race against the clock had taught him how to cut corners; he didn't believe in spending huge amounts of time on elaborate setups.

No amount of time in film school would have given O'Hara the liberal education she got "on the hoof" with Ford, right down to the details, like the way he asked his cameraman to blow up the shadow of a chair on a wall to give a scene life. "You looked and you saw and you said, 'Son of a gun, that's beautiful.' Before it was just a scene, now it's spectacular. When he got Monument Valley to photograph, I think he just forgot about the actors. Monument Valley was really the star of all his Westerns."[17]

O'Hara reminisced years later with McDowall about Ford's unfussy way of working: "We'd read the lines and read the lines and read the lines. He'd listen and he'd say, 'All right, now let's go out and go to work.' And we'd go out and rehearse once or twice, and then the positions were marked, and before you blinked an eye it was lit, and before you knew it you shot it and it was done and he said, 'Next set-up.' And you thought: Wait a minute, I was only getting started."[18]

"He was the boss on the set," O'Hara pronounced, "and nobody dared step out of line, which gave the performers such a sense of security."[19] He gave his cast confidence in themselves even on the days when he was "cutting you up into little bits."[20] In some ways, they even fed off the negative energy. If an actor was out of favor with Ford, it was called being "in the barrel." "Every day the cast members would ask each other 'Who's in the barrel today?' If it was yourself, you were going to have a terrible, miserable day because he would never let up nagging you and insulting you and hurting you. But it didn't mean he was necessarily mad at you. It meant that out of the corner of his eye he was watching somebody else until he got him in the mental condition he wanted him in. Then he would shoot the scene."[21] It was a "divide and conquer" strategy that fired people up.

O'Hara witnessed Ford's demonic side the day she pointed out an anachronism in his choice of a modern cheese basket. She was sent to the "sin bin" for this declaration and was removed from the scene he was shooting. After serving her time on a hillside, having bitten her lip, she was "allowed" back.

How Green Was My Valley opened to positive reviews, and O'Hara was singled out for special mention. She appears almost like a force of nature in some scenes, subsumed under an endemic purity. Joseph Mc-Bride thought Ford's "immediate and powerful" affinity with O'Hara was evident in her "luminous" close-ups, filmed with an emotional intensity not seen in his work since he'd directed Katharine Hepburn in *Mary of Scotland*.[22] Bosley Crowther was one of the few reviewers to pounce on the fact that the film had too many stories, becoming a kind of patchwork quilt rather than a straight-up narrative. He felt that in spite of its brilliant detail and its "exquisite feeling for plain affectionate people," it never really formed a concrete pattern of their lives.[23]

The film was nominated for ten Oscars and won three, including Best Picture. This was no mean achievement, as it was up against Orson Welles's *Citizen Kane*. Welles's film has subsequently been acknowledged as one of the greatest ever made, if not the greatest, but his precocious talents weren't fully appreciated at the time. Also, Ford's strong embrace of family values at a time when the United States was at war struck a chord with the Academy. (Welles accepted the decision philosophically. "I like the old masters," he said when asked who his favorite directors were, "by which I mean John Ford, John Ford and John Ford.")

Many people felt O'Hara deserved a nomination, but it wasn't to be—not for this role or for any other. She took it hard, but she wasn't the only talented actress to be snubbed by the Academy. Barbara Stanwyck, Greta Garbo, Marlene Dietrich, Judy Garland, Gloria Swanson, Jean Simmons, and many others never won an Oscar. Stars who weren't even nominated in their careers—like O'Hara—included Jean Harlow, Ida Lupino, Veronica Lake, Rita Hayworth, Lucille Ball, Lauren Bacall, Claire Bloom, and other notables. Joan Fontaine won that year for Alfred Hitchcock's *Suspicion*.

Donald Crisp won for Best Supporting Actor, and Sara Allgood was nominated for Best Supporting Actress. Ford won for Best Director but didn't turn up to accept his Oscar (Wayne collected it for him). He hadn't attended the ceremonies for his previous wins either. (As has often been remarked, it's amazing that of the four Oscars he won in his career, none was for a western, the genre he is generally associated with.) He explained his reasons for being a no-show to fellow director Robert Parrish: "Once I went fishing, another time there was a war on, and on another occasion,

I was suddenly taken drunk."[24] It probably doesn't matter which circumstance applied to which Oscar. The point was clear: he didn't like formal occasions or encomiums. The work was what mattered, just doing it.

Oscar or no, O'Hara was now a lady to contend with. People were starting to say that she could become a major star. She'd made two interesting movies with Charles Laughton and then two indifferent ones, but now she was entering a different league with Pappy. Signs looked good for the future.

She'd been slated to star opposite Tyrone Power in another Zanuck film, *Son of Fury*, earlier in the year but had to pull out due to illness: she had her appendix and two ovarian cysts removed in Reno Hospital. This didn't please Zanuck, who thought her chemistry with Power would have worked a treat. Zanuck didn't appreciate the seriousness of her condition and sent a top doctor from Twentieth Century–Fox to survey her medical records. After he did this, he remarked, sneeringly, that the ovarian cysts were "probably just a fragment left over from an abortion."[25] Today, a comment like that might have landed him in court, but these were different times. Although his remark drew no visible reaction, O'Hara felt like hitting him, but in the end, she did nothing but simmer.

This was a difficult time for her in other ways. Shortly before her operation she'd applied to have her marriage to George Brown annulled. In fact, the annulment deposition was taken from her hospital bed. How could she care about movies in such circumstances?

O'Hara started dating a man named Will Price around this time. A native of Mississippi, he had been the dialogue director on *The Hunchback of Notre Dame*, after performing the same function on *Gone with the Wind*. O'Hara met Price the first day on the set of *Hunchback*, and she was feeling poorly. Her hair and makeup had been done wrong, and she felt uncomfortable in the clothes she was wearing. Also, her "natural shyness" was making her feel awkward with people. All of a sudden, a man appeared with a "round jovial face" and a pair of blue eyes that seemed to say, "Welcome, Maureen, come on now, smile—things aren't as bad as they seem." He was her dialogue coach and "one of the finest-looking men I had ever seen." He assured her that her voice was fine and rich and would record beautifully: "It wasn't the usual phony praise. He seemed to mean what he said." Suddenly her awkwardness disappeared. "I knew I had found a real friend. . . . Somehow the gentleness of the strange Mr. Price, his hospitality and warmth, had changed everything."[26]

He helped her "immeasurably" in the following weeks as their friendship grew. Then one day he asked her to go to the Hollywood Bowl with him. She agreed. He also asked to meet her mother. This touched her. It reminded her of what an Irish suitor might have done. The friendship became something else: "I realized I had travelled half way around the world to find the one man I could love."[27] Just seventy-five days after her marriage to Brown was annulled, she married Price. She called their wedding "one of the most exciting things that ever happened to me." In him, she had found "the man with whom I can be completely happy."[28]

But what about Brown? She told Wolfe Kaufman of *Modern Screen* magazine that marrying him had been "the honest, the sincere, the right thing to do." But now, after not seeing him for four years, and after thinking it over carefully, she had decided it was unfair to continue being George's wife because "I don't love him."[29] The fact that she hadn't seen her husband since their wedding day is mentioned almost casually!

Her marriage to Brown she dismissed as a comedy of youth. The one to Price, in contrast, evolved as a tragedy of inexperience. With Price, her desperation to make things work all but blinded her to his demonic behavior, at least early on. O'Hara was a virgin, and the wedding night was an anticlimax. "I knew the experience wasn't special for me," she wrote in her autobiography, "because I don't remember it. All I remember is thinking: What the hell have I done now?"[30] This set the tone for their future together. Shortly after the honeymoon, she saw something that would become a familiar sight: Price drunk as a skunk.

He disappeared for long stretches but disclosed little about his movements to his bride. When he was home, he played the genial host, riding shotgun with his popular Dublin wife. In most of the photographs taken of them in the early 1940s, Price is sporting a Falstaffian grin and O'Hara is either gazing at him adoringly or throwing her head back in laughter. She lights his cigarettes, walks arm in arm with him, kisses him lightly on the cheek. Who could have believed there was trouble in paradise? But then, she was a good actress. (And he was a good actor.)

For Price, O'Hara was his ticket to Easy Street. He never really took an interest in projects, except in fits and starts or as the mood struck him between binges. In time, drink became too available and too affordable. Married to a pauper, he might not have become such a lounge lizard. Like many men who chafed at the notion of work, he had expensive tastes. He wanted servants for their apartment, and he usually got what he wanted. O'Hara supported him in the manner to which he thought himself entitled. She worked almost nonstop in the studio and, more often than not, came home to find him unconscious on the floor. After the first few months, it became clear that their marriage was on a slow but unremitting path to divorce court.

Work took her mind off her problems at home. *To the Shores of Tripoli*, produced by Zanuck, was her first color film. (During every subsequent color feature she made, a bouquet of flowers would be delivered to her dressing room by a representative of Dr. Herbert Kalmus, inventor of the Technicolor process.) It was directed by Bruce Humberstone, who was regarded as a vulgarian by some. He was nicknamed "Lucky" because of the number of successful B movies he had helmed. This was another one.

In the film, John Payne plays a pampered marine—a "worthless young pup," according to his father—who falls for O'Hara, looking lovely as nurse Mary Carter. But it isn't long before Mary realizes he isn't exactly marriage material. His recruiting officer, played by Randolph Scott, is a good friend of the young marine's father, but after sampling some of the soldier's "lip," he toughens up with him. The insolent manner in which Payne speaks to Scott would hardly have been countenanced in any naval institute, but it all comes right when Payne prepares for the front line in the final reel. This means that Mary, who has now warmed to him, will have to wait for some tender loving care. Or will it be that tender? In an earlier scene, the marine explains to a rookie that a rifle is "just like a jealous woman. You gotta hold her and squeeze."

Nobody in the film seems to have lived life. The characters' emotions, like their uniforms, seem too streamlined. The scene in which Payne tries to ingratiate himself with O'Hara by pretending he's been knocked down by a jeep might have found a better home in a *Carry On* caper. Even the title is a misnomer. We don't reach the shores of Tripoli, or anywhere else. The last scene might appeal to gung-ho viewers: the reformed Payne throws his civilian clothing to the wind and promises to send Dad "a few Japs for Christmas."

O'Hara was back to black and white in Henry Hathaway's *Ten Gentlemen from West Point*, a film about the founding of the U.S. Military Academy. She becomes part of a love triangle involving patriotic George Montgomery and pampered John Sutton. Laird Cregar plays the cruel major knocking the sparks out of the cadets. She would have enjoyed making the film infinitely more if John Payne, its intended star, had been there. But only a week into shooting, Payne's wife, Anne Shirley, walked out on him. It was a bolt from the blue, and it hit him hard. "He came into my dressing-room," O'Hara poignantly recalled, "and sobbed like I've never seen a man sob. Without any knowledge that anything was wrong, he woke up to find that Anne had left and was getting a divorce. He was totally heartbroken. He kept saying, 'Why didn't she ever tell me she was unhappy?'"[31]

Montgomery wasn't a very gentlemanly replacement, at one point giving O'Hara "an open mouth kiss and damn near choking me to death." She walked off the set for the only time in her career and reported him. The matter was dealt with discreetly, and for the rest of the picture he behaved "like an angel." O'Hara justified her action by saying, "I know today they practically lick each other's faces clean, but back then it just wasn't done."[32] She had no problem laying down the law about acceptable behavior from a screen lover. She didn't like men who were too cocksure of themselves or who prolonged a kiss after the director shouted "Cut." "It's the ones that lallylag over you for the kick they get out of it that I classify as Grade A non-gents."[33] O'Hara had a foolproof way of dealing with this breed. "You bore me," were the kiss-off words she chose.[34]

During the course of filming, she bought herself a house in Bel Air. She couldn't really afford it, but she needed something to take her mind off the disaster zone that was her marriage. Price continued to spend her money: one day she came home to find a brand-new Cadillac in the driveway—another of his "little" extravagances.

One night, Price and O'Hara went to a party attended by Ava Gardner and Mickey Rooney, whose marriage was also on the rocks. At one point, O'Hara heard Gardner ranting, telling two reporters that life with Rooney was mental torture. They advised her to stick it out because the longer the marriage, the more alimony she'd receive. O'Hara was actually eavesdropping on this conversation: she was sitting in a basement kitchen with the lights out. Perhaps she should have indicated her presence in some way, but she didn't. She stayed in the dark as the revelations unfolded outside the door, writing in her autobiography, "Ava listened as the couple coached her on what to do. She took their advice and left Mickey just a year later. I should have told Mickey that he was about to be taken but I didn't and I have always regretted it."[35] Gardner always denied that she was after his money.

One night not long after the party, O'Hara received a call from a prostitute asking her to come and collect Price. The woman roared into the phone, "I've got your husband here. Come and pick the son of a bitch up and get him the hell out of here!"[36] By now, O'Hara had stopped caring. She found him drunk in a brothel at the seedy end of town and dragged him home. A few days later, he went off to boot camp in San Diego. The marriage was only two months old.

O'Hara didn't tell anyone how miserable she was during this time, pacifying intrusive journalists with bland comments about her lifestyle. *Jamaica Inn*, she said, had been "lucky" for her, "because that was the movie that brought me to America and if I hadn't come to Hollywood I would not have met Will."[37] And once she met him, she "never had a date with anyone else, man or boy, not ever."[38] *She* may not have dated anyone else, but he certainly did, time and again. Few knew this. Being a homebody, O'Hara poured her heart out to only a few family members, who wondered at the strange world of Hollywood, where irresponsibility seemed to be a given.

On the first anniversary of her ill-fated wedding, December 29, 1942, she wrote a letter to her "service husband" that was published in *Movieland* magazine. It outlined the "wave of pain" she suffered when she realized her darling man wouldn't be there with her to do the things they always did together—driving to the San Fernando Valley, eating in the Chinese restaurant on Hollywood Boulevard, going back to the house "Will bought for me" (the phrase "with my money" isn't appended), playing badminton, eating the shrimp Arnaud he cooked so well, lighting the fire, sitting on his lap, and going to bed at the end of a "perfect year." (It could hardly have been more imperfect.) If she could change the world, she speculated, there would be "no war, no Hitler, no Japs." She would continue to adore her husband and forgive him for grooving to boogie-woogie music, which she hated. She would even forgive him for not coming promptly to dinner when she served it and for the shambles he made of the bathroom with his garden clothes and messy boots.[39]

So deep was the "wrenching" pain of her loneliness, she went on, that she spent the day of their anniversary scrubbing floors, polishing the nickel, puffing the pillows up to "fat, bloomy balloons," even scouring the toilet. When the phone rang, she tripped over brooms and mops, thinking it might be him, "But you did not call." She cleaned the birdcage and the doghouse and even spruced up the maid's room to take her mind off herself and her grief. And yet in a strange way, it was a happy day, for she thought: "Will, my husband, is fighting to protect the things I want. . . . That is why I am happy—because this is what Will is fighting for, this house."[40] She had to pretend to be happily married for her parents; she was terrified of putting them through the shame of another divorce so soon after the George Brown debacle.

She finally starred opposite heartthrob Tyrone Power in *The Black Swan* in 1942. It was shot in a watery area behind the Fox studios named "Tyrone Power Lake," in tribute to him. Based on a novel by Rafael Sabatini, the film is a robust tale of rival pirates in the Caribbean. O'Hara, as Lady Margaret Denby, daughter of the governor of Jamaica, is in her element playing "an Irish wildcat for the first time, but certainly not the last."[41] Power is Jamie Waring, the dashing pirate who kidnaps her. Her attitude toward him oscillates between affection and anger, in a kind of prelude to her similarly ambivalent roles opposite John Wayne in the following decade. George Sanders is almost unrecognizable as a red-haired villain. All the performances are suitably overripe, and Henry King directs with his customary pizzazz.

Power is trying to rid the Caribbean of rival pirates—and to gain O'Hara's hand. Along the way, he has to contend with Sanders, Laird Cregar, and Anthony Quinn, a familiar trio in O'Hara films, though usually not all together. There are thrills and spills a-plenty and lots of abrasive set-tos between Power and O'Hara. Power is less chivalric than usual and more brash, which allows O'Hara's natural feistiness full play as the pair of them engage in swordplay and passionate clinches. In the end, Power's dash wins the day, but O'Hara is more than a match for him. Sanders is also a revelation, camping things up in a way we're unaccustomed to, based on his previous oleaginous roles. It's as if the red wig frees him up to be outrageous.

The film was tosh, but high-grade tosh. A critic conceded: "Henry King made what might have been a third-rate pirate formula into a celebrated cutlass-wielding romp."[42] Leon Shamroy went on to win an Oscar for his cinematography, the first of four he would accumulate in his career. It's a record that still stands today.

"Ty was a wonderful person to work with," O'Hara cooed to Kevin Lewis, "but Technicolor and his magnificent good looks very often prevented him having the roles he should have had and was absolutely capable of doing. I felt the same way about myself. I was very well trained. I wasn't discovered in an ice cream shop."[43]

O'Hara held her own during the action scenes, as Sara Hamilton found out when she visited the set. "They kept telling me what a nice girl Maureen O'Hara was," Hamilton recalled bemusedly, before she saw Power nursing a swollen lip outside the sound stage. "Maureen hit me," he mumbled helplessly. A few moments later she ran into George Sanders "twirling around like a waltzing mouse" as he held his head. "Maureen hit me with a bottle," he burbled.[44] She left a veritable trail of destruction in her wake, but she wasn't experiencing any pangs of guilt. "I had to smack him [Power] in the face seven times," she admitted, "and I know how to smack. He just fell back and sat there on the bed, staring at me as if he didn't believe the evidence of what senses I had left him."[45] She seemed almost proud of herself.

One scene that surprisingly escaped the censor's scissors has Power and O'Hara tucked up in bed together, pretending they're married. She's in a petticoat and he's bare chested. Many pulses were set racing here. In another scene, he had to hit her. He slapped her so hard, according to King, he "pretty near knocked her out" (payback for the split lip?). O'Hara took this in stride and was glad to see Power enjoying himself. It was as if he was breaking out of a mold. "His great downfall," according to King, "was that he would get with directors who would want him to be strong and Ty would force that." This made things seem false. "It's like playing golf," he surmised, "If you force it, you can't eat your hat."[46]

O'Hara was concerned about a scene in which Power throws her into the sea in her underwear, so she wrote a letter home to her parents to warn them: "While I'm a career girl, and married, to my parents I am still their baby." She continued in this vein: "I'm not prudish but my training was strict. Dublin is conservative. I have a list of 'Don'ts' and am my own Hays Office." She went on to describe herself as the "Don't" girl of Hollywood: "Newspapers carry gossip lines saying Maureen O'Hara won't drink, won't smoke, won't wear revealing evening gowns, or *negligées*, or sweaters. Maureen O'Hara won't take a bath before the camera, or appear in a bathing suit. Or show her legs." All this was true. "Luckily, I've not had to portray smoking or drinking on the screen and I hope I never shall because I don't do either in personal life." [47] (She liked to see her films as an extension of her own personality, rather than the taking on of a new identity, in contrast to other stars who delighted in such transmogrifications.)

For instance, a scene in *To the Shores of Tripoli* called for her to meet John Payne in a cocktail lounge, but she asked the director to change the locale to a terrace; he happily complied. At real-life cocktail parties she opted for lime juice and seltzer rather than alcohol, which resulted in "a lifted eyebrow or two," but this didn't bother her: "This is a good time to brush aside the follow-the-crowd ideas, for the world is changing, and the new independence is bringing more freedom from social traditions."[48] It's difficult to grasp her logic here. Surely the "new independence" for women meant precisely the ability to indulge in habits, such as drinking and smoking, that were traditionally approved of only for men. Her "conservatism" went even further: for a scene in *The Black Swan* she refused to take off her wedding ring, so some clips had to be designed to make it look like a dinner ring (she was married in real life, but not in the film).

As the years went on, O'Hara relaxed her ban on smoking and drinking onscreen. If she hadn't, she might have been out of a job. But, like the pure Catholic girl she was, she always refused to disrobe: "I'm an actress, not a model, so I won't wear clinging negligées, revealing play suits, nor pose for 'cheesecake' art. . . . Anyway, suggestion stimulates the imagination and often soft materials following the lines of the body, and sheer chiffon yokes and sleeves create a seductive glamour that nudity would destroy."[49] Her admirers had to content themselves with photographs of her in elaborate finery, and call on their imaginations to do the rest.

4

Saluting Uncle Sam

Tyrone Power enlisted in the Marine Corps after *The Black Swan* wrapped. Henry Fonda, who would become O'Hara's next costar, also signed up. He became an apprentice seaman in downtown Los Angeles and then headed off to boot camp in San Diego. When he arrived, though, he was sent back to Hollywood, where he discovered that Darryl F. Zanuck had figured out a way to "squeeze one more movie out of him, by convincing Washington that a potboiler called *The Immortal Sergeant* would help the mobilization."[1]

Fonda doesn't play the title character; that refers to his commander, Sergeant Kelly (Thomas Mitchell), a whimsical Irishman. Fonda plays Colin Spence, a raw recruit who's in love with Valentine Lee (O'Hara), the beauty he left behind in London. They've had a few dates, but he's unsure of her—or unsure of *himself*. Before joining the army, Spence is so timid he doesn't even complain when a waiter ruins a dinner reservation. He worries about losing Valentine to their mutual friend Tom Benedict, played by Reginald Gardiner. (The day Henry Fonda loses Maureen O'Hara to someone like Reginald Gardiner, it's time to eat one's hat—or one's war helmet.)

Spence is part of a regiment crossing the Libyan desert. They're a jolly bunch, but after an enemy plane crashes into one of their jeeps, panic sets in. They begin to run short of food, petrol, and men. Every time something goes wrong, though, Kelly looks on the bright side (immortal, maybe; optimistic, definitely). He grooms Spence to take over for him, should tragedy strike. When it does—a bullet rips into the sergeant's groin—he feels like a liability to the other soldiers, so he shoots himself, leaving Spence to carry on. But Spence had earlier confessed to Kelly, "I can carry out orders but I can't give them." Kelly disagreed; he saw something in the "wartime educated amateur" that made him believe Spence had what it took to lead the men to safety. Kelly's confidence is rewarded. Spence gets his men out of the desert and receives a hero's medal for his troubles. He also gets the girl. Being a hero has its perks, we see. The moral of the film is that war has made a man of him (hardly an original conceit). We now know that, having succeeded in leading his troops across a war zone with only a pineapple for sustenance, Spence will have no trouble at all dealing with an incompetent waiter. Valentine can look forward to many meals with her soft-spoken sergeant in the poshest of restaurants.

The production values are satisfactory, but there's little we haven't seen many times before. The film revives Fonda's milquetoast image, but he looks rather ridiculous when, on the verge of delirium, he starts talking to himself. The flashbacks to his interlude with O'Hara don't work either, mainly because there are too many of them. Fonda was one of the few minimalist actors O'Hara starred with—that is, he conveyed moods through his expressions rather than dialogue. Working with someone like this (in contrast to the broad brushstrokes of, say, a Douglas Fairbanks Jr.) brought out the best in her. She told many interviewers over the years that Fonda was heaven to share a film with. When his eyes teared up in emotional scenes, so did hers. He made it easy for her to generate emotion without fabrication. He was so convincing to play opposite, she even forgave him for sitting on the steps of his trailer every day, "working like a dog" on his mathematics and other skills he would need in the navy.

His last line dutifully delivered, Fonda entered the service much later than intended. He went to the Pacific the following year and became an air combat intelligence officer. He didn't see any action but served with distinction. He was elevated to the rank of lieutenant before his discharge.

O'Hara wondered where her next film would come from. Hollywood's output between 1942 and 1945 decreased from 533 films to 377. Because of wartime shortages, directors couldn't afford to reshoot scenes, except in rare instances, so everyone had to be line perfect. A price ceiling was also placed on the construction of sets. Rubber and steel were in short supply, so sets were often painted to look realistic. Ammunition for the firing of blank cartridges was rationed, which affected mainly westerns and gangster films. Many directors went on location in an effort to achieve the authenticity that was so elusive under such conditions.

RKO lost a total of 847 people to the armed forces, including 13 women.

Key technicians were replaced by assistants or hurriedly trained substitutes, resulting in delays and extra production costs. The moguls denied that the situation would result in lower-quality films.

Because so many great actors were in the trenches in real life, O'Hara was lucky to find quality costars in her "reel" life during the war years. Actors who stayed in Hollywood did their bit by appearing in propaganda films and selling war bonds at functions to boost national morale. O'Hara became a pinup girl under the moniker "Big Red." She was often photographed in off-the-shoulder evening dresses that emphasized her patrician bearing, a shadowy backdrop underscoring her features to create a semierotic charge. In such poses she became the thinking man's sex symbol. She refused to smolder, leaving that for more obvious beauties. Instead, she seemed to outstare the camera, a formidable Cleopatra clone that challenged all comers with those huge, rarely blinking eyes.

She made a bevy of adventure films during this time. There were three in 1942 alone: *To the Shores of Tripoli*, *Ten Gentlemen from West Point*, and *The Black Swan*. She followed these with *The Immortal Sergeant* and then made *Buffalo Bill* and *The Spanish Main*. None of these films were classics, but they brought in the money and kept her profile high. They also gave her a chance to develop an acting style; rather than being a stumbling block, typecasting became an advantage for her, a mode of identification. Actresses were called on to *do*; stars, to *be*. It helped if audiences knew something about a star before they entered the theater, like a brand that defined her, a calling card. In an industry driven mainly by money, the studios knew O'Hara would bring in audiences by swashing her buckle. She was happy to sign on the dotted line for these largely indistinguishable films. She was building up a following based on her persona as a stubborn lass who stood up to villains but was content to play the maiden in distress to her leading man—often after fighting him.

She wasn't averse to rolling up her sleeves or going down on all fours to escape danger. That's what stars like Tyrone Power and John Payne loved about her. She didn't mind getting her hands dirty when the occasion called for it. She wasn't prissy or demure. She didn't give the come-hither look, like so many of her predecessors in this genre. Love was something that happened when the business of saving the fleet or the garrison was expedited. Duty came before passion, just like the head ruled the heart.

She returned to RKO after a two-year absence to reunite with Charles Laughton in 1943 for *This Land Is Mine*, a World War II story set "somewhere in Europe." One imagines it's France, but none of the town's inhabitants make any attempt to put on a European accent, unless it's a British one (a newspaper in one scene even has an English headline). It was directed by Jean Renoir, whom Laughton had met at Elstree Studios in 1937. Renoir was sufficiently impressed with O'Hara's previous performances with Laughton to sign her, and she was looking forward to getting her teeth into another potentially meaty endeavor with her old tutor. The script was written by Dudley Nichols, who had famously refused an Oscar for *The Informer* in 1935. Nichols also coproduced the movie with Renoir.

Laughton plays Albert Lory, a cowardly teacher whose mother (Una O'Connor) dominates him. He's in love with Louise Martin (O'Hara), another teacher at the school, but he's too inhibited to express his feelings for her. Louise's brother Paul (Kent Smith) is a member of the Resistance movement in town. The occupying Nazis have a cozy attitude toward the townsfolk. In one scene, Louise refuses to shake hands with the very jolly Nazi commander, Major von Keller (Walter Slezak), and he takes no action against her. It's difficult to imagine this happening in real life—people were sent to concentration camps for less. Even when Paul sabotages a train, von Keller is reluctant to take action. He prefers to recruit informers like Georges Lambert (George Sanders), who's engaged to be married to Louise. Louise isn't aware that her brother is an activist at the beginning of the film, and when she finds out, her affections cool toward the Nazi-friendly Lambert.

Mrs. Lory, like Lambert, believes that cooperating with the Nazis is the best course of action. She suspects Paul is the saboteur and tells Lambert, who in turn informs von Keller. Paul is then shot. Lambert has turned against his own people, and he has lost Louise for good, so he kills himself. (Sanders would do the same in real life.) Lory discovers his dead body, with a gun beside it, and is accused of murdering Lambert because of his jealousy over Louise. Lory undergoes a catharsis in prison that isn't totally credible, and he signs his death warrant by giving a speech in court against the Nazis. It's very noble, but for some reason, this scene doesn't work. O'Hara is effective in it, crying and smiling at the same time as Lory does his bit for the cause beloved by her dead brother, but Laughton's throwaway delivery is anticlimactic. The fact that there's only one Nazi in the courtroom also beggars belief. Where's von Keller? Lory is acquitted on the murder charge and returns to his classroom. The pupils who once intimidated him are now rightly respectful, agog as he reads the American Declaration of Rights to them. After he's taken away by the Nazis, a fate he accepts with stoical calm, Louise continues to read the declaration, and the film ends there. Viewers are entitled to have mixed feelings about all this. Renoir has tried to do too much and ends up confusing his audience.

Laughton saw *This Land Is Mine* as a love story between Lory and Louise, the two of them reaching heroic heights in different ways. "As I go to my death at the end of the picture," he wrote to a friend, "Maureen kisses me, not in daughterly devotion but with physical passion." This heartened him, even if the plotline meant he could never possess her. Laughton told the same friend he had once espied a note on Irving Thalberg's desk that said, "Laughton must never get the girl." It was upside down, but he was still able to read it. "I've trained myself to do that," he blithely informed his friend.[2] The content of the message failed to faze him.

The Fallen Sparrow (1943) also has a Nazi undercurrent. RKO was not shy about cashing in on the anti-German fever sweeping the United States at the time. It was directed by Richard Wallace and again costarred Walter Slezak. John Garfield plays Kit, a man who was tortured by Franco's zealots during the Spanish Civil War and for two years afterward while being held captive. A friend helps him escape but is then murdered; the murder is passed off as a suicide. Kit makes a connection between the murder and a Civil War flag the Nazis are looking for, and he knows its location. Why is it so important to them? This information is never disclosed.

Something else we aren't told in this enigmatic drama is why the morally compromised Toni (O'Hara) is working for the oleaginous Dr. Skaas (Slezak). He delights in telling Kit about the latest developments in torture techniques, the most sophisticated of which involves making the tortured person complicit in the process. Kit greets these discourses with a mixture of apprehension and nonchalance, catching the balance well as he tries to keep his posttraumatic stress in check. Toni is also conflicted. O'Hara portrays this well—so well, in fact, that one wonders why she didn't take these ambivalent roles more often. All she has to work off is a close-cropped hairstyle and her instinct for duplicity. It's a finely nuanced performance, and she keeps us guessing just how much—or how little—she cares for Kit right up to the last frame. She tells Kit she's working for Dr. Skaas, "the man who limps when he walks," because she has a daughter in a concentration camp in Germany. Is this the truth? We doubt it, but our curiosity is aroused.

Garfield wasn't the first choice for the part—James Cagney and Cary Grant both turned it down—but the film's politics appealed to him. He'd always had left-wing sympathies, so playing a character who opposed Franco's totalitarian regime was right up his alley. The fact that Franco and his cohorts aren't specifically named is strange. Why would the Nazis be propping up the government and not the Spaniards? Obviously, the script was tailored to tap into Americans' anti-German sentiment. As a result, Garfield's battle is described as being "between me and the little man in Berlin" rather than the little man in Madrid.

O'Hara liked Garfield, referring to him as a "sweetheart." He didn't really rate her as an actress, but the pair of them played off each other effectively. Their characters conceal secrets from each other as they quietly evaluate how much the other knows, scene by scene. This gives an added frisson to their would-be romance. The film may not have the same resonance as *Casablanca*, but no false notes are struck, apart from one trivial scene early on when Garfield has O'Hara try on a string of hats to punish her for being offhand with him; it maintains the tension admirably.

Kit always seems just a step away from sliding back into the psychic pit he inhabited in Spain. Toni eyes him warily, trying to discover why he's so protective about "a little piece of cloth, a dirty rag that you wouldn't even pick up on the street." O'Hara wears an almost permanent look of anxiety in the film and gives a delicate performance; all her broad reactions evinced in less subtle films are scrubbed out of this one, as Wallace opts for a nuanced mien that perfectly suits the material. In some scenes she doesn't have any dialogue, so we watch her expressions for clues as to why she wants to pick Kit's brain. O'Hara hints at more emotions than she expresses, and Garfield picks up on this with equally telling glances and gestures.

This Land Is Mine and *The Fallen Sparrow* were two important films for O'Hara, adding to her growing prestige in the film industry. They helped her crawl out from the gimcrack melodrama of adventure films. Offscreen, though, her life was as miserable as ever. She continued to bamboozle the public about how happy she was with Will Price, while her heart was breaking inside. In an interview conducted after *The Fallen Sparrow* wrapped, she sang his praises, claiming to be offended if anyone was "tactless enough" to ring their home and ask for "Miss O'Hara." In such instances, the caller was informed he had the wrong number. As she explained, "I never intend to embarrass my husband by having someone call me Miss O'Hara in front of him. If the lesson has to be driven home, I do it."[3]

As a little girl, she took pleasure in humoring her father; now the compliant housewife delighted in doing the same for her husband. "When you have pleased him you have really accomplished something. I can't tell you how much fun it is to do things for Will because he is so appreciative."[4] She expressed satisfaction over the fact that Price put a "shiny brass" knocker on the front door and also put the keyhole at eye level, like the one she had in her house in Dublin—presumably so she could look through it and vet visitors. She indulged him by cooking "strange and delectable dishes." She drew a line between her screen persona, for which she adopted a more formal guise, and her "at home" one, where she could "put my feet on the coffee table or dangle from the living room chandelier." She looked forward to calling her baby Maureen if it was a girl.[5] (It was, but she didn't.)

She gave an interview to *Motion Picture* magazine in which she talked about her relationship with Kathryn Grayson, her neighbor in Bel Air. The article described Grayson as O'Hara's "only movie star friend." Apart from acting, they shared an interest in opera, went shopping and walking together, and spent hours discussing what constituted a good or a bad film. Grayson, like O'Hara, was married to a man named Price. This caused much confusion among mailmen and grocery deliverers. One day Grayson got O'Hara's milk bill. Another time, O'Hara's lamb chops were delivered to Grayson's house. They laughed about these mix-ups. O'Hara enjoyed Grayson because she was natural, a homebody like herself. Neither of them needed the falseness of the party scene. Their comfort zone was the home, far from the madding crowd. In that interview, O'Hara claimed her husband was important to her "for the very selfish reason that I want someone I love in the other chair by the fireplace later on when I am old and fame has gone."[6] This was an unusual pronouncement, considering it was made so early in her career. Few stars would have looked so far into the future for an emotional insurance policy.

In between filming *This Land Is Mine* and *The Fallen Sparrow*, O'Hara was asked to speak at a function in Texas geared toward selling war bonds. The man seated beside her that night was Errol Flynn. In accordance with his wild-man image, Flynn spent the evening sipping whiskey from a teacup and making lewd suggestions to her. As someone who lived with an alcoholic, she found this behavior hard to take. She eventually warned Flynn she'd knock his block off if he didn't stop. He got the message and slid from his chair, going down on all fours to crawl under the table as he made his way to the exit, giving her a little wave at the door. Flynn had also been scheduled to give a speech that night, but not surprisingly, it didn't happen.

Price, who was drinking more than ever by now, decided to join the marines. O'Hara couldn't believe her luck: it meant he would be out of her hair for a while. Although she was relieved he was gone, she wore her heart on her sleeve in public utterances. "I shall never forget the gnawing loneliness—and perhaps the fear—that I felt when my husband was in Iwo Jima. It was so easy to draw up terrifying images in my mind. But I knew that I must not dwell on these things. Not if I was to dignify the work my husband was doing in the war, or my own responsibility as his wife and the mother of his child."[7] She crossed the line of believability when she talked about missing the raggedy towels he used to leave in the bathroom. "Nothing is any fun any more," she said. "When I get all dressed up to go to a premiere I'm empty inside. When people say, 'How nice you look' it doesn't mean a thing. Will didn't say it."[8] In ruminations like this, she seems to be trying to convince *herself* that she had a loving marriage. It's possible she believed it at the time, but it's hard to accept when compared with passages like this from her autobiography: "Will returned from battle in August 1943. . . . Unfortunately, war had only made him worse. He had turned angry and mean. This new dark side came out whenever he drank. In the morning, however, he wouldn't remember any of it."[9]

She said she wrote to Price three times a day and vowed to be a better wife after his wartime duties were over: "When he comes home he will find that I have progressed and have widened my horizons, both mentally and materially."[10] His actual homecoming, on a furlough, wasn't quite what she expected. He fell in the door of their home one night, accompanied by a minister friend, and passed out. The minister made a pass at her, which she spurned, but he told her not to worry about being faithful to Price: her wandering husband had been with a woman the previous night and had asked the minister to marry them! After hearing this, O'Hara ordered Price to leave the house, but he said he was too drunk to drive. She allowed him to stay under her roof with this proviso: "If you so much as come one step toward my door, I'll report you to the police and to your base immediately. Then I'll kill you."[11]

She became pregnant by him that year too. The bigger the child grew inside her, the more he seemed to rage. On a film set, she could have reported him to the producer or even to the front office, but what could she do in her own home? She was a prisoner of her fame, her marital status, and her strangely inhibited self. She viewed her life as though outside herself, wondering how she'd managed to exchange a happy home in Dublin for this house of horrors.

Yet in June 1944, not long before her baby was due to be born, she praised Price in *Photoplay* magazine. He had guided her through her pregnancy, she said, and he had been there for her during the medical complications of recent months. It was also Price who had decided the baby would be called Bronwyn, not Maureen, because "there's only one Maureen in my life and there'll not be another."[12] Did he really say that? It certainly sounds out of character. She fretted that Will might be gone to war when the baby was born. "And yet I'll not be really alone, for I shall know that no matter where Will is, our love will be the voice through which we shall speak to each other."[13]

Shortly before the birth, Price turned up on another furlough, roaring drunk and in a "particularly nasty mood." He looked at her prized collection of antique dolls and snapped, "You and those goddamned dolls. They're everywhere." When she told him they were dear to her, he said, "Well I hate them. Get them out of here." When she refused to do so, he smashed them to bits and burned them. One night he "buried his fist" in her stomach when she tried to stop him from going out drinking.[14] His mother witnessed the incident, advising her daughter-in-law to go to the police if it happened again. The blow actually endangered the life of the baby. Nights like this were almost commonplace, but they were too revolting to relate to the world or even her family. Instead, she dusted herself down and did what she did best—make movies.

By now, she worked primarily for Fox, with the proviso that she do one film a year for RKO. Her first film under the new arrangement was *Buffalo Bill*, directed by William Wellman. She plays Louisa, spouse to Buffalo Bill Cody (Joel McCrea). There's a discernible lack of depth in this plot-driven farrago, and O'Hara was understandably unhappy with it. Event follows event as the film chases its tail in an episodic search for something significant. The famous scout is trying to live peacefully with the Indians, but Chief Yellow Hand (Anthony Quinn) is having none of it. Louisa marries Bill despite her aversion to the hard life of the frontier. She undergoes a dark night of the soul when their son dies of diphtheria, but she rallies. Bill gets his second wind with a Wild West show set up by Thomas Mitchell. It all resembles a poor man's epic, a mixed grill of buffalo hunts and tenuous peace with the Indians.

McCrea gives an almost somnambulant performance. He rouses himself briefly, such as when O'Hara whispers that she's pregnant, but then reverts back to that deadpan sense of frontier calm. Quinn does his best with his lines: "It is a bad thing for man to starve; there are better ways to die." But the film's sense of earnestness is pedantic. Too many things happen too fast for comfort. The voiceover does not help. One has the sensation of viewing a comic book on film. The emotions are tabloid, the characters' reactions out of proportion to their actions. It's a tribute to O'Hara's professionalism that she maintains any semblance of credibility. She portrays a lady of simple charm, and it works—almost. Sadly, McCrea gives her little to work off. She has no lines to help her scenes reach liftoff, so she must content herself with being part of his reflected glory.

Wellman made a gallant effort to create a seminal biopic, but this is more a dutiful exercise in staid storytelling than the purported panegyric on white supremacy and westward expansion we were promised. By the time we get to Cody's Comeback Special, we're all a little weary. It's a pity the film is remembered primarily for this "overly sentimental" section, as Todd Robinson notes.[15] Wellman admired O'Hara's performance, but she characterized the film as "forgettable." She was surprised it turned out to be a box-office success, a fact she attributed mainly to the "masterful use of Technicolor" by Wellman and cinematographer Leon Shamroy, the pair of them teaming up to provide "an outdoor panoramic feast for the eyes."[16]

O'Hara had her first and only child in 1944. She called her daughter Bronwyn. After she was born, O'Hara wrote a kind of "Prayer for My

Daughter" in which she outlines her hopes for the child. Looking far into the future, she expresses the wish that Bronwyn will find a man who kisses her "first thing in the morning and last thing at night," brings her candy and flowers, and never lets the sun go down on an argument. Price and O'Hara followed that last rule: they always apologized before they slept if they were in the wrong.[17] She advises "Bron" to don "fancy nighties and fabulous *negligees*" for her man, but says it's okay to go around the house in a robe and slippers and with her hair tied plain if he isn't home. O'Hara warns Bronwyn that she'll be bringing her up the hard way, with no sparing of the rod, because children today are "spoiled rotten." O'Hara wants her daughter to have a steady job when she grows up: "I want you to know what it means to get up in the morning and go to work and have a boss yell at you and come home tired out. Then you will know how your husband feels and won't nag him, but will be understanding, sympathetic and tender, as a wife should be."[18] She doesn't advocate acting as a career, but if Bronwyn chooses it, it must come second to her marital duties.

Price was uncharacteristically busy with work at this time. According to O'Hara, he was a "producer-director" on the film *Woman on the Beach*, starring Joan Bennett and Robert Ryan.[19] O'Hara's own next venture was *The Spanish Main*, but she almost lost the role due to a vicious rumor spread by an unnamed actress. Just before she was due to report to the set, she received a phone call from Joe Nolan, an executive at RKO. He said he had heard from an up-and-coming actress that O'Hara was "as big as a horse" since giving birth. She informed Nolan that this was totally untrue, and he believed her. But it was a reality check for her, a timely reminder that any number of young hopefuls were only too willing to do whatever it took to usurp her place on the totem pole.

In *The Spanish Main*, O'Hara shows her determination not to leave her sexuality at the birthing stool. She looks deliciously fragrant in the splashy histrionics on view here, in RKO's first film in the three-color Technicolor process. She plays Contessa Francesca, the daughter of a Mexican viceroy in the Caribbean. Paul Henreid is Laurent Van Horn, the Dutch sea captain who captures her. She's engaged to be married to the corrupt governor, Don Juan Alvarado (Walter Slezak), but Van Horn wants her for himself. She reluctantly marries him, but they fight on their wedding night in a prefiguring of a similar scene in *The Quiet Man* (although O'Hara doesn't try to stab John Wayne with a knife). Francesca gradually softens to Van Horn, as O'Hara does to countless leading men in these costumers. Alvarado isn't perturbed when he learns that his fiancée has married Van Horn; he assumes he'll have no trouble hanging the lowly pirate. What he hasn't factored in is the minor detail that the beautiful Francesca is unlikely to choose an overweight beast like himself over Van Horn (even if Henreid is woefully miscast as a laughing rogue).

Binnie Barnes provides some light relief as Anne Bonney, a chirpy buccaneer. She makes fun of Francesca, who isn't as adept with a sword as Lady Margaret is in *The Black Swan*. Nor does she know how to handle a pistol. There are minor giggles in a scene in which Francesca and Bonney engage in a mock duel and end up with coal dust on their faces instead of gunpowder. This is Van Horn's idea of a joke, and it's about as riotous as he gets. (His nickname in the film is "Barracuda," but he looks more like a goldfish.) At one point he refers to Francesca as an "ornament." She's peeved at the slight, but she doesn't show much more emotion in her green bodice and elegant pigtails. She rescues Van Horn from Alvarado in a protracted narrative, and they engage in a sunset embrace at the end, in a scene reminiscent of the finale of *The Black Swan*. The whole plot is disconcertingly similar to the earlier movie, but Henreid is no Ty Power.

One day while *The Spanish Main* was being shot, John Ford came to the studio to see O'Hara, but he wasn't admitted. The guards at the gate thought he looked shabby. (O'Hara explained that he always wore old clothes because whenever his wife bought him new pants, he'd promptly burn holes in them with his cigars.) Ford left in a temper, but O'Hara called him and explained what had happened. She assured him that if he returned the following day, a red carpet would be rolled out for him. And it was. He drove his car over it and then made his way to her room. He was there to offer O'Hara a "handshake" deal on *The Quiet Man*.

It would be many years before it became anything more than that. They couldn't get the project off the ground, despite their best efforts. "All the studios turned us down," O'Hara lamented in interviews. "They said it was a little nothing Irish story that would never make a penny."[20]

O'Hara was a frequent visitor to Ford's yacht the *Araner*, which he kept at Catalina Island, off the California coast. The *Araner* was a 130-foot-long double-masted sailboat that Ford had bought in 1934 for $30,000;

he named it after the Aran Islands (situated off the coast of Galway, where his mother had been born). O'Hara spent many days on the yacht with Ford and his children, and she always brought Bronwyn with her. O'Hara would take down various drafts of the screenplay for *The Quiet Man* as Ford, wearing an old hat O'Hara's father had given him, dictated from his scribbled notes. "He'd send the kids ashore to swim," she remembered, "then put on his Irish records and chew on his handkerchief while I took notes in my Pitman shorthand and typed them up later on. I could make no comment. I just had to take down what he said and give it back to him."[21] There wasn't much small talk on such excursions, and she wasn't invited to contribute. She was a secretary, pure and simple.

O'Hara became close to Ford during this time, but he was notoriously unpredictable. Toward the end of the year, while attending a party at his house, Ford socked her in the jaw for no reason. She was too stunned to react. Had she said something to upset him? She didn't know. An interviewer once asked her why she didn't hit him back. Her response: she wanted to show him that she could "take a punch."[22]

As she waited for *The Quiet Man* to be green-lighted, she continued to feel shackled by unappetizing swashbucklers. Her frustration was obvious: "Almost every letter I receive asks why Hollywood doesn't take me out of these silly Technicolor features and give me dramatic pictures."[23] Why did she put up with such hymns to trivia? "Every one of us has to pay the groceries at the end of the week," she said. "You're cast in a film and you go, 'Mother of God, this is awful, how am I going to do it?' But you have to, whether you like it or not. You would be suspended if you turned down a script. You would be put off salary."[24] Lew Wasserman's old words of warning had burned themselves into her soul.

However, the stars who were willing to risk suspension created better roles not only for themselves but also for their colleagues. They created a groundswell of discontent, a spirit of rebellion against the dictatorial warlords of the studios. After Olivia de Havilland made *Gone with the Wind*, she was given a succession of worthless scripts and refused them all. Jack Warner suspended her each time, but after the seventh suspension, she filed suit in the Superior Court of California, as this was the maximum number of times an employer could force a contract on an employee. Warner blacklisted her with every studio in Hollywood, and she didn't work for three years as a result. But in March 1944 a decision was handed down whereby stars could refuse roles without having the resulting layoff period added to the duration of their contracts. It was a limited victory, but an important one. Everybody, including O'Hara, benefited from this ruling, as it took away part of the fear of saying no to a role, thereby weakening the patriarchal studio system.

Her next film would prove to be one of her most memorable ones, albeit for all the wrong reasons. In *Sentimental Journey* she plays Julie, an actress with a fatal heart condition. She doesn't tell her husband Bill (John Payne), for fear of what the revelation will do to him. He dearly wants a child, so Julie decides to "adopt" one so he'll have something to remember her by after she's gone. One day while she's walking along the beach, she meets a little girl called Hitty (Connie Marshall). They become friendly and start to bond. Julie adopts Hitty, without telling Bill. After Julie dies, Bill is inconsolable, and he neglects the child, who almost drowns on the beach where Julie first met her. Payne rescues her and then realizes his future now resides in this little girl, Julie's posthumous gift to him.

The trade papers lambasted the film, but it appealed to the "six Kleenex brigade," who tended to flock to soapers like this one. Marshall bore the brunt of the abuse. A critic described her as "just another one of those precocious Hollywood juvenile products who in workaday life would benefit from a good hiding."[25] *Sentimental Journey* was voted the Worst Film of All Time by Harvard. Bosley Crowther accused it of being "a compound of hackneyed situations, maudlin dialogue and preposterously bad acting." From the moment O'Hara clutches ominously at her heart after being told by Sir Cecil Hardwicke that it's weak, "the gradient to blubbering bathos begins." From the moment the "vaporish" O'Hara meets the toddler Marshall on the beach and is mistaken for the Lady of Shalott, the treacle begins to flow. It becomes more viscous when Marshall babbles to Payne about sea horses and unicorns, and it "plainly solidifies to taffy" after O'Hara takes her leave of the world.[26]

Few could quibble with this estimation, but critics don't pay actors' wages. The public does. And the public went for it hook, line, and sinker. It became a "honey" for audiences worldwide. O'Hara wasn't too troubled by the critics' reactions; she fed off the film's goodwill for years. Often when she traveled to foreign countries, people would come up to her and sigh

"Oh, you were in my favorite movie." She would be expecting them to say it was *The Hunchback of Notre Dame* or *The Quiet Man* or maybe *How Green Was My Valley*, but they often named *Sentimental Journey*.[27]

Payne enjoyed the experience of working with O'Hara. He spoke of the film in glowing terms, citing it as the favorite of his whole career. "I played a grieving widower," he exulted to a reporter, "and when I tell you that my late wife was played by Maureen O'Hara you'll know why I was grieving." This was high praise indeed.[28]

She was less happy with her costars in *Do You Love Me?* (1946), neither of whom was a "real" actor: Harry James was primarily a trumpeter, and Dick Haymes a crooner. It was her first starring role for Fox, and the film is typical of the lightweight, postwar fripperies Hollywood was churning out with astonishing regularity at the time. Shortly after shooting began, O'Hara was groped by the film's producer, George Jessel, and screamed holy hell. In the simpler era of the 1940s, that was all it took. She didn't need to file a lawsuit or delay work on the movie. She yelled so loudly, she recalled in her memoirs, "You could hear my voice echoing outside my trailer." The incident hit the trade papers, and Jessel backed off.[29]

The plot has O'Hara playing the bespectacled dean of a Philadelphia music academy who decides to trade prissiness for glamour when she takes an interest in swing music. Her superiors at the academy aren't impressed and fire her, but she won't be deterred, teaming up with James to perform on campus. Common sense prevails, and she is reinstated as dean. In addition to James, Haymes is now sniffing around her as well, along with the school's business manager, played by Richard Gaines. O'Hara has her pick of men, and she chooses Haymes in the end. The film's director, Gregory Ratoff, wasn't satisfied, so he thought up a new ending: James gets into a cab occupied by his real-life wife Betty Grable—consolation for losing O'Hara.[30]

Jeanine Basinger sees the film as the story of "a mouseburger who becomes a sexpot" as a result of being "jeweled and gowned." Basinger goes on to note that character transformation in a "woman's picture" is often a function of sartorial splendor—or what we might call "power dressing" today.[31] It's a moot point. O'Hara felt underused in the role, and she didn't even get to sing. She should have, although the songs are nothing special. Haymes covers the cracks in the plot and dialogue with a kind of sleek professionalism, but even he can't rescue this limp revue.

Darryl F. Zanuck offered O'Hara a part in *The Razor's Edge* while she was shooting *Do You Love Me?* He warned her not to mention it to anyone, but she couldn't keep the secret and blurted out her news to Linda Darnell while the two were having lunch, not knowing that Darnell was Zanuck's mistress. That afternoon, she was asked to call Zanuck. "I told you you were not to discuss our meeting," he roared down the line, "but you did and you're now out of the picture."[32] Darnell didn't get the role either. It went to her friend Gene Tierney. The score between O'Hara and Tierney was now one each, considering O'Hara had edged Tierney out of the running for *How Green Was My Valley*.

Regardless of talent, success often depended on a roll of the dice or who one knew. Another role that escaped O'Hara was the lead in *The King and I*. Zanuck wanted her instead of Deborah Kerr, but when Richard Rodgers (of Rodgers and Hammerstein) heard she was in the running, he threw his hands in the air and roared, "A pirate queen to play my Anna? No!" O'Hara pined, "They never even listened to my recording."[33]

She was also offered a role in *The Paleface* with Bob Hope, "but at the time I was going through a difficult period of my life and I didn't think I would be able to laugh every day and have fun. Against my better judgment but feeling I was being honorable and fair to Bob Hope, I turned it down. Jane Russell got the job and I've regretted it all my life. It was a terrible mistake. I should have kicked myself in the rear end." One can understand her frustration at losing a classic like *The Razor's Edge*, but hardly a lightweight comedy like this. She became philosophical about such losses, reflecting, "There's many who regret the parts they didn't get, but there's some who regret they didn't get mine in *The Quiet Man*."[34] (According to author Darwin Porter, she also turned down a potentially career-changing role in Frank Capra's *It's a Wonderful Life*. This is hard to believe, and one must be dubious of Porter's credibility, considering some of the outrageous allegations he has made in his many biographies.)

One reason she lost plum roles, in her view, was her refusal to sleep with Hollywood's power players: "I wouldn't throw myself on the casting couch and I know that cost me parts. I wasn't going to play the whore. That wasn't me."[35] She also felt her squeaky-clean lifestyle worked against her; she lacked the "edge" directors wanted for the spicier parts. "Hollywood won't consider me anything but a cold potato," she complained, "until I divorce my husband, give my baby away and get my name in all the papers."[36]

When her frustration over not getting quality parts reached the boiling point, she gave an interview to the *Los Angeles Times* to vent. "Producers look at a pretty face," she griped, "and think: 'She must have got this far on her looks.' Then along comes a girl with a plain face and they think, 'She must be a great actress, she isn't pretty.' So they give her the glamour treatment and the pretty girl gets left behind."[37] There was a price to pay for everything: "Because I photographed well in color, I missed out on all the great roles that were still being done in black and white."[38] People missed the forest for the titian tresses. An old Hollywood adage goes, "There's no poverty in Technicolor." It proved true for O'Hara. The gloss of color cut her off from a good 50 percent of the meaty parts. But, she said, "I proved there was a bloody good actress in me. It wasn't just my face. I gave bloody good performances." She was now at the pinnacle—or nadir—of what she referred to as her "hoop skirts and bonnet" period. "No more duchesses, countesses and great ladies with bangs and parasols," she pleaded. "Instead the kind of women that Greer Garson and Irene Dunne play. Women who are alive. Not living today, necessarily, but alive."[39] By now, the sense of thwarted potential had become a running sore with her. But she might as well have been talking to the wall.

Her tirade was answered with yet another ocean opera, *Sinbad the Sailor*. A riot of color, it chronicles the eighth mission of the nautical hero. O'Hara is Princess Shireen to Douglas Fairbanks Jr.'s Sinbad in a razzmatazz of fun and frolics. Anthony Quinn is the villain, and the ubiquitous Walter Slezak—appearing opposite O'Hara for the third time in four years—is equally entertaining as an eccentric Mongolian barber.

The quality cast handle their lines well, but they are encumbered by a stilted plot and a set that looks more like a painted tapestry than the ninth-century Orient. For all their sumptuous color, the props, like the characters, never become more than cardboard cutouts. For an action film, there isn't much action; Sinbad doesn't sail much, either. He spends most of his time orating, as do most of the cast. O'Hara looks splendid and gets to wear some of the most stunning costumes of her career—a different one in almost every scene—but her dialogue is floridly empty. She exudes potential in the early scenes, where her air of sybaritic slyness seems to promise she'll be something more than window dressing, but the film is almost totally lacking in drama until the fairly sensational death of Quinn's villain. The fight scenes are overly orchestrated—as false as the sets on which they're shot.

Fairbanks had just come back from performing high-level strategic intelligence work during the war. He was entranced by O'Hara's beauty, particularly in the scanty apparel she wore here, but found her physically distant, in line with her "Frozen Champagne" sobriquet. The fact that she had resisted the casting couch and extramarital affairs even led to a rumor that she was a lesbian. That allegation was so ridiculous she could only laugh at it. As for the Frozen Champagne tag, this was her reaction: "How do you want champagne, piping hot?"

Dr. Paul Singh, RKO's technical adviser on *Sinbad*, was impressed by O'Hara's sexual coyness. "Women should never walk around completely undressed in front of their husbands," he opined. "That's the quickest way to lose him. He'll look for somebody who keeps part of her figure a mystery." O'Hara, he concluded "wore just enough to be tantalizing."[40] Her garb, he felt, was even more sexual than nudity. Perhaps these costuming decisions were due to a directive issued by Will Hays's cohort Joseph Breen. Breen had read a report stating that O'Hara's outfits for *Sinbad* would make her costumes in *The Spanish Main* look positively puritanical.[41] By now, her outfits were garnering more interest than the plots. The *New York Times* intoned snidely, "The costumes worn by Miss O'Hara are most fetchingly displayed by Miss O'Hara and most fetchingly display Miss O'Hara, which exhausts the subject of O'Hara."[42] One is reminded of Constance Bennett's self-denunciation: "I'm a lot more sartorial than thespian. They come to see me and go out humming costumes."[43]

O'Hara continued to laugh all the way to the bank, but deep down, she knew something was wrong. "If you receive too many compliments on the costume you're wearing," she espoused, "it's a failure. The important thing is for people to find you attractive without knowing why." Inner beauty was what she sought—and a way out of being a slave to fashion: "I know women who always wear what is new, yet they look like the devil."[44]

Back at the ranch, she continued to maintain an aura of connubial bliss as she drifted farther and farther away from Price. Bronwyn was the only light of her days. Price's extravagance gnawed at her, as did his bluff good cheer. The games played by Bronwyn, coupled with her quirky comments on the world opening up before her, made O'Hara's days go round. They helped her forget the bad stuff, or at least put it to the back of her mind.

When Sheilah Graham came to interview O'Hara for an article in *Photoplay* magazine in 1947, the gossip columnist met Price in the driveway. He was carrying a saw because he was about to build a doghouse for their Great Dane, Tripoli, and joked to Graham, "I'm the only husband in captivity who builds his own doghouse."[45] This is one of the few recorded comments from Price about his marriage. Is it conceivable that he saw *himself* as the victim, rather than O'Hara? (He died long before she wrote about the "real" Will Price in her memoirs, so her allegations against him went unanswered.)

O'Hara seemed the picture of contentment as she chatted with Graham about Bronwyn, who sat beside them chortling into a make-believe phone. She insisted that she wanted more children, and if they didn't arrive naturally, she was going to adopt some: "A fortune teller in Ireland told me I'd have two redheaded sons."[46] (The fortune teller was obviously way off.) She stressed the importance of family over career, indicating a desire to make only one movie per year so she'd have more time at home. "We're very family people. Will has a million cousins and we like to have our relatives around." She didn't even like dining out. "It kills us to go out because we'll be missing something good at home. Will sometimes gets up in the middle of the night and I'll find him in the kitchen eating cold beans with homemade mayonnaise."[47] Was this meant to conduce to the excitement, or was she just trying to be funny?

The interview ended with O'Hara informing Graham that she'd lost weight when Price was in the marines due to worrying about his welfare. "The girl nearly lost her mind with anxiety," Graham wrote, warming to her theme. O'Hara went on to say that she was now building a swimming pool, "not to impress Hollywood. Just for Will and me." Graham's last sentence completes the rose-tinted picture: "And there you have the keynote to Maureen O'Hara. It's 'Will and Me.'"[48]

In truth, the keynote to Maureen O'Hara was "Bronwyn and me." Her life at this time was a succession of manic work schedules followed by equally manic mothering. After each day's filming, she removed her makeup as quickly as she could and prayed the traffic lights would be with her as she rushed from the studio so that she could get home in time to give the little girl her bedtime kiss. If Price was sober, she'd tell him the day's news; if not, she would read or telephone a family member or catch up on the household chores. If she was entertaining, which didn't happen often, the house would be scrubbed clean, with everything laid out to perfection. Guests would arrive, and the talk would turn to politics, religion, or show business. O'Hara would defend traditional values, cajole her company, and enthrall them with stories from the "Old Country"—tales of fairy rings, leprechauns, ghosts, banshees, and black cats—and superstitious fables, some of which she even believed herself. On such evenings, her guests knew enough not to enter into debates with her. She held strong views but preserved a sense of levity—in contrast to the image of hauteur she seemed to exude on the set.

It was an action-packed life, but one that was empty at the core. The days and nights became a metronomic continuum of fulfilling work and idle play, her need for emotional stability uneasily welded onto the ambitiousness that had been driven into her as a young woman. As the years passed, she became inured to such contradictions. Movies were her protection against falling into the same pit as Price. Work was more therapy than art by now, a way of coping with an inane and insane marriage.

This was her attitude when she stepped onto the set of *The Homestretch* in 1947. She plays a refined Boston beauty, Leslie Hale, who lives with her maiden aunt and is engaged to a dull diplomat named Bill Van Dyke III. But when Leslie meets raffish racehorse owner Jock Wallace (Cornel Wilde), he turns her head and sweeps her off her feet. Before she knows what's happening, she's left her boring life behind and is tripping the light fantastic with Jock. Another woman from his past, Kitty Brant (Helen Walker), is still on the scene, but Leslie isn't unduly worried about her or about Jock's drinking. She marries him, confident that love will conquer any potential problems. Jock offers liberation to Leslie, but at a price. He's unlikely to settle down after marriage. Bill would obviously be a safer bet, but a life with him would lack excitement.

Zanuck felt the film failed "because we told the story of human beings and not the story of a horse." People usually believe the converse about films that feature animals, but he had a point. He thought the film was compromised because it tried to mix the two stories: "The people who want to see Cornel Wilde and Maureen O'Hara in a bedroom do not want to see the problems of a cow pony. And the people who want to see the problems of Smoky do not give a damn whether Cornel Wilde is in or out of the picture, and they're certainly not interested in his problems with a society girl."[49]

O'Hara received this dubious praise for her performance: "Her perfect clearcut features register no shades of emotion and her poise in any circumstance remains correct and undisturbed. She is ravishing in Technicolor. Who can give a thought to horses when she adorns the screen?"[50] She could be forgiven for detecting a tinge of irony in these comments.

Disenchanted with her career, she contemplated her own "home stretch" as she planned a trip back to Dublin. She hadn't been home since the beginning of the war—or, as it was referred to in Ireland, the "Emergency." Her family was hoarding whatever meager rations they could accumulate, planning to pamper her upon her return. She was really looking forward to seeing them, and when she received permission to fly home in 1946, she "jumped at the chance."[51] Who could blame her?

By this point, her sister Margot had also become an actress, appearing in *I Know Where I'm Going!*, a British romance, in 1945 and *The Captive Heart*, a war film, the year after. Both parts were negligible. Her other sister, Florrie, had a bit part in *Hotel Reserve*, another war movie, in 1944. Florrie was based in Montreal now, and Margot in San Diego.

O'Hara's decision to return to "Erin's green shore" embroiled her in a fracas that ended up on the front pages of newspapers on both sides of the Atlantic Ocean. When she applied for an American passport, she was informed she would first have to renounce her allegiance to Britain. This confounded her, since she didn't have such an allegiance. Thus began a lengthy process of patriotic to-ing and fro-ing. She refused to allow American authorities to list her nationality as British on her citizenship application and took her case to court. Her refusal to recognize Ireland's old colonial enemy as her native home forced the United States to acknowledge Irish citizenship for the first time. It was a huge campaign on her part and received massive media coverage. Ireland's then-president Eamon de Valera, who had fought in the War of Independence in 1916, hung a photograph of O'Hara on his wall as a tribute to her fighting spirit. She remained rightly proud of her part in shaping the future history of her fellow Irish citizens abroad, the so-called green army.

The captain of the plane that brought O'Hara to Ireland was Charles Blair, the man she would eventually marry. For now, though, he was just a family friend.

She felt emotional being home. She had left as a would-be starlet and was returning as a seasoned professional of the screen. But that didn't matter to her. She was Maureen FitzSimons again, making a "sentimental journey" back to the people who loved her. The prime motivation was to introduce her daughter to the family. Bronwyn ended up getting even more attention than her mother. All the way from Shannon Airport to Dublin, Maureen's father sang Irish songs to the toddler. In the following days, her parents and siblings oohed and aahed over Bronwyn, and O'Hara had to tell them to stop, for fear of spoiling her.

The talk turned to movies. Her brothers Charles and Jimmy expressed a wish to go back to Hollywood with her. She promised to organize some tests for them with Warner Brothers. Her parents were dubious, however, being suspicious of the life of a movie star. They thought Maureen looked awful, that she needed to eat more. "They had forgotten how Hollywood stars are supposed to look," O'Hara concluded, "all slender and not too well padded. They were used to the womanly curves of the Irish lasses."[52]

A reporter asked her if she thought Ireland had changed, and she responded that she lamented its increasing urbanization. Ranelagh and Milltown had once been like the countryside; now the conurbation of postwar housing made everywhere look the same—the suburbs had become part of the inner city by proxy.

She attended the premiere of *Do You Love Me?* and it proved to be a gala turnout. So many people were there that some of them ended up standing on the stairs (in contravention of fire regulations). After the movie ended, she found a gaggle of children engulfing her car. One official told her he hadn't seen so many fans since Gene Autry had visited Dublin years before. But in general people left her alone, unlike in Hollywood. If they passed her on the street they just said hello and went on their way. The Irish were less frothy than Americans when it came to seeing film stars in the flesh.

Her vacation was spoiled by a call from Twentieth Century–Fox requesting her presence back on the lot. They wanted her for a film called *Miracle on 34th Street*. It would become one of the most memorable of her career, but she couldn't know that at the time. She was infuriated at the studio's impatience. "I just got here," she pleaded, "I don't want to go back."[53] She'd waited many years for her trip home, and now it looked to be ending prematurely. Because it was a low-budget movie, Fox couldn't afford to waste any time. Either she came back immediately, or she was out of the picture. So she signed for the film without knowing anything about it. "I didn't know what the script was about," she gasped. "I didn't know anything except I was ordered by my boss to be back in New York."[54] She was furious. Maybe that was why, during a radio interview in Ireland, she described being an actress as "a hard physical and mental life, and completely unglamorous."[55]

She departed Ireland grudgingly but got full value from her visit. As she alighted from the plane in New York, she was carrying five coats in one arm and Bronwyn's toys and a miniature vacuum cleaner in the other. Bronwyn herself had dolls, pandas, and teddies all tied together by a string, a total of fifteen items in all.

When she reached the studio a few days later and read the script, her spirits picked up. She also learned she would be working with a quality cast: John Payne, Edmund Gwenn, Thelma Ritter, William Frawley, and Porter Hall. "When these people did their scenes," she enthused, "you didn't go and lock yourself in the dressing-room. You'd stay around and watch."[56] She was particularly enraptured by Gwenn. He immersed himself so completely in the role he *became* the character.

The film's story begins when an actor playing Santa at Macy's department store is discovered to be drunk by a man who actually looks the part (Gwenn). O'Hara plays Doris Walker, Macy's special events director, and she persuades the man to take the drunk Santa's place. But he creates a stir when he tells people his name is Kris Kringle. More ominously, he tells customers that anything Macy's doesn't have, Gimbel's might. Doris sacks him but later has to reverse her decision when his eccentricity starts to drum up positive publicity for the store. The personnel manager, Granville Sawyer (Porter Hall), believes Kringle should be committed to an institution. John Payne plays Fred Galley, the attorney who romances Doris and ultimately goes to bat for Kris, who is having fun with the whole business. Doris has raised her daughter Susie (Natalie Wood) to believe in only what she can see and touch, so Susie tells Kringle, "You're just a nice old man with whiskers." But then things change. Kringle introduces Susie to a whole new world of wonder when he tantalizingly asks her, "How would you like to be able to make snowballs in the summertime? Or drive a great big bus right down Fifth Avenue? How would you like to have a ship all to yourself that makes daily trips to China or Australia? How would you like to be the Statue of Liberty in the morning, then in the afternoon fly south with a flock of geese?" We're getting way beyond the issue of the existence of Santa Claus here, but this film was never really *just* about Christmas, despite the zealous TV program planners who foist it on us every Yuletide. It's more a parable about getting in touch with our better selves.

There are problems with O'Hara's character. The reasons for her hardness aren't properly explained; her alcoholic ex-husband was virtually eliminated from the plot on Zanuck's instructions. Zanuck dearly wanted to be "Capraesque," but he succeeded only in making Doris's insistence on "life's harsh realities" less credible to the audience.[57] She's cold to Susie, and we don't really know why.

Shirley Temple supposedly stopped believing in Santa Claus when she sat on his knee in a department store and he asked for her autograph. Something similar could have happened to Natalie Wood if she hadn't met Gwenn. On the set, she really believed he was Santa. At the end of the shoot, though, there was a party, "and I saw this strange man without the beard," she recalled, "and I just couldn't get it together."[58]

O'Hara bonded with Wood in the same way she would with another child star years later: Hayley Mills in *The Parent Trap*. Natalie called her "Mama Maureen," she reminisced fondly, "in a very happy young girl's way." She used to make ceramic figurines and give them to O'Hara as gifts.

The top brass at Fox were so dubious about *Miracle* that they decided to "dump it on the market," to use Wood's phrase, in the middle of summer. They had little hope for a film with a "portly, white-whiskered geriatric patient" as its hero, so they "smuggled" it out.[59] Imagine their surprise when it became such a hit that Gimbel's took out a full-page ad in the *New York Times* to congratulate its competitor.[60] Maybe we shouldn't be surprised to learn that for many years after its release, Gwenn received letters addressed to him as "Santa Claus, Care of MGM."[61] The public vicariously allied itself with the film's central motif.

As so often happened in O'Hara's life, celluloid success warred with domestic strife. Her home life continued to go downhill, the elation of the Irish trip and the movie undercut by Price's discharge from the Marine Corps. This meant he would come home for good, decimating her bank account as he partied like there was no tomorrow.

In an interview with *Screen Stars*, O'Hara claimed money didn't matter to her. She probably should have said that it did matter, but not as much as love. Most Hollywood insiders were aware of how frugal she was. Living with the extravagant Price, maybe she had to be. She spent hours ferreting out auctions and discount stores. "I feel very happy when I get a bargain," she revealed. "I turn out the lights when I leave the room: I don't let them burn all night. I never throw out food. We have one 'left-over' meal a week."[62]

Covering for Price's poor earning power, she tried to spare him embarrassment by telling the interviewer, "I make more money than Will now but I'll make it for a shorter period of time. Will's career will be longer than mine. Fifteen years from now, the overall picture will show that he was the person who put the most money in the bank." She must have known this projection of events was laughable. Equally incomprehensible was her declaration that Price had "built" her house for her: "Not a cent of my money went into it. He pays the household expenses, the utilities, the grocery bill, the nurse's, cook's and gardener's salaries, the upkeep of the cars—everything."[63] In contrast, she wrote in her autobiography: "All the bills for running the house continued to be paid out of my account while Will ran around town like a high-rollin' playboy."[64]

After being demobbed from the marines, Price bought a house in Bel Air for the pair of them—with her money. It was a palatial mansion with five bedrooms, five bathrooms, and a four-car garage with its own gas station in the basement. O'Hara was now earning a salary of $2,000 a week, but "it wouldn't be enough to cover the costs of the new house, nanny, cook, maid, laundress, chauffeur, gardener, pool man, and Will's special talent for blowing money on booze, dames and the races."[65] Lew Wasserman managed to get her a hefty raise to $4,000 a week to help cover her expenses. Price was thrilled at this news, and he hired a business manager named Bill Duce. Duce promptly opened a separate bank account for Price, and half of O'Hara's salary was deposited into that account every week— nice work if you can get it. (For reasons even she could not fathom, O'Hara continued to employ Duce after her marriage to Price broke up.)

She was reunited with her sisters Florrie and Margot after the war and treasured their company. After all the years they spent apart, she enjoyed even the most trivial revelations from them; her virtual starvation of news from the "shamrock patch" fed her enthusiasm as she pumped them for information about family and friends from home. They responded in kind, quizzing her for details about her own radically different lifestyle, rubbing shoulders with the great and the good of Hollywood. The only time the sisters weren't talking was "when we're asleep," she said delightedly.

O'Hara's two sisters were both military wives. Florrie had married a Canadian serviceman who went into business in Montreal, and Margot had married a marine major she met at the British embassy in London. All three sisters had children under three years old and were committed homemakers. One evening when Price took them all to a nightclub, the women went home early to play Patience as they watched over their babies. Florence looked so much like Maureen that Bronwyn thought she had "two mommies."[66] A similar confusion assailed her years later when, visiting her aunt Peggy, who was a nun, she concluded that the convent was full of Aunt Peggys!

We can see history starting to repeat itself here, the insulated nature of O'Hara's upbringing in Ireland being transposed onto the glitzy tableau of Hollywood. Whether one was in Bel Air or "Bel Eire" (Ireland's nickname for the playground of its stellar expatriates), some things never really changed at all.

5

Civvy Street

Postwar Hollywood underwent many of the same cultural shifts as the nation at large. A new conservatism assailed it, combined with what Jesse Lasky Jr. called "dislocation": "We felt unable to pick up the pieces of our old life, unready to plant seeds for the new. We were like emotional tumbleweed. Some younger GIs who had been wild and loose before the war rushed back to seize the stability of children, marriage, mortgages to be paid off." Solid life patterns ensued, and a vote for "Daddy-loves-you" Eisenhower.[1]

For O'Hara and Price, however, things went on as before. He continued to live lavishly and she continued to fund him. That course of action was marginally less problematic than all-out war with him, or divorce. She was getting so much satisfaction out of her work that his extravagance (and his frequent dalliances with other women) could be put aside, at least in the short term. As for what lay down the road, she would deal with that when she had to. The fact that their marriage was over in all but name gave her a strange kind of relief. She knew there was nothing worth saving, so she didn't have to think about it.

O'Hara had never been a particularly sociable person, being decidedly averse to klieg lights and the paparazzi. In 2000, when Larry King suggested that life in the 1940s must have been phenomenal for an actress in "this town" (i.e., Hollywood), she replied, "The *town* was phenomenal. It wasn't the people."[2] "I never made many friends," she admitted in 1940, "and I don't make many now. I don't like parties and I don't like nightclubs. I like my radio and I like my own fireside. I like one or two close friends, only one or two."[3] She suggested to Helen Weller of *Motion Picture* magazine that her "sit-by-the-fire" personality resulted from a pronounced awkwardness in the company of others, an inability to make small talk. She claimed to have overcome this shyness at the instigation of a friend, Stephen Ames, who warned that her inferiority complex could be misinterpreted as precisely the opposite unless she did something about it. As a result of this advice, one night at a party she forced herself to join a group of people. Before she knew what was happening, she was laughing away with them. From that moment on, she never looked back, having lost her "dread" of being in the midst of large groups.[4]

She may not have been a big player on the party circuit (an important part of networking for any actress), but she had a healthy rapport with the studio bosses, which was a different kind of advantage. She didn't give them "lip." Harry Cohn had a special regard for her. One day, he broke down and started blubbering like a baby because his wife and children were about to convert to Catholicism. He confided in O'Hara because she was, in his view, the only person he knew who understood both Catholicism and Judaism. She was astounded by his emotional vulnerability (not a quality Cohn was known for) and by how much he knew about her family, including that they were in the clothing business and that her mother was a singer and her father a soccer fan.[5]

O'Hara also knew how to ingratiate herself with Darryl F. Zanuck, when she needed to. Zanuck had a terrible sense of style, but that didn't stop him from bullying people about their wardrobes. One day O'Hara was wearing a beautiful green chiffon gown for a role she was playing. Zanuck didn't like it, which threw her, so she said she would change it (but didn't). The following day she purred, "Mr. Zanuck, you were so right, look at the dress now." He said, "See? See? It's perfect!" But O'Hara hadn't changed a stitch.[6] Her psychology worked.

She usually rose to the moguls' defense when they were attacked. A familiar tirade of hers was, "People don't want to hear wonderful things about those old boys and want to make them out to be monsters. They were tough but there was a unity and you were taken care of. It was a system where you knew you were cared for, and about."[7]

After the elation of *Miracle on 34th Street*, she sank herself in a routine historical drama, *The Foxes of Harrow*, playing opposite Rex Harrison, an actor she grew to despise. A stodgy Frank Yerby mini-epic, it's set in antebellum New Orleans and documents the fortunes of an illegitimate Irish philanderer (Harrison) who's expelled from a riverboat for cheating. He then seduces the wealthy Odalie Lillie D'Arceneaux (O'Hara) and gets her to marry him. (The pomposity of her screen name prepares one for what's to come.) Afterward they live in a mansion he won in a card game. The marriage is a disaster from the outset. He is more interested in her social status than anything else, and her defiance of him clashes with his ice-cold sneering. Their life together is like one long bleat of mourning. After their child is born, he advocates tough love, but that isn't her way. They grow further apart, and then tragedy strikes. One night he threatens to hit her, and their son rushes to her defense, resulting in a fatal trip on the stairs. Can life get any worse? Yes: Harrison loses his fortune too. But, purified by suffering, he edges toward a tenuous reconciliation with his wife at the end.

O'Hara struggled with the meretricious excesses of this cardboard *Gone with the Wind*. She flattered the material with a solid performance, her strength of character shot through with her disdain for Harrison, but he gave little back. The irony is that this could have been one of her most highly acclaimed performances, were it not for the overblown dialogue and the creaky characterization. Frankly, my dear, nobody really gave a damn about her upper-crust pretensions.

The relationship between O'Hara and Harrison was fractious through-out the shoot. He thought she disapproved of him simply because he was British. To pay her back for her rudeness, he belched in her face during their dancing sequences. He also accused her of making anti-Semitic remarks on the set. (Lilli Palmer, his wife at the time, was Jewish.) O'Hara strenuously denied these allegations.

Harrison became a figure of fun for the film's crew, who dubbed him "Sexy Rexy" in ironic mode. He seemed to have little trouble getting wom-en, but a lot of trouble holding on to them. Two of them, Carole Landis and Rachel Roberts, committed suicide after their relationships with him turned sour. Most biographies of Harrison testify to a thoroughly vain and self-obsessed individual whose patina of sophistication hid a ruthlessly ambitious edge.

O'Hara confirms that estimation of him in her memoirs, ending her ruminations on Harrison by claiming his career was "never the same" after Landis committed suicide.[8] In contrast to her ungraciousness to him in her book, he says nothing against O'Hara in his, merely remarking that he'd been miscast in the film. "They dressed me up in all sorts of elaborate clothes," he propounded self-deprecatingly, "and for the first and only time

I can remember, gave me a moustache. This did not do for me what it had done for David Niven or Ronald Colman."[9]

The film didn't endear itself to either the public or the critics. Bosley Crowther demolished it in the *New York Times*, accusing it of being over-stuffed with "the fattiest of romantic clichés."[10] Maybe so, but its message of the virtues of domestic harmony appealed to O'Hara, as she explained in an interview: "Take any girl you see on the street—ask her what she wants to be. She'll say, 'Secretary, teacher, artist, model' or any number of other professions. Not one will say, 'I just want to be a good wife.'" O'Hara believed family values were on the decline: "Happy husbands and wives are considered dull news. The divorces are given the glamour treatment."[11]

While she was filming *The Foxes of Harrow*, Price's brother Kenny, a lawyer, was discharged from the navy and was invited to stay with the family. Bronwyn liked him, and so did O'Hara. She hoped he would help get his brother off the drink. (Kenny was a teetotaler.) When Kenny expressed an interest in Nancy Gates, an actress friend of O'Hara's, she introduced them, and soon they were dating. Then, before she knew it, they were en-gaged to be married. But Kenny had developed a problem with alcohol that turned out to be just as serious as his brother's. Instead of Kenny getting Will *off* the drink, Will got Kenny *on* it. Kenny was also diagnosed as being manic-depressive. O'Hara felt guilty for inadvertently dragging Gates into her vortex of misery.

Gates broke off the engagement, and Kenny went into therapy. He admitted he only wanted to marry her so he could be a kept man, like his brother. Luckily, she escaped that fate. But Kenny's life went further down-hill after she ended their relationship. He had electric shock treatment for his depression, but it didn't work; he ended his life by smashing his car into a wall—deliberately. O'Hara was devastated. Alcoholism, she concluded, obviously ran in the Price family.

She always worried that her husband would crash his car, too (par-ticularly when Bronwyn was with him). Price had nearly killed the two of them once when O'Hara was driving and he tried to wrest the steering wheel from her on a dangerous bend. She narrowly averted disaster on that occasion. He didn't seem to care whether he lived or died sometimes, which made him doubly dangerous to herself and "Bron." But brooding on such scenarios was fruitless: who knew what the future held?

She started work on a new movie, a suburban comedy called *Sitting Pretty*, featuring Clifton Webb as a male babysitter called Lynn Belvedere. The plot is thin, but the verbal asides are spot-on. Audiences had already witnessed Webb's facility with acerbic one-liners in the films *Laura* and *The Razor's Edge*. O'Hara plays Tacey King, the wife of lawyer Harry (Robert Young). They live in the fashionable Hummingbird Hill suburb, but she and Harry are having trouble controlling their three wild sons, who specialize in driving successive nannies round the twist. She advertises for a mature, live-in maid, expecting to hire a woman, but the redoubtable Belvedere answers the ad. He deals with the Kings' brood as one might expect W. C. Fields to handle it: with undisguised indifference. Tacey is happy when he dumps a bowl of oatmeal over one of her son's heads. If she had tried it herself, she probably would have had the same done to her, but coming from Belvedere, the gesture works. The boy is rendered submissive, and Belvedere is a living example of the practical benefits of tough love.

Things get awkward for Tacey when she starts to indulge her hobby for sculpture, using Lynn as a model. A gossipy neighbor played by Richard Haydn puts two and two together and gets five. Noticing that Tacey and Lynn are spending an inordinate amount of time together, he deduces they're having an affair behind Harry's back. This is exactly what Lynn wants him to believe. Since his arrival at the King household, he's been spending an inordinate amount of time in his room, and nobody knows what he's up to in there. In fact, he's writing a book about the bitchiness of suburban gossip. Harry almost loses his job as a result of the rumormongering, but it all ends well. The community becomes famous as a result of the sardonic book, and the nosy neighbor gets his comeuppance.

Webb steals the film with his affectations of roguish omniscience, and Young and O'Hara have the good sense to allow him to do so: anything less would have been churlish. Belvedere rocks Hummingbird Hill to its foundations as he unseats prejudices and exposes peeping toms. His dissembling of the bourgeois values of small-town America is enacted with acidic glee. Some of his one-liners ("Money is the root of all evil, and I have the greatest possible respect for it") are almost Groucho-esque in tone. When Tacey tells him at the end that he can't stay because she's expecting a baby, he replies, "Then you will find me of great service, Mrs. King. I was also an obstetrician."

Webb hadn't been looking forward to making the movie, according to a recent biography by David L. Smith, as he'd heard O'Hara was difficult to work with. Happily, this proved not to be the case, and he found her most affable.[12] O'Hara won the Redbook Gold Medal for her performance, but Webb went one further with an Oscar nomination. (He might have won but had the misfortune to be up against Laurence Olivier for *Hamlet* that year: a David and Goliath encounter.) More important, a significant amount of work came his way on the back of the movie, including two sequels.

Offscreen, O'Hara was living in her own version of Hummingbird Hill with Price. She allowed few people to know how miserable she really was, a poor little rich girl drying up her tears behind lace curtains. "You can't whine," she exclaimed, "I don't like whiners." As it did for many others in her predicament, motherhood came to her rescue. She transferred all the love she might have given to a husband to her child. In February 1948 she chatted merrily with Herb Howe about how wonderful it was to be married to Price, even giving him credit for landing her the part of Angharad in *How Green Was My Valley*.[13]

Another interview around this time had her trotting out the uxorious niceties that came with being "Mrs. William Price," wife of the master of the house.[14] When the phone rang, she said, it had to be answered with the words, "This is the Price residence." She mentioned that although she'd had a nurse for Bronwyn during the war years, she'd had to forgo some of her servants and close down some rooms. "If we were without servants I could and did clean my own house."[15] The picture emerged of a bountiful hostess ingratiating herself with the hired help: "Housekeeping became a habit with me and it certainly pays off in peace of mind and a happy house. The servants too have more respect for a mistress who knows how to clean a bathtub thoroughly, to scrub and wash and iron."[16]

O'Hara made *The Forbidden Street* in 1949 (it was released in Britain as *Brittania Mews*). But she didn't have her heart in it, and she admitted her performance was under par. The film was saved from disaster by its fine supporting cast of Sybil Thorndike, Wilfrid Hyde-White, and Fay Compton.

It's a Victorian melodrama set in the 1870s. O'Hara plays a wealthy widow, and Dana Andrews costars in the dual roles of artist and lawyer. O'Hara becomes entranced with struggling artist Andrews, and she subsequently marries him. One day they have an argument, and she pushes him. He has been drinking, and he falls down a staircase and dies. Thorndike, playing the waspish neighbor, witnesses the incident and blackmails O'Hara, threatening to tell the police that she was responsible. Time passes. One night another man appears at the bottom of the staircase, looking remarkably like the deceased artist, but this man (also Andrews) is an actor-cum-barrister. He and O'Hara become romantically entangled, but they have to find a way to deal with the meddlesome Thorndike. Andrews impersonates the dead man, leading to a number of situations that director Jean Negulesco treats half humorously.

O'Hara was being unduly hard on herself when she debunked her performance. She acted well under difficult circumstances, and the only obvious flaw was a familiar one: her accent. It goes from cut-glass to cockney and back again without any explanation. The film flopped on both continents. The reason may have been the film's mixed mood, with Negulesco threatening to go down the baroque road in the scenes with Thorndike but then switching gears as inexplicably as O'Hara switches accents.

Maverick director Nicholas Ray was behind the camera for *A Woman's Secret* (1949), which was equally problematic. O'Hara was reluctant to appear in it because she didn't like the book on which it was based, Vicki Baum's *Mortgage on Life*. Nor could she see herself as the "plain little frum" the part seemed to call for.[17] Producer Dore Schary persuaded her to take the role, but O'Hara agreed only on the condition that Will Price be given a contract to direct a film at RKO.

Ray, too, had little faith in the project. "RKO didn't care if the picture was good or not," he moaned. "They were acting in response to their bookkeeping, which controls so much of our art."[18] The Algerian setting looked false, and there were problems with the censors: some of O'Hara's postures in the rushes were deemed far too revealing.[19] It is difficult to be a sex symbol without showing flesh.

O'Hara plays Marian Washburn, a faded singer who is grooming starlet Susan Caldwell (Gloria Grahame) to take over for her on the sound stage, but things don't go as planned. Washburn winds up shooting Caldwell in a scuffle over a gun. The older woman was trying to stop the younger from committing suicide, but this isn't what Washburn tells the police. In an effort to save Caldwell the stigma of her "intended suicide," Washburn pretends she shot her intentionally, a lie bolstered by a flashback at the beginning of the film. Would a woman risk the electric chair merely to save somebody's reputation? It's a highly unlikely premise on which to base a film. There's also a flippancy in the direction that works against the nascent melodrama of the plot. But O'Hara is excellent, which goes to show that with a quality director, she could be relied on to deliver. She also *looks* as beautiful as ever, her pale skin flattered by the monochrome (it was sometimes a novelty to see her without those famous titian curls). Other than O'Hara's, the performances are inconsistent. Melvyn Douglas is bland as a pianist, and Victor Jory, playing a lawyer with a romantic interest in Grahame's character, is almost comically over the top. But Grahame herself—an actress genetically disposed to playing bad girls, even when they were good—is as engaging as ever.

A *Woman's Secret* flopped at the box office. The muddled pace confused audiences, as did the skewed motivation. Nor did the multiple flashbacks help. O'Hara licked her wounds, taking solace from the fact that even if Ray didn't deliver for her, at least Schary did. He was a man of his word and offered Price a directing job on a noir movie called *Strange Bargain*, starring Jeffrey Lynn and Martha Scott. A timid bookkeeper (Lynn) is experiencing money problems, so he asks his boss for a raise, only to be informed that he's about to be fired because the company is going bankrupt. But there's a twist in the tale: his boss is planning to commit suicide, and he offers Lynn $10,000 to make it look like a murder so his wife can collect the life insurance. Lynn tries to talk him out of it, without success. The man dies, but he actually *is* murdered, and because Lynn is at the scene to collect his money, he becomes a suspect. Harry Morgan plays the eagle-eyed cop trying to put the pieces together. The intricate plot is interesting, but Price didn't have enough stamina to flesh it out beyond a teleplay length of sixty-eight minutes. Once again, an opportunity was lost, and the film disappeared in the vaults of B-movie archives.

O'Hara's next feature, *Father Was a Fullback*, was equally forgettable. It is one of those fluffy family films Fred MacMurray fell into when he wasn't making classics like *Double Indemnity*. Natalie Wood plays O'Hara's daughter again, but their chemistry from *Miracle on 34th Street* is lacking. As a result, the film implodes in a welter of bathos.

Using the hackneyed formula of a down-at-the-heels football coach

(MacMurray) as a kickoff point for a lightweight tale of parental angst, this is a second-rate attempt to cash in on the success of *Sitting Pretty*. Sadly, it lacks the sparkle of the earlier film. More important, it lacks Clifton Webb. MacMurray is George Cooper, and O'Hara is his wife Elizabeth. They have some mildly amusing exchanges on the woes of parenthood, such as when George says, "Next time, dear, why can't we have a nice cocker spaniel?" and Elizabeth replies witheringly, "They shed." She then confides, "If I ever have another child it will be a government project. . . . I'll raise the next one scientifically." Their main worry is their elder daughter Connie, played with a well-timed sense of dreamy frustration by Betty Lynn. They're concerned because Connie can't seem to get a boyfriend, and Elizabeth frets that she will develop an inferiority complex. George is more bothered by his team's abysmal performance on the football field.

One of the main problems is that MacMurray looks more like an accountant than a sports coach. He also dresses like one, even on the playing field. Did the budget not extend to a tracksuit and cap? As things stand, he seems to have only a nodding acquaintance with his players, commiserating with them after a loss much as a distant fan might. "I was going to invite you around for cider and doughnuts," he drones after a 33–0 defeat, "but I thought the doughnuts might remind you of the score." He seems more interested in drafting plans from home or shooting out self-deprecating one-liners to Elizabeth. "You're a good loser," she consoles. "Almost perfect," he agrees.

Picturegoer magazine denounced the film for its unhappy mixture of "Freud and football."[20] Most of the Freudian material centers around Connie, who is at that "difficult" teenage stage, when adolescents demand meals in their bedrooms to soften the blow of spurned love. One is put in mind of a latter-day Ophelia—without the soliloquies.

Elliott Nugent, the original director, was having personal problems, so he was replaced by John M. Stahl, who would work often with O'Hara. Stahl brought in a crew of screenwriters to tighten up the script: Richard Sale, Mary Loos, Aleen Leslie, and Casy Robinson. Sale thought highly of O'Hara, describing her as "solid, never a fuss, and so beautiful."[21]

She had problems with Stahl, however. He shot so many takes—sometimes up to fifty—that she was bewildered. She'd say, "Mr. Stahl, is there something we should change?" and he'd reply, "No, no, do it again," without telling her what was wrong. "Then you'd be shocked because he might print Take Three and you'd think: What was he looking for? He would be the same with Natalie as he was with me and Fred MacMurray."[22]

O'Hara found Wood just as easy to work with as in *Miracle on 34th Street*. "You'd just sit around and have a good time," she gleamed, "and enjoy each other and gossip and chat and tease. It was different from today."[23] It's a pity their camaraderie couldn't lift this fudge to another level.

After *Father Was a Fullback*, O'Hara was back to sandy terrain with *Bagdad*. By now, she was queen of the B-adventure picture, as well as queen of Technicolor, so she knew exactly what energies to harness. She plays Princess Marjan, the daughter of an Arabian sheikh, who is returning to Bagdad after being educated in England. Upon her homecoming, she discovers that her father, the leader of the Aremlak tribe, has been murdered by a band of outlaws known as the Black Robes. She entreats the aid of Pasha Ali Nadim (played by a shifty Vincent Price) to avenge his death, but he insists he has to stay neutral. She then meets Prince Hassan (Paul Hubschmid), whom she suspects of being the leader of the Black Robes. Is he? Or is Nadim really the culprit? Or is it his cousin Raizul? Do we care?

This was the kind of film in which "Maureen Sahara," as her siblings dubbed her, was most comfortable. Though described as "a woman of a hundred moods" in the trailer, petulance is uppermost. She also turns her mischievous side to good effect as she plays cat and mouse with Price in an effort to divine the circumstances of her father's murder. (Not even she, however, can wrench the truth from that crushed-velvet voice.) The sets look artificial, but the studio got more than its money's worth from O'Hara. She sings, dances, fights, and loves in a tale of derring-do that ticks all the requisite boxes for an opulent history lesson. It is unashamedly formulaic in its triad of hero, villain, and sumptuous leading lady caught in the middle, but one isn't bored as the exotic intrigue unfolds. O'Hara throws herself into the action with ardent conviction, managing to deliver lines like "Be silent, brother to a barrel!" with a straight face, for which she deserves much credit.[24] Other women who tried costume drama came across as mannequins with cleavage, but O'Hara gave such roles that extra vim and vinegar. Audiences might have tut-tutted when she finally succumbed to the charms of the men she initially slapped when they got out of line, but no one was quite as committed to the (often ludicrous) exigencies of the plotlines. And when it came to dexterity in action, O'Hara was a nonpareil. Much of this dexterity resulted from an active childhood. She explained: "When you do stunts where you fall, and in fight scenes, you use a lot of judo. The things you learn in judo give you the agility to make it look believable. I worked at judo when I was a teenager in Ireland."[25]

She was willing to do whatever it took to make *Bagdad*, and the harem films in general, look as credible as possible. Such films flourished during the war years, when few audience members were likely to be critical. Jeanine Basinger writes: "Their excesses in color, clothing and design were appreciated during a time of rationing. These escapist fun fests were in happy contrast to many of the movies that were democratic and realistic."[26] During World War II, Basinger believes, these films allowed audiences to escape the daily grind. It was easy to dismiss them as piffle, "but this overlooks an essential fact about movies: the clever way the story could both conceal the troubles of the day and yet explore them in a safer mode."[27]

O'Hara's exceptional beauty had doomed her to this expedient subgenre. Her thinking was: if you're going to be in a substandard movie, at least be the best thing in it. It was like making a virtue out of necessity. Dressed in opulent garments and mouthing lines that seemed to emanate from a particularly poor Arabian Nights page-turner, she'd built up a reputation as a purveyor of the formulaic. Not acting superior to her material was the first rule for an action heroine. No matter how fatuous the dialogue was, she delivered it with conviction. As a result, audiences empathized with her predicaments. They wanted her to be rescued from the swirling seas, the vertiginous cliffs, the nefarious brigands. They wanted her to ride into the sunset with the hero as the final credits rolled, a green-tinted testament to what John Wayne might term "true grit."

Hence another peppery swashbuckler followed. *At Sword's Point* was produced by Howard Hughes, a man O'Hara found to be as cold as ice. She made it in 1949, but Hughes didn't release it until 1952, for reasons unexplained. It was a spin-off of the Three Musketeers story, featuring the sons of the musketeers and one daughter (guess who?) in the thick of the action. The sets were leftovers from *The Hunchback of Notre Dame*, the plotline a leftover from a hundred penny-dreadful divertissements.

Sometimes referred to as *Sons of the Musketeers*, it begins with the queen of France (Gladys Cooper) sending rings to the original musketeers to let them know she's being held prisoner in her castle by Duc De Lavalle (Rob Douglas). He wants to kill her son the prince (Peter Miles), marry the princess (Nancy Gates), and claim the throne for himself. Cornel Wilde is the young D'Artagnan, the male lead. (Wilde was one of the main male pin-ups of the 1940s, being on the cover of more movie magazines than either Van Johnson or Tyrone Power between 1945 and 1947.)[28] Dan O'Herlihy is the young Aramis, Alan Hale Jr. the young Porthos, and O'Hara the daughter of Athos. Booted and suited, she's ready for action as she and her three compadres rally to the queen's call. But the queen is betrayed by her lady-in-waiting (June Clayworth), and they're all captured as a result. To save their lives, the queen allows De Lavalle to carry out his demonic plan. O'Hara impersonates the princess at the subsequent wedding, in an attempt to outwit him, but the lady-in-waiting interferes again and scuppers things.

It's all very sophomoric, but O'Hara performs serviceably in the parry-and-thrust stakes. Her acting is another matter—but maybe good acting is a hindrance in charades like this. It barrels along on a tide of its own infectious energy and somehow manages to tie up all the loose ends. An *Irish Times* reviewer summed up its shortcomings: "Maureen O'Hara and Irishman Dan O'Herlihy work hard to make their presence in the film really necessary, and Cornel Wilde and Gladys Cooper go about their roles with a sort of I-hope-my-friends-don't-see-me-now air. Can't say I blame them."[29]

At Sword's Point probably represents the acme of O'Hara's career as a swashbuckler. Her character proves herself the equal of the men in every department here, including brainpower. As well as jousting like a woman possessed, she comes up with many of the ideas to outwit the villains. Nor does she sacrifice her femininity, managing to look sexual as well as athletic. It isn't surprising that two of the musketeers fall in love with her. "Her sword is the equal of ours," the young D'Artagnan informs the queen. When one of the villains says, "We will not fight with a lady," she rasps back, "I am no lady when I fight."

Jeanine Basinger points out that when Wilde is being tortured, O'Hara doesn't break down and give the torturers the information they're looking for, unlike her generational forebears. This is another notch on her feminist belt. For Basinger, the entire film is "about" women. She notes that the royal figure is a queen rather than a king, that her lady-in-waiting is the chief villainess, and so on. "Women are everywhere," she pronounces. O'Hara's character has to be a woman because she impersonates the princess in one scene, and in another she uses her feminine wiles to trick a bunch of soldiers by pretending she's a barmaid.[30]

Lewis Allen, the film's director, didn't think O'Hara would be able to handle the fencing scenes. She didn't like him as a director—or as a man. On the day of her big scene, she gave it her all, while being cheered on by a crew that also disapproved of Allen. "I fenced the ass off the whole lot of them," she bragged. Allen was astounded. "After I finished the scene there was just one word: 'Print.'"[31] She'd justified her "manhood." It was a sword she wielded, not a curtana. At the end of the scene, four stuntmen "sank to their knees" in recognition of the fact that they had been bested.[32] The gesture told Allen that he had woefully underestimated her proficiency.

The fact that Hughes waited so long to release the film, in the opinion of James Robert Parish, "made it clear that he was underwhelmed by Maureen's high-priced presence on the lot." As far as he was concerned, any role for which she might be considered "suitable" would certainly be offered first to his protégées Jane Russell and Faith Domergue.[33] O'Hara took the unsubtle hint, packed her belongings, and promptly left RKO for Universal. (She doesn't allude to any of this in her autobiography.)

O'Hara had met Hughes while she was making *Ten Gentlemen from West Point*. During dinner one night at John Farrow's house, Hughes ignored her for the whole evening, refusing to answer any question she asked him. For a while, she gave him the benefit of the doubt, imagining that one of his many plane crashes might have caused partial deafness. This was a myth Hughes himself circulated for his own convenience. Veronica Lake surmised, "I suppose he found it advantageous in business dealings, a technique to keep others off their guard while he took in everything they said."[34] It was also an excuse for rudeness. O'Hara got tired of it when she noticed that he could hear Farrow's questions perfectly well and responded clearly to them. She realized his "deafness" was a mere ploy, so she decided to take him on. "I hear you've been in a lot of plane crashes," she taunted. "Is it true you're held together with wire and string?" The room descended to silence, but Hughes kept his poker face, refusing to react even to this.[35] The night, as a result, ended on an anticlimax.

Hughes's last crash changed him utterly. Gene Tierney, who had dated him for a time, chronicled the transformation: "There had been a boyish, clear-eyed quality about him. Now the eyes had turned beady, the face had tightened. Rather than adding character, the scars only aged him."[36] She also said, "I don't think Howard could have loved anything that didn't have a motor in it."[37] It comes as little surprise that O'Hara didn't get on with him. He liked his women demure and feline and was used to snapping his fingers at them.

Hughes did call O'Hara on one subsequent occasion, shortly before St. Patrick's Day 1949, to ask her to open a hotel for him in Houston. He was "networking," as she saw it, and she politely refused, claiming it clashed with her film schedule. Panic ensued. Word got back to the top brass at the studio, and all the relevant buttons were pushed to free her up to open Hughes's hotel. She acceded in the end—but under her terms. The postman had to ring twice.

O'Hara felt optimistic about moving to Universal after *At Sword's Point*. She was confident it signaled a change in the kind of material she would be offered and the way she was viewed by the press. One critic gave an honest summation of the way she'd generally been portrayed in the media: "Most of the journalistic attention paid to Maureen O'Hara was dedicated to finding new and less interesting ways of telling us that she has red hair. At times it must have seemed to her that an equal inspiration was applied to selecting her roles. Her actual credits notwithstanding, she seemed forever adrift on a studio-created galleon. Someone wrapped in black silk and blacker moustache would wheel her away, then someone with lots of teeth and no shirt would bring her back again. There is no record of an awful crime committed against her studios that warranted punishments like *The Black Swan*, *Sinbad*, *The Spanish Main*, *Bagdad* or *Against All Flags*."[38]

Derring-do was also in evidence in *Comanche Territory*, a western in which O'Hara is called on to be proficient with a bullwhip. In her first pairing with Macdonald Carey, she plays sharp-tongued saloon propri- etress Katie Howard, a woman conspiring with her crooked brother Stacey (Charles Drake) to scupper a peace treaty with the local Indians so they can get rich mining silver. The Comanches are portrayed as pacifistic, which usually wasn't the case in Hollywood films made at this time, but other- wise, the characterization is one-dimensional. The movie, which runs for only seventy-six minutes, was more matinee fare than anything else—like many O'Hara films. It was hardly *Bury My Heart at Wounded Knee*.

Comanche Territory was directed by George Sherman. Sherman made four films with O'Hara, but he apparently didn't make much of an impression on her: she doesn't mention him in her autobiography. As Katie, she's on fire from the word "go," spitting out lines like cannonballs ("You call me a lady once more and I'll fill you full of lead!") as she negotiates the trajectory from Calamity Jane–style spitfire to Carey's unlikely love interest. She even gets to stop a saloon fight at one point by putting her fingers in her mouth and emitting an almighty whistle. All that's missing from the semicomedic proceedings is John Wayne. No matter how many punches get thrown, the chorus girls continue to dance onstage. O'Hara also manages to trill what the Irish call a "come-all-ye" song in one scene. Whether speaking or singing, her brogue is as broad as it's ever been, even in *The Quiet Man*. (Maybe she was getting herself in the mood for that movie: it was finally about to be made.)

O'Hara had lead billing over Carey, who plays it for laughs as a tame Jim Bowie. It's a reflection on his performance that one remembers his famed knife more than anything else about him as the film canters toward its supercharged climax. He even has to be enticed into kissing O'Hara in the dying moments by a laconic Will Geer, a man who at least has the courtesy to remember the brand of perfume she favors as she shoots him.

As a result of her frustration over forgettable fare like this, and a desire to have at least a modicum of control over her career, O'Hara announced the formation of her own film company, Price-Merman Productions. She set this up with Price and John Payne, as well as investor L. B. Merman. She planned to make seven films with the company, a tall order that was dependent on Price staying off the sauce.

He both wrote and directed the first one, *Tripoli*, a military story based on Price's time in the marines. O'Hara plays the daughter of a French diplomat. She disguises herself as a dancing girl so she can accompany a tough lieutenant (Payne) as he forages through the Libyan desert, engaging in battle with some thoroughly nasty pirates in the process. She didn't enjoy making the film; her main emotion was relief that Price managed to remain sober for the shoot. When it was finished, she informed a reporter that Price had treated her exactly the same as he would have treated a stranger on the set.[39] She meant this as a compliment, but one could take it two ways. She also mentioned that they were totally in tune with each other regarding their priorities.[40] Contrast this to her autobiographical recollection of the *real* story:

> The day he left for San Francisco to write *Tripoli* I took Bronwyn
> to Mass and prayed to God to keep Will sober long enough to
> complete the film. . . . A few days later, a box was delivered to the
> house. It was from the hotel where Will was staying in San Fran-
> cisco. It was addressed to our home at 662 Stone Canyon Road
> but had Will's secretary's name on it. I opened it anyway. Will had
> bought her the most beautiful lingerie you have ever seen but mis-
> takenly sent it to his own address. (I learned later that whenever I
> went on location to make a movie, Will moved her, and others, into
> my house and my bedroom. Our staff even served them breakfast
> in my bed every morning.)[41]

She followed *Tripoli* with *Flame of Araby*, another "tits and sand" opera. She almost could have phoned in her performance by now. This time, she's cast as the fiery Tunisian princess Tanya, "a wench with temper," as costar Jeff Chandler dubs her. He's Tamerlaine, a Bedouin chief. They begin proceedings in a fiery fashion, with Tamerlaine whipping Tanya after she ruins his chances of capturing a wild black stallion he craves. He appears to value the stallion much more than he does Tanya. "Never have I seen such strength, such beauty, such fighting spirit," he exclaims—about the horse. When he eventually gets around to kissing Tanya, he does so only after perusing her up and down like a trinket one might purchase at a market stall. "Shapely head," he notes, "long of limb, shoulders well formed and in proportion and soft of muscle." "You have much to learn," she responds ruefully, rebuffing his kiss. At which point the elusive horse appears from his hiding place behind a waterfall. (Does the title of the movie refer to the horse or to O'Hara? Either is possible.) Tamerlaine and Tanya fall in love after she's kidnapped by "Corsair dogs" who want her hand in marriage, but otherwise, the story focuses mainly on racing the black steed. As for the future, Tanya will have to enjoy "the simple blessings of Allah" with Tamerlaine, far from her palatial riches. He, in turn, will have to learn to stop talking about horses.

It moves at a rip-roaring pace from the moment the credits roll and gathers momentum after Tamerlaine goes on the run. Lon Chaney and Buddy Baer are entertaining as the leering Corsair brothers, and O'Hara shows her fiery charm to good effect as she parries with them. Yashmak-clad and sumptuously gowned, she slots herself full-bloodedly into the proceedings (even if one can see the resolution a mile off).

O'Hara despised the film and all it (mis)represented. She complained about it but was told to just get back on her horse and do her scenes. Nor was she over the moon about Chandler as a costar. The only thing that sustained her was the thought that she'd be making *The Quiet Man* soon. She even did wardrobe fittings for *The Quiet Man* on the set of *Flame of Araby*. If Chandler had any doubt about her lack of commitment to the movie, this confirmed his suspicions. Certainly, her diverted concentration contributed to their lack of chemistry.

Meanwhile, John Ford had gone to Ireland to do some preproduction for *The Quiet Man*, spending much of his time socializing with O'Hara's family and getting the feel of the "old country" in the process. Afterward he flew to Honolulu to film a documentary on Korea for Republic. From there, he started to write O'Hara love letters filled with slushy sentiments: "Arrah Máisín ma chree how much happiness you have given me & how little I've given you but girleen I love you so much."[42] They were all transcribed in a stream-of-consciousness style with little punctuation, as if he wrote them while drunk. (He probably did. Sober, he might have been too inhibited to express his feelings.) He signed them "Seán," as if he was already immersing himself in the spirit of *The Quiet Man*. O'Hara was astounded by the letters. They were almost a contradiction of the devilish way he generally behaved to her face. They were also, of course, delusional and wildly incoherent. She told only a few close friends and her brother Charles about the letters.

She had to make another film before *The Quiet Man*, so the agonizing wait continued. *Kangaroo* is set in Australia—a long way to go for so little. It's an enigmatic film that quirkily zigzags its way to an oblique denouement. It begins with a drunk Michael McGuire (Finlay Currie) in a doss-house, screaming about his lost son. Richard Connor (Peter Lawford) hears him and claims to be McGuire's son. Connor then strikes up a relationship with another ne'er-do-well, Gamble (Richard Boone), and the two of them carry out a robbery that turns into a murder. Gamble isn't unduly bothered about this development, but Connor is. When McGuire sobers up, they pretend he struck a cattle deal with them while he was in his cups, so he takes them back to his ranch to meet his daughter, Dell (O'Hara). After this, things go even more haywire. Dell doesn't know if she can trust the men, and when Connor starts to succumb to her charms, she's reluctant to allow herself to fall for him. But how *can* she fall in love with him? If he's really her brother, as he claims, wouldn't this be incest? Director Lewis Milestone doesn't appear to be overly concerned about such minor details, or indeed about anything else in this muddled misadventure. It's a potentially interesting movie, but whenever things start to get lively, Milestone breaks off the story to show us cattle drives, dust storms, aboriginal dances, and hopping kangaroos: it moves from drama to travelogue with beguiling nonchalance. Matters are not helped by performances that range from stage Irish (Currie) to would-be riverboat gambler (Lawford). (Complicating the situation, in the middle of filming, O'Hara had to rescue Boone and Lawford from a boy brothel. The less said about this, the better. Afterward she took to calling Lawford "Peter Awful.")[43]

During production O'Hara was offered a gift of some land from the Australian government. She turned it down because, as she explained to Conor Power in the *Irish Examiner* years later, she came from a country "where the people lost their lands through political reasons and I'd worry about who owned the land."[44] It proved to be an unwise decision, as oil was eventually found there. She threw away a fortune due to a misplaced principle.

Once *Kangaroo* was completed, she was that much nearer to *The Quiet Man*. It was now more than six years since she'd made the "handshake" deal with Ford. So much time had elapsed, she used to joke with John Wayne that when the cameras finally rolled, they'd have to play the old couple in the movie instead of the romantic interests.[45]

The Quiet Man was being made by Republic, a minor studio specializing in B movies. Ford wasn't accustomed to such parsimonious conditions: the cost of one of his usual films almost equaled the annual production budget for Republic. But the fact that Wayne was under contract to Republic gave the studio a significant bargaining chip. Wayne had cut his celluloid teeth with the studio, making *Westward Ho*, its first feature, back in 1935. Herb Yates, Republic's owner, agreed to lend Wayne out only if Ford made a western for him first. As far as Yates was concerned, this would be the cash cow that compensated for the money he believed he'd lose on *The Quiet Man*. That movie turned out to be *Rio Grande*.

Rio Grande is the third installment in Ford's highly acclaimed cavalry trilogy. It's never been given the credit it deserves, perhaps because of the excellence of its two predecessors: *She Wore a Yellow Ribbon* and *Fort Apache*. Ford is in a pastoral mood and seems to be in no hurry to get on with the plot as he tells the story of hard-bitten Lieutenant Kirby Yorke (Wayne), who's been forced to burn the plantation of his wife, Kathleen (O'Hara), on orders from his commanding officer, General Sheridan (J. Carroll Naish). It was the first screen partnership for Wayne and O'Hara, and though they were paired under some duress, as a promissory note for *The Quiet Man*, they don't let it show. (O'Hara was originally supposed to appear opposite Wayne in *Tycoon* in 1947, but she had so many other projects that year, the part went to Laraine Day instead.) What Wayne liked most about O'Hara in the film, in the view of Harry Carey Jr., was the way she looked at him so intently. "Duke liked you to really look at him," Carey observed, and O'Hara had that strong gaze in all the movies they made together.[46]

Wayne is never more comfortable onscreen than when he's fighting marauding Indians, and *Rio Grande* is no exception. The Apaches here engage in vicious raids before hightailing it back across the Mexican border, where they've been granted immunity. The situation can't continue, so enter John Wayne to do what a man's gotta do. As the film begins, Kathleen hasn't seen her husband for fifteen years, never having forgiven him for burning her plantation. Her reason for visiting him is that she is trying to buy their son Jeff (Claude Jarman Jr.) out of the army. Jeff would prefer that she didn't, and when he joins Kirby in an attack on the Indians (both of them risking a court-martial for doing so), he achieves heroic status. Kathleen forgives her alienated spouse for his past indiscretions, and everything is wrapped up a mite too tidily in the end. But Ford's commitment to the project, along with the undeniable chemistry between O'Hara and Wayne, rescues the film from its hard-crusted overtones. "You've grown more thoughtful,"

Kathleen tells Kirby in one scene. In some ways, the film is the story of a lonely man's search for his humanity, which he finds through the softening influence of his wife and son. "What makes soldiers great is hateful to me," Kathleen says elsewhere. She also gets to utter the wry toast: "To my only rival, the United States cavalry."

It's a brooding, bittersweet piece, with Ford in the same kind of contemplative mood he used in films like *The Searchers* to such good effect. The cavalry scenes look very majestic. As Leonard Maltin observed, there's majesty even in the title of the film.[47] Combine that with its music, the monochrome minimalism, the quiet dignity of the opening scene of the dust-blown cavalrymen returning from battle, and the equally subdued finale in which Ford breaks with tradition by having his hero stop an arrow, and you've got a unique western by any standards.

Carey believed Ford was uncomfortable with the romantic aspects of the film. He refused to shoot the love scene between Wayne and O'Hara until the very last day, even though it occurs, chronologically, much earlier in the film. Did it mean too much to him? Or too little? Carey etched in the circumstances behind it: "Maureen looked so gorgeous it took your breath away to see her every morning: I wished I was a leading man and could do a love scene with her like Duke did. Uncle Jack put off that scene until the last day of shooting."[48] Wayne predicted this would happen, saying the previous week, "Christ, we're right here on the set. We could shoot that scene easy now where I have to take her in my arms and kiss her. He's duckin' it. He hates to direct a love scene. You watch—he'll put it off till the last goddam day."[49] And so he did. Was there something Freudian going on? Was he jealous?

In another scene, Kathleen tells her son he's "stubborn and proud," just like his father. He replies, "Just like you are, Mother." Here again, we have the familiar scenario of two people who are too forthright to get along. They admire each other's strength of character but can't live together because they're too similar. Although Kirby and Kathleen haven't seen each other for a long time, an "erotic longing" permeates the movie's texture, underpinned by the musical interludes, particularly the heavily redolent "I'll Take You Home Again, Kathleen."[50] This creates a captivating mood.

Lee Pfeiffer thought O'Hara's role was "probably the least demanding" of any of her five films with Wayne, in terms of acting.[51] That may appear to be the case, and perhaps she hadn't nailed down her trademark fieriness yet, but in another sense, this makes the performance richer. Less is more. In fact, one could argue that in *Rio Grande*, the chemistry between Wayne and O'Hara is at its most charming. O'Hara excellently conveys Kathleen's underlying feelings for Kirby, just as Ford excellently nuances their gradual growing together against the backdrop of Kirby's grudging acceptance of their son's military prowess.

Lindsay Anderson notes that the tension between Wayne and O'Hara in *Rio Grande*—"North and South, duty and emotion both passionate, both stubborn in their pride"—prefigures the same clash of equally independent spirits in *The Quiet Man*.[52] From this point of view, the two films aren't markedly different in tone. It could even be said that Ford flexed his muscles for *The Quiet Man* on the *Rio Grande* set. The film also gave Wayne and O'Hara an opportunity to see how they would square up against each other, even if the western is a much more restrained offering than the Irish caper. Victor McLaglen also seems to be preparing himself for *The Quiet Man* by hamming up his role to comic effect.

O'Hara recalled the tough working conditions during the movie: "We were in what was supposed to be the Rio Grande. They used to say it was too thin to plow and too thick to drink. The heat was unbearable. It was so bad they dug a huge pit in the ground and cut steps in the side, then put some metal camp beds down there and a tarpaulin over the top. Victor McLaglen and all of us, when we'd have an hour or so off when we weren't needed, we'd go down in the pit just to stay cool and not die in the deadly heat."[53] It was also a way of avoiding Ford's abstruse moods. As if to compensate for this, they had entertainment in the evenings, with Ford prevailing on O'Hara to sing Irish songs. He got Wayne to sing too, even though he couldn't hit a note. O'Hara was infuriated by Ford's constant ribbing of Wayne. Maybe that's one of the reasons he persisted. In O'Hara's favor, she was more upset by Ford's treatment of Wayne (which was so offensive that it made her throw up in the bathroom, on occasion) than of herself.

Lindsay Anderson once asked O'Hara what she considered to be Ford's special quality. She replied that it was his ability to spur stars to "rise above the mediocre." How did he achieve that? "He seems to know just what's necessary to get a good performance from anyone," she explained. "Some people he'll be entirely gentle with and with others he'll be a brute." Anderson then asked if the mischievous ending to *Rio Grande*, where she "provocatively twirled" her parasol after Wayne gives her this olive branch, was Ford's idea or hers. It was Ford's, she admitted.[54] He suspected it would work better than a mawkish finale, and he was right.

Rio Grande came in on schedule and received positive reviews. It also posted a healthy return at the box office, so Yates was happy. O'Hara bathed in its glory and heaved a huge sigh of relief that it had gone so well. She also licked her lips in anticipation of returning to Ireland to see her loved ones and finally make the "silly little Irish film" that had been simmering on the back burner for so long. Would it live up to expectations? All she could do was hope.

O'Hara was feeling as good as she had in years, but in March 1951 she was hit with a thunderbolt when she learned that Price had totally cleaned out her bank account. She'd made thirty films by this time, and suddenly she was broke. She wasn't the only star whose fortunes were frittered away by irresponsible people. It happened to John Wayne, Tyrone Power, and Teresa Wright, among others. O'Hara wanted to mobilize a large contingent of stars to finance a lawsuit against their financial abusers, but it never happened: they were afraid of looking "not too intelligent." O'Hara's attitude was: "It wasn't that we were stupid. It was that we were so busy earning the money and we trusted these people." She told her friend Roddy McDowall in a 1991 interview in *Premiere* magazine that she once approached some "top politicians" to do something about it, but "they just laughed at me."[55]

That wasn't all. Price had supposedly been drying out in a rehabilitation hospital, but when O'Hara visited his doctor, she discovered that the "hospital" was more like a luxury home where the residents cavorted with floozies and continued to drink to their hearts' content. She sacked the doctor, needless to say, but soon afterward he showed up at her house with Price and told O'Hara she had a serious medical condition. She severely doubted this but agreed to give a urine sample for analysis, which confirmed the doctor's worst suspicions: she had a growth on her kidney that needed to be removed immediately if she didn't want her body to resemble a man's! Her own doctor rejected this diagnosis and told her the operation proposed by the other doctor had a high fatality rate. Was Price trying to kill her? She couldn't rule anything out, so she hid his guns in a gap in the wall and slept with a baseball bat beside her bed. Her life was turning into Grand Guignol.

Even so, she continued to deliver the patter about her happy family for the media. In an interview that appeared in *Photoplay* in 1953 she did one of those "At Home with the Stars" fillers that was more about her house than herself. It was described as being "as Irish as the traditional sham-rock," with green (her favorite color) everywhere—the sofa, chairs, a love seat (surely not for herself and Will), and even the draperies. She informed the interviewer that Price had bought her a picture of a small seaside town in Ireland at an auction. She then said to him: "You couldn't find anything to please me more. How did you know?" For good measure, he also pre-sented her with two altar plates he'd dredged up on a trip to Dublin.[56]

One could be forgiven for imagining that the pair of them were the happiest couple in Hollywood on the strength of this conversational fluff, but Price was getting ready for a final onslaught after his bride's career "honeymoon" in Ireland.

6

Sojourn in Cong

The Quiet Man isn't so much a film as a brand. Call it shamroguery or pad-dywhackery if you wish, but it put Ireland on the world's stage—for better or worse. John Ford sent up his homeland in his unashamedly stage-Irish vignettes. He was well aware that he was making an amiable farce. What he couldn't have predicted was its immortality.

Ford had already been forced to make *Rio Grande* to persuade the cash-strapped Herb Yates to green-light his Irish venture. To sweeten *The Quiet Man* pill, Ford brought Yates to the most picturesque part of Conne-mara in Galway and showed him a small whitewashed cottage with shutters and a thatched roof. "There it is," Ford blubbered, with tears running down his cheeks, "the house where I was born."[1] Ford was actually born in Portland, Maine, but the trick worked. Yates started crying too, and the deal was done. He budgeted the project at $1.5 million. According to O'Hara's brother Charles, Ford never got over the fact that he wasn't born in Ireland. He saw it as his "one great emotional tragedy."[2]

Ford was unhappy with what he considered a paltry budget. When he told Yates he needed an additional $250,000, Yates balked, saying that was way out of his league. To keep costs down, Wayne agreed to do the part for a flat fee of $1 million and waive his usual percentage of the gross. O'Hara pocketed an even more modest $65,000.

The film is based on a short story by Maurice Walsh. Ford bought the rights to the story shortly after he first read it. It concerns a boxer called Sean Kelvin who leaves the United States to seek out his Irish roots after accidentally killing a man in the ring. He falls in love with an Irish girl named Ellen O'Grady, but her brother, the bullish Liam, doesn't take to Sean and withholds his sister's dowry, hoping to upset the relationship between them. Sean and Ellen marry anyway, and he eventually has to engage in fisticuffs with Liam to attain the dowry for his frustrated wife.

Up until now, Republic had made mainly low-budget films. Artistically, it was a step down for Ford, but it was a step he was willing to make. Old Herb Yates was the only man in Hollywood willing to touch Walsh's short story with a barge pole. Ford originally wanted to set the film in Spiddal, Galway, where his parents were from. This proved impractical, so he settled instead for the small Mayo town of Cong, although certain scenes were filmed in and around Galway and Connemara as well. Ford also brought eighty regulars from Republic to Ireland with him.

O'Hara traveled to Ireland with her daughter and her brothers, stopping off in Reykjavik, Iceland, en route. There, she found John Wayne, stranded from an earlier flight. She gave him her bunk on the next flight so he could get some much-needed shut-eye, and she shared one with Bronwyn. The bonding between O'Hara and Wayne had already begun, and not a spool of film had been shot. Wayne was with his then-wife Chata, but they weren't getting on and would soon divorce.[3] One of the reasons Chata traveled with her husband was that she was worried he might have an affair with O'Hara. This was never going to happen, for a number of reasons. First, both of them were married and took their vows seriously. Second, they never had that kind of attraction to each other. Wayne thought of O'Hara as someone to accompany him to the bar, not the boudoir. (The fact that she wasn't a drinker didn't seem to matter to him.)

After O'Hara touched down at Shannon Airport, she told reporters excitedly, "This is a film I've really wanted to do. The debate has been going on since the mid-forties and thankfully we've succeeded. It's a really great script with no attempt at stage-Irishism."[4] Many people, this writer included, would quibble with that last sentence.

Ford put his two brothers, Francis and Eddie O'Fearna, in the film, as well as his future son-in-law Ken Curtis. All of Wayne's four children appeared in it, as did O'Hara's two brothers Charles and Jimmy. Charles played an Irish Republican Army (IRA) commandant; Jimmy, using his mother's maiden name of Lilburn, played the part of the curate, Father Paul. Charles also helped scout locations for the movie and, in his capacity as a solicitor, drew up many of the cast members' contracts.

Ford commissioned Richard Llewellyn, the author of *How Green Was My Valley*, to expand Walsh's story into a novella (Frank Nugent would later replace Llewellyn). He then changed the names of the two main characters to Sean Thornton (Wayne) and Mary Kate Danaher (O'Hara). Ford's real name was Sean, and he was well acquainted with a number of Thorntons, which might explain these amendments. As for Mary Kate, Ford's wife's name was Mary, and the Kate could have been for Katharine Hepburn (whom Ford had worked with and was very fond of) or for the character in Shakespeare's *Taming of the Shrew*.[5] O'Hara discounted the theory that the name Mary Kate was a nod to "Kate" Hepburn. She preferred to think Ford chose the name because her own father had wanted to call her Kate. "My baptism was held up because of this," she declared to all and sundry.[6]

Ford's old friend Victor McLaglen was playing O'Hara's brother, who would now be called "Red" Will. Ward Bond, another member of Ford's stock company, played a priest, Father Lonergan. The quirky Irish stage actor Barry Fitzgerald took on the role of the tipsy matchmaker Michaeleen, and his real-life brother Arthur Shields played a Protestant minister, Reverend Playfair. Fitzgerald and Shields were established Irish performers.

Before a foot of film had been shot, the *Irish Times* predicted that Ford would win an Oscar for it.[7] Yates kept a close eye on the production, anxious that it not go a penny over budget. He practically wore out the Cong switchboard with daily phone calls from Hollywood about Ford's progress. Reels of film were sent from Shannon Airport to Yates after each day's shoot, for his perusal.

A reporter in the *Connacht Tribune* documented the "Hollywoodization" of the picturesque village: "What with cigars, chewing gum, dollar bills, American accents and brilliant sunshine, Cong has taken on a Californian look. When you put your nose outside the door you have an equal chance of bumping into a film star, a director, a property master, a stuntman or an ordinary native Irishman."[8] Almost every villager seemed to have been co-opted into the cast. Pat Cohan's grocery shop, occupying a key location in the center of town, was swiftly transformed into a public house. This caused confusion to at least one thirsty local, who had to be informed that the pub sign was just a prop.[9] Never mind—they could drink the town dry again after the cameras stopped rolling.

Electricity came to Cong during the shooting of the film. It was the first time many locals had seen a lightbulb, never mind an electric generator. They were delighted to be wired for electricity, one writer joked, but when they found out they had to pay for it, they asked the Electricity Supply Board to take it back.[10]

Interest in the production came from far and wide. Representatives from various newspapers decamped in Cong for sound bites from the cast and to draft location reports. Tourists flocked to the town like never before. People lined up to be extras. A flood of Maureen O'Hara look-alikes dyed their hair red in the hopes of becoming her double or stand-in.

The *Connacht Tribune* described the cast's easy manner with reporters: "Victor McLaglen wakened out of a snooze on a deckchair to offer a warm handshake. John Wayne was like an old friend you had known for years. Maureen O'Hara hopped down from a sidecar in which she had been on her first date with the returned Yank and spoke of the film as if it was something happening to her in real life. She wore a summer frock and tweed jacket, the very antithesis of a temperamental, neurotic star."[11]

For Ford, the film was both a literal and a metaphorical homecoming. He could explore his roots and also immerse himself in a culture that had been simmering in his subconscious for most of his life. He wanted to film Ireland's "forty shades of green" in a manner that would be both winsome and enchanting.

The basic thread of the plot rests on two misunderstandings. The first is that Sean thinks Mary Kate wants the dowry for its financial benefit rather than its symbolic one. The second is that she attributes his failure to fight Will to cowardice rather than confusion. The film spends two hours trying to work out these misunderstandings and has great fun doing so.

The church used in the film was Protestant rather than Catholic, which posed a problem for some of the extras. They were supposed to come through its doors in the scene in which Wayne offers O'Hara holy water from the font. Such was the religious zealotry of the parents of one of them, Bridie Hopkins, that they suggested she mention her denominational indiscretion the next time she went to confession. The religious conservatism of the locals was also evident in an anecdote told by Ford's friend Lord Michael Killanin: A woman berated Ward Bond for playing a scene with his hand in his pocket. "No Catholic priest ever puts his hand in his pocket," she attested. Ford snapped back, "Ma'am, you're absolutely right. Only in other people's."[12] He could never resist the urge to hurl a salvo at the church.

The atmosphere on set was more congenial than on most Ford movies. Every evening after the day's shooting, the cast and crew would congregate in nearby Ashford Castle. Ford sat at the head of a long table, and when he started to eat, it signaled everyone else to do the same. He looked like a bedraggled Henry VIII presiding over a motley crew of Hollywood's elite—and some local color. The food often consisted of fish caught by the crew in the nearby rivers. More often than not, a singsong would start up after dinner. "He would make all of us sing, even Duke," O'Hara informed journalist Stan Gebler Davies, "but he [Wayne] would make us sing out of tune."[13] Ford himself had a "tin ear" but could carry a tune when the occasion called for it (which happened only once in a blue moon).[14] It was like a rehash of evenings on the set of *Rio Grande*. Ford always had to have someone to mock as well as praise, the former more so. Afterward, in the absence of elevators, O'Hara made her way up various stairways to get to her room. The activity, she consoled herself, "kept the muscles in your legs good and strong."[15] The hotel room Ford booked for her was a shambles (there were holes in the carpet, and the paint was peeling off the walls), whereas Wayne's was luxurious by comparison. But she didn't complain, because he probably would have given her a worse one if she did.

O'Hara's double was Etta Vaughan, a young girl spotted by Ford's brother-in-law Wingate Smith while having tea in Ashford Castle one day. She hadn't even applied for the job—unlike the hundred hopefuls who had applied and been summarily rejected. She told him she'd have to ask her mother's permission, even though she was in her twenties at the time. Her mother eventually said yes, with the proviso that the girl be allowed to stay in her native Galway for the duration of the shoot rather than in Cong with the rest of the cast. This was agreed to, and she was driven to the set in a limousine every day. One day Bronwyn ran into Vaughan's arms, thinking she was her mother. The fact that she couldn't tell the difference between them reveals how little time O'Hara was spending with her daughter due to the pressure of work. (Strangely, Vaughan isn't mentioned in O'Hara's autobiography, and she never spoke of her in interviews.)

Ford was possessive about every detail of the movie but grudgingly allowed some innovations. On one particular day, the field where they were about to shoot was covered in seagulls. O'Hara thought it would be a good idea if the birds were allowed to remain in the shot until Wayne walked through them, scattering them to the four winds. She didn't dare broach the subject with Ford directly, though, because all suggestions had to be submitted "through the back door."[16] Otherwise, they would most likely be thrown out. Not only that, "He'd make fun of you afterwards and you'd be mad for falling into the trap."[17] Ford used the suggestion because he wasn't pressured into it.

In one of the fight scenes between O'Hara and Wayne, he's supposed to drag her through the fields; then she throws a punch at him but misses, spins around, and he kicks her on the bottom. They carefully choreographed it and rehearsed in secret to get it right. They knew Ford was spying on them, but he played dumb. "Well now," he chuckled, after they had it down cold, "you see how wonderful a thing can be when it's totally spontaneous."[18] "We could have cheerfully killed him," O'Hara said. "We knew he knew we'd been rehearsing it all along because he'd been peeking through the bushes at us."[19]

Even though Ford behaved reasonably well toward O'Hara, they still had their moments. In one scene, she was in a cart with a wind machine behind her, which made it difficult for her to see. Ford asked her to open her eyes wider a few times, but she couldn't do it because of the machine. Finally he roared, "Open your damn eyes!" and she flipped. She shouted back at him, "What would a baldheaded son of a bitch like you know about hair lashing across his eyeballs?"[20] It was one of the few times she ever stood up to him, and everybody gasped. "I watched him," she reflected years later, "and I saw him take in every face on the set and make his mind up whether he was going to kill me or laugh."[21] Thankfully, he decided to laugh, and the cast and crew followed suit. "Watching him make his decision was fascinating," she allowed.[22] It was as if nobody had permission to laugh unless he did.

In the film, Wayne first sees O'Hara herding sheep through a sunlit glade and utters the immortal words, "Hey, is that real? She couldn't be." This first sighting isn't so much realism as a figment of the Irish diaspora. To quote Martin McLoone: "What we're seeing here is a vision of Ireland that was sustained by the Irish-American community that Ford was brought up in; the romantic excesses of this vision are attributable to the power of the exile to embellish memory with fantasy."[23] The faraway hills were truly green in this sense.

Lindsay Anderson had this to say about the Wayne-O'Hara love scenes:

Ford has eschewed the directly sensual close-ups of love-making which audiences today have been taught to expect: instead he has imaged their passion in the wind that sweeps over them as they embrace, in the thunder that breaks into their courtship in the churchyard, and in the rain that drenches down as they stand in each other's arms, wetting the girl's upturned face and soaking the man's shirt so that it clings, transparent, to the flesh. Never, perhaps, has the delicacy, the essential decorum of Ford's style been more in evidence than in this film. His camera never sensationalizes or draws too near. Even in the climactic fight he's careful to stand at the proper distance, to keep the violence in its proper perspective.[24]

This distancing creates an atmospheric mood that acts as an impressive counterpoint to the more manically frivolous antics of the cast.

Apart from everything else, the movie is a visual treat. Filmed through a diffusing mist, rural Ireland has "the sunless, remembered look of a surrealist painting."[25] O'Hara noted that the country had never been shown onscreen in Technicolor before, and she thought Ireland was the real star of the movie. "All you do is turn a camera on it," she claimed, "and it smiles on you."[26] The Irish Tourist Board, which has made a fortune from the film in the past sixty years, surely would have agreed with her.

O'Hara was quick to debunk certain stories surrounding the shooting of the film, one of which concerned the amount of boozing that went on (after all, it's Ireland we're talking about). She noted, "Somebody gave an interview saying John Wayne and John Ford drank all the time. That is not true. On the entire shooting of *The Quiet Man*, John Wayne had a couple of drinks one night, and one night only. John Ford never drank during the entire picture."[27] She undoubtedly believed this to be the case, but some of the extras begged to differ. Etta Vaughan said she saw Wayne nipping in to a pub for a "quick one" one day when "the chief" (Ford) wasn't about. "For whatever reason, every glass in the pub had been smashed the previous night and they'd been served their porter in jam jars. This really tickled John, who laughed about it for days afterwards."[28] An extra, Robert Foy, said he saw Wayne "footless" one day after going on a bender and claimed he was unable to stand at other times.

The relationship between Sean and Mary Kate is clearly the film's centerpiece. During the famous scene in which she kisses him for the first time in the cottage, O'Hara injured herself trying to hit Wayne. It was supposed to be a fabricated attempt, but he had annoyed her on the day in question, so she lashed out at him for real.[29] She remembered the scene like this: "I thought, I'm going to break his neck, I'm going to kill him. I hauled back and I let go but he saw it coming. He put up his hand and my hand snapped against the tip of his fingers."[30] A pain shot up her arm, but she was too proud to tell anyone about it. She hid her hand in her petticoat, but Wayne knew something was up. "Damn it," he demanded, "let me see your hand. You'd have broken my jaw if I hadn't blocked your blow." By now, her fingers had swollen up like sausages. Wayne said to Ford, "She's always doing something to herself."[31] She was taken to a nearby hospital, where X-rays revealed she had cracked a bone in her hand.

Wayne enjoyed seeing her in rages. He thought anger only highlighted her beauty. One is reminded of his comment to Vera Miles in *The Man Who Shot Liberty Valance*: "Hally, you look awful purdy when you get mad." Anger intensified O'Hara's strong spirit and made those hazel eyes burn.

Ruth Barton observed that O'Hara is seldom seen in repose in the film: "At mealtime she flounces around her family kitchen dishing out potatoes and scolding her brother and the other men, all of whom are seated at a lower level to her. She almost dances around Wayne and she flits around her own house when they move into it, refusing the conventional pose of the Irish woman seated at the hearth."[32] It's this incessant fidgetiness that makes her character come alive.

Steven Spielberg is an acknowledged admirer of the film, as evidenced by the fact that he featured a scene from it in *E.T.* He enjoyed the confused parameters of the Wayne-O'Hara relationship: "I've always loved that moment with the wind blowing and the way he held her by the hand without forcing her. He just allowed her to allow herself to come in for the kiss. Well he kind of forced her. He put her in a half-Nelson actually."[33] Spielberg's confusion here seems to mirror the polarities Ford was trying to access.

Wayne had a problem with the scene in which O'Hara locks him out of their bedroom. The way it was written, he reacts simply by picking up his boxing gloves and throwing them into the fire. But Wayne felt the scene was seriously underwritten for a man of his pugilistic credentials. He went to Ford and told him he was fed up "cowdogging" and saying "Yes, Ma'am" and "No Ma'am" all the time. He was wondering when Ford was going to let him, as he put it, "show some balls." Ford wasn't impressed with this tirade and gave the actor a dirty look, but he must have taken Wayne's complaint to heart, because a few days later he made this offer: "Duke, I'm going to let you do what you always do when a broad locks you out. I'm going to let you kick the fuckin' door down!"[34] And so it came to pass.

"There'll be no locks or bolts between us," Sean tells Mary Kate as he breaks it down, "except in your mercenary little heart." The line betrays his total misunderstanding of her motives. When Michaeleen (Fitzgerald) espies the wreckage the following morning, he exclaims querulously, "Impetuous! Homeric!" as if the damage had been caused by a marital romp. The audience knows this isn't the case, but the Irish film censor, Richard Hayes, still saw fit to delete those words. He also censored Jack MacGowran's earlier comment about the (extra large) bed: "Ah, a man'd have to be a sprinter to catch his wife in a bed like that." The eradication of "comic and mild references to sexual relations, even between married people," was nothing unusual in Ireland in the 1950s.[35] Both these lines were subsequently reinserted. Ford was toying with the censors, making sex into an athletic display rather than something sacred to be spoken of only in hushed tones. "I'm certainly not against sex on the screen if it's done in the right way," Ford declared. "Many Westerns have a gutsy sort of sex, and I think I made the sexiest picture ever in *The Quiet Man*. This was all about a man trying to get a woman into bed but that was all right. They were married."[36] Here we see the two sides of Ford: the conservative and the rogue.

Wayne told Barbara Walters that what he liked most about his onscreen relationship with O'Hara was that it was "healthy and strong and sensual but it wasn't degrading."[37] Many people might disagree, considering the way he drags her through the fields toward the end. But it's important to temper our sociological invective with common sense. As Joseph McBride makes clear, "The ironic amusement with which Sean, Mary Kate and Ford approach the marital donnybrook is lost on humorless viewers who consider *The Quiet Man* an appalling demonstration of the problem of spousal abuse in rural Ireland."[38]

The *Sunday Independent* advised a suspension of normal critical faculties with this input: "Mr. Ford is chuckling from his director's chair as he gives us in burlesque all the colorful codology solemnly accepted with wide eye and open mouth by the foreigner who believes the pig is the guest of honor in the parlor."[39] The film doesn't so much endorse loutish behavior as send it up. The animals grazing around Ashford Castle at that time weren't pigs at all, incidentally, but sheep, so it was sheep droppings O'Hara was dragged through.[40] She tried to disperse the droppings before the scene was shot, but Wayne and Ford kicked them back into place. Afterward, Ford gave orders that she wasn't to be given a towel or water to clean herself, so she sat like that for most of the day. For O'Hara, this was just Pappy being Pappy.

She did, however, suffer damage to her back as a result of the scene, and she subsequently spent two years on "flat surfaces and operating tables" trying to get various disks back in the right places.[41] In fact, the problems continued long after the movie; she had an operation to repair a ruptured disk as late as May 1957.[42] It was a high price to pay for being humiliated in a Mayo field. And yet, of all the scenes she ever did, it's probably the one people remember best. It's also the one she herself remembers most fondly. "I had to have a laminectomy after the damage done to my back because of it," she complained. "I was mad but it didn't do me any good. You learn to smile and laugh and let the men have their way."[43] (How ironic that in a film with so much fighting, she was the only person who suffered a long-lasting injury—in a scene that wasn't even in the original script.)

Is the scene as demeaning to women as it appears? Perhaps not. Wayne's biographer Garry Wills points out that Mary Kate's indignities serve to underscore Ford's main point, which is that, in the end, she usually gets her way: "Against her brother's wishes she marries the man she wants. Against her new husband's wishes she gets him to fight her brother. Against her brother's wishes and her husband's complete indifference, she makes her husband demand, and her brother give over, the dowry that symbolizes her independence."[44] Looked at this way, the momentary discomfort of her trawl through the mud turned out pretty well.

Along with the memorable action, the script still sparkles after all these years on, giving us such delightful speculations as, "He'll regret it to his dying day, if he lives that long." Another great line is Barry Fitzgerald's: "It's a fine soft night so I think I'll join me comrades and talk a little treason." You can almost hear Ford's raucous horselaugh behind that one.[45] His republican sympathies are on display here, but otherwise, few political notes are struck. Ford originally wanted to set the film in 1921, at the height of Ireland's armed struggle against Britain. He even considered having Thornton "come home from the United States to do his bit in the fight for freedom."[46] He eventually rejected this notion, realizing that the film's main strength lay in what we would now call its "rom-com" element.[47]

Politics hasn't totally been excised, however, as Louisa Burns-Bisogno makes clear in her book *Censoring Irish Nationalism*.[48] Although IRA references are skittish in the main, the script is littered with them from the moment Wayne arrives in Innisfree and has his bags appropriated by an IRA commandant. Another line redolent of Ford's mischievous attitude toward politics and crime is this: "His grandfather died in a penal colony in Australia and his father was a good man too." It's a choice non sequitur. When Sean and Mary Kate get married, they're toasted with the words "May they live in peace and national freedom" by the IRA commandant (played by O'Hara's brother Charles). Significantly, Ford edited out the word "national" for fear of being accused of making a jingoistic point. There's a slight blip on the lip-syncing as a result.[49]

The much-heralded fight between Sean and Will that closes the film is played more for laughs than anything else. Ford takes great pains to contrast it to the kind of fight Thornton would have had in the ring, where winning is paramount. Here, there are two winners because it's really more of a brawl—a kind of male bonding ritual in which throwing a punch is almost a term of endearment. Wayne engaged in many of these fights in his screen career, with the likes of Robert Mitchum and others.

This is what Mary Kate has been hoping for all along, a set-to that proves Sean's manliness both to her and to all the other inhabitants of Innisfree. The fight is an elongated encounter (the scene runs for eight and a half minutes) that starts in the fields and continues across meadows and even a river before the two pugilists take a time-out for some liquid refreshments in the pub, thereby proving "the Irish-held belief that even during a matter of life and death there's plenty of time to stop for a pint along the way."[50] Part two begins as Sean sends Will hurtling through the wall of the pub. Things get even more hectic, until both men finally fall down exhausted. The scene took four days to film, with Ford getting the best out of McLaglen by "lambasting the actor unmercifully for giving a poor performance up to that point."[51]

It's now time for Mary Kate to return to the kitchen, thereby accepting "a traditional wifely role despite all the thunder and bluster of her earlier revolt."[52] Her last words, "I'll have supper ready for you," leave little doubt about her capitulation to her man. Men fight and women cook: that's the deal. All that remains now is for her to whisper a message in Sean's ear before the final credits roll. Is she asking him into her bed here? People have spent more than half a century pondering this. O'Hara told Des MacHale: "Only three people know what I whispered. The first was Pappy and he's dead. The second was Duke and he's dead too. The third is myself and I ain't telling."[53] She even refused MacHale's request that she leave the contents of the whisper in a sealed envelope to be opened by him upon her demise, should he outlive her. MacHale employed some expert lip-readers to try to decipher her words, but they were stumped because the camera films only the side of her face. The closest she ever came to revealing the secret was when Larry King asked her if it was "sexual or cursing." "A little bit of both," she teased.[54] The exact words she used, according to one writer, have now acquired the enigmatic resonance of the Third Secret of Fatima for many film scholars.[55]

She did admit that when Ford told her what to say, she balked at first because it was too rude. She also confirmed that if she'd said it out loud, she would have been in trouble with the censors. She informed MacHale that Wayne himself didn't know what the line was until she spoke it. This was intentional on Ford's part; he was seeking the shocked expression on Wayne's face. Wayne liked to say, "Maureen makes me act because she makes me react."[56] He certainly did that here.

The "curtain call" at the end of the film, whereby the characters "take their bow," is a throwback to films of a much earlier, even pre-talkie era. It emphasizes its "theatricality"—not that there is any doubt about this anyway.[57]

Location work was completed in July. The crew flew back to Hollywood to film the interiors, and by the following month, they were all done.

After Ford and his crew left the sleepy Irish village, the local newspapers suggested it would be a long time before it got over the experience. According to one writer, "It never did."[58]

Ford was feeling pretty emotional. After six weeks of self-imposed sobriety, he went on a massive bender, getting so drunk on the plane back to America that he had to ask the pilot to do a U-turn and allow him to disembark in Dublin.[59] Only John Ford could have gotten away with that.

He knew he had a winner on his hands by now. His film had music, poetry, and the Irish love of the *craic* (Gaelic for "fun"), as well as quality-studded performances from his gilt-edged cast. Yates, however, remained unconvinced and was worried that the film would overrun the 120 minutes he'd allocated for it. In fact, Ford's final cut ran 129 minutes, but he didn't divulge this to Yates. On the night of the test screening for the studio bosses, he had a secret plan to get Yates to agree to the longer running time. Ford started the movie, and almost from the outset the "suits" were charmed by its pastoral nature. Even Yates—the "king of the cheapies," who had spent most of his life cutting films to the bone—warmed to it. But he became nervous as the 120-minute point grew near and the film showed no sign of ending. When it hit the two-hour mark, in the middle of the mock-epic dustup between Wayne and McLaglen, the spool ran out and the lights went up. The studio executives jumped out of their seats and demanded to see the end of the fight. Ford looked over at Yates and crowed, "There you are, Herb, exactly 120 minutes. I couldn't figure out how to cut nine minutes out without ruining it so I figured, what the hell, why knock myself out. I just cut the fight." Yates had to admit the extra nine minutes were needed, so Ford got his way.[60] (Yates did have one gripe with the final cut: "Everything's all green. Tell the cameraman to take the green filter off."[61] What did he expect from Ireland?)

After the screening, Yates's native caution kicked in, and he decided to release the film in midweek with a backup stage show to "rescue" it in case it bombed. He needn't have worried. *The Quiet Man* did better business than any John Ford film since *How Green Was My Valley*. People waited in long lines to see it, many of them returning four or five times to see it over and over. In some theaters it played for as long as two months. After seeing the profits roll in, Yates had to admit his radar had been on the blink in the early stages. It became the most financially successful film in Republic's history and the most critically successful as well, drawing rapturous praise from the most unlikely sources.

O'Hara received the best notices of her career thus far. There was even some noise about an Oscar nomination. One critic wrote of her partnership with Wayne: "Their quieter scenes together are a triumph of emotional growth and control, their fussing and feuding a glorious riot. They're like Laurel and Hardy in a field full of leprechauns."[62] The *Irish Times* blithely jibed, "It's probably fair to say that O'Hara's character contributed to exporting a few myths about the Irish female: namely, that all Irish women are redheads, and they come with a mighty temper attached to them."[63] More than sixty years later, Ireland is still trying to live that reputation down.

Maggie Armstrong thought O'Hara's beauty was the film's standout element: "her burnished red hair, her porcelain skin, her voluptuous figure clothed in Virgin Mary blues." Wayne, in contrast, was just plain old Duke: "a little chauvinistic, wooden and superannuated."[64] Brandon French thought Mary Kate epitomized the qualities of both goddess and shrew, which eventually "cancel each other out and clear the stage for the introduction of a real woman who is neither."[65] This is a point worth noting—particularly since nothing else in her canon of work can lay claim to such complexity.

The film was nominated for seven Oscars: Best Picture, Best Director, Best Supporting Actor, Best Screenplay, Best Cinematography, Best Art Direction, and Best Sound Recording. It won two. Ford got his second statuette, and the other award went to Winton Hoch and Archie Stout for their cinematography. It was Hoch's third Oscar in just four years. Both O'Hara and Wayne might have expected at least nominations, but clearly the Academy saw it as a director's film. (The Academy was also notorious for ignoring comedies on Oscar night.) Victor McLaglen might have won for Best Supporting Actor if he hadn't already got an Oscar for *The Informer* in 1935. In the event, Anthony Quinn edged him out with his passionate turn as Marlon Brando's brother in *Viva Zapata!* (Having said that, McLaglen's accent is the most suspect one in the film, sounding more like cockney London than Mayo. He was actually born in Tunbridge Wells in Kent.)

Denis Myers thought the film gave O'Hara a chance to escape from "the brocades and *coiffeures* of those Technicolor storms and masquerades through which she sailed a decorative passage." Instead, she became "a barefooted shepherdess on the rolling turf."[66] Myers found her transition from "frightened maid of the pastures" to "self-assured shrew" too quick for comfort, until he realized that everything in the film was fabricated, including the "typical" Irish village. So why should she be different?[67] Another critic agreed, claiming O'Hara looked like a "wild Irish girl" one minute and "as if she had just come from a ladies' finishing school" the next.[68]

O'Hara rarely gave an interview without mentioning that this was her favorite film. No matter what aspect of her life was under discussion, she would find some way to bring it up. For her, it was the terminus a quo and terminus ad quem of her career trajectory. She described the film as "lightning in a bottle." She usually told interviewers she deserved an Oscar for her performance. Maybe she did. In no other role were her classic qualities more embedded: the resolute charm, the pale beauty, the temper, the stubbornness. While the film itself may be a collage of outmoded scoundrels and Synge-song dialectics, O'Hara's immersion in it was a career capstone and gives it a different kind of ballast.

Most of the cast are dead now, but people still flock to the film's Irish locations or stay in Ashford Castle for "a rub of the relic." The "White O'Morn" cottage has been dilapidated for many years, but tourists still visit in great numbers annually. One of the problems with its upkeep is that people remove stones from the cottage to keep as mementos. Because it was so expensive to maintain, the cottage was put on the market in 1986 and bought by American Gregory Ebbitt for the modest sum of $27,000. The understanding was that he would restore it to its former condition, but that didn't happen. O'Hara joined the "Save The Quiet Man Cottage" Facebook group to lobby politicians and conservationists to do something, but little could be achieved without Ebbitt's backing, which he refused to give. He also refused to sell it. As some consolation, tourists can see a reconstructed version of the cottage in the Cong Museum. The film is also shown there at regular intervals. (Some people have watched it up to 200 times.)

Time has been good to *The Quiet Man*. In 1996 readers of the *Irish Times* voted it the greatest movie of all time. Three years later it came in sixty-sixth in an Internet survey of the top movies of the millennium.[69] In 2001, its fiftieth anniversary, Galway launched a nationwide search for the best Mary Kate Danaher look-alike in Ireland, and a winner was finally selected from a short list of twenty.

The place where O'Hara herded sheep is now the third fairway of the Cong golf course.

7

Back to Bread and Butter

By 1950, people were snapping up TV sets, buying more than 7 million that year alone. Movie attendance sank to 50 million a year, almost half the previous tally. Many people moved to the suburbs, where geography also became a problem, along with mortgages and the cost of raising children. Some theaters raised prices to cut their losses, but this created a different kind of barrier.

Billy Wilder professed to be delighted with the so-called one-eyed monster of television. "It used to be that films were the lowest form of art," he said. "Now we've got something to look down on."[1] More than 3,000 theaters closed between 1950 and 1953. To try to halt that trend, Cinerama was introduced in the fall of 1952. This wide-screen format required three projection booths and a huge curved screen that provided almost 160 degrees of vision. It was expensive, and not all theaters could be restructured to accommodate it, but the profits were tempting.

The contract system was also changing. Stars began to ask for percentages of the gross. Some of them even farmed themselves out to other studios. James Stewart's contract with MGM ran out during the war, and when he came home, his agent (Lew Wasserman) advised him to go freelance. (Stewart practically became a millionaire on the strength of his earnings from *Winchester '73* because Wasserman's deal gave him a chunk of the gross.) Other stars began to set up their own film companies.

As noted earlier, O'Hara tried to get in on this particular action, although her company, Price-Merman, seemed doomed from the start. In a last-gasp effort to revive it, Price accompanied O'Hara to Mexico in 1951, hoping to procure financing for a film he wanted to make. She was going there for another reason as well—to receive an award at a film festival. As soon as they arrived, he started to hit the bottle, and that was the last she saw of him for the whole festival. One night at a restaurant, she met a man who would have a huge impact on her future: wealthy financier Enrique Parra. They formed an immediate bond, despite his limited English, and danced the night away. The following day they met again. Price finally reappeared, but the financing for his film fell through due to his drunkenness, and Price-Merman was finished as a company.[2]

O'Hara had been wiped out financially by Price at this point. He had run up debts in her name in excess of $300,000. She'd decided to file for divorce some time previously, but before she could do so, they received word that Price's mother had died. She put everything on hold out of respect for his bereavement.

O'Hara became more involved in Parra's life as time passed. She felt comfortable in his presence. The obvious stumbling block to their relationship was that they were both married, although both were estranged from their spouses. He had a son and daughter, Quico and Negrita. Negrita resented O'Hara, although the two never met. Negrita also suffered from diabetes and was prone to diabetic coma as a result.

The more time O'Hara spent with Parra, the more she considered a long-term commitment to him. Could they marry one day? He was living apart from his wife, but he feared a divorce could exacerbate Negrita's condition. O'Hara felt helpless. At times, Parra seemed like an escape from her situation with Price; at other times, it seemed that a life with Parra would invite more problems than it would solve. She let things slide in the hope that a resolution would come somewhere down the road.

On December 29, 1951, their tenth wedding anniversary, Price "staggered" out the door, suitcase in hand, and never came back. "I still don't know why he left," O'Hara confided to the *Los Angeles Times* some months later. "He didn't tell me he was leaving."[3] But she wrote in her autobiography: "I know what made him leave. The party was over and Will knew it. Charlie Fitz and Jimmy were at the house all the time now and he wouldn't dare treat me the way he had before in front of them."[4] His departure opened the door for divorce, and for Parra. Or did it? Many people disapproved of her relationship with Parra, including John Ford. Ford also disapproved of O'Hara divorcing Price. His generation believed that a bad marriage was better than none—it was the Catholic way.

Her mind aswirl with marital tension, O'Hara was offered another movie directed by George Sherman, this one starring Errol Flynn. The last time she had seen Flynn, he'd been down on all fours, sneaking away from a war bond function after draining a bottle of whiskey. She didn't imagine things had changed much in the interim.

Against All Flags is a fast-paced trifle. Flynn, nearing the end of his golden age as the derring-do supremo, plays Brian Hawke, a British naval officer on a secret mission. O'Hara plays the aptly named Spitfire Stevens, and Anthony Quinn is—again—the villain of the piece. Sherman directs as if he's running for a train. Flynn's character is working undercover, pretending to be a deserter in order to infiltrate Quinn's pirate gang in Madagascar. The two men fight for O'Hara. She enjoys their attentions but becomes enraged when Flynn briefly shifts his focus to an endangered Indian princess (Alice Kelley). O'Hara saves his life when Quinn tries to kill him. After Flynn's cover is blown, it's time for more thrills and spills, but nobody doubts that he will get the girl—and the ship—in the end.

O'Hara was well aware of Flynn's legendary charm, and she worried that he would endeavor to lure her to his bed during the making of the movie. Rumor had it, very few of his leading ladies had escaped thus far. The feared seduction didn't happen, thankfully.

O'Hara didn't approve of Flynn's penchant for eating vodka-laden oranges between scenes, but at least he was punctual. Because he was receiving a percentage of the profits, with no salary up front, he was motivated to make the film as good as it could be.[5] With this in mind, he demanded that work finish at four every day because, as biographer Michael Freedland noted, "people would work harder if they knew they were going to get away early."[6] (Freedland might have added that Flynn wanted to shut down production at four so he would have more drinking time.) Everything went fine until Flynn refused to use a stunt double and broke his ankle in a fight scene; shooting was held up for five months.[7]

Flynn was reluctant to do a scene in which he challenges O'Hara to a duel. He asked Sherman, "Do you think this is going to work? You know I'm supposed to be the bravest guy on the screen. How could I fight a woman?" Sherman allayed his fears by telling him he'd worked with O'Hara before and warned, "You'd better be in shape."[8] Flynn found that out as soon as the scene began. Steve Jacques contended that O'Hara outdid Flynn in the bravado department, and "to protect Flynn's image, many of her most skilful scenes didn't make it to the final cut."[9]

Sherman praised O'Hara's improvisational ability, something one doesn't normally associate with her. She was able to "ride with the scene," he averred, if he suddenly did something that hadn't been rehearsed: "She'd be quick enough to grasp the change without missing a beat. You couldn't rattle her."[10] He also praised her for being proactive in scenes, often coming up with ideas that denied her "face time," to use the contemporary idiom. She was sensitive to the story line of a movie, Sherman observed, "even when it meant taking a scene away from her."[11] The organic development was more important to O'Hara than her ego.

O'Hara disclosed to Larry King that Flynn was fine to work with in the morning, but by four in the afternoon, he was unable to function because of all the vodka he was drinking. Because of this, he was usually advised to go home and sleep it off.[12] As a result, O'Hara's declaration of "I love you" was delivered not to him but to "an X marked on a black flag that was supposed to be Errol Flynn."[13]

Maybe the experience of working with such a broken-down man led to O'Hara's ruminations to *Photoplay* magazine in 1952: "I've been looking for some time at the motion picture stars who have lived sensibly and modestly in Hollywood and are living comfortably now. I've also looked at the stars who spent all their money, lived high and rich. Many of these, too many, are working as extras today." She thought there was "nothing in life more forlorn than the big ex-star. There's nothing more forgotten. I feel so sorry for them I'll stand there until my feet ache listening to them as they talk about their 'day.' Just recently, on the set of *Against All Flags*, one of them told me, 'In my day I wouldn't have done this scene as Flynn did it.' My heart begins to ache as they go on and on about their 'day,' which is their yesterday. Don't they realize that every day must end?"[14]

O'Hara and Flynn were like two sides of one coin. Each was identified with swashbuckling roles in which they fought fiercely and usually did their own stunts. In his autobiography Flynn blustered, "Dammit, I said to myself, I'm not going to be a phony. The reason behind it was I had fear and I had to go out and meet it. If I'm afraid to do something I move in on it and try to tangle with it and lick it."[15] It almost could have been John Wayne talking.

O'Hara appreciated his attitude. In fact, she reprised it. Future generations of actors would see things differently. Some action heroes and heroines insist on performing their own stunts, but thanks to computer-generated special effects, they don't have to. They define fear and courage in other ways—like coming to grips with their characters. There's a famous anecdote about James Dean: He urinated in front of a crowd while filming *Giant* to free himself up to do a scene. If he could do that, he boasted afterward, he could do anything.[16] That was his definition of courage.

This is one reason O'Hara had little respect for the finer points of Method acting. Actors were exhorted to dig down into their deeper recesses to access some neurotic impulse or memory that might act as a catalyst to interpret the characters they were playing. She was far too well adjusted to have any neuroses in the first place.

O'Hara's rival around this time was Rhonda Fleming, another effervescent redhead who was drop-landed into one action movie after another. As O'Hara was jousting with Flynn in *Against All Flags*, Fleming was playing an English noblewoman posing as a pirate in Sidney Salkow's Caribbean blockbuster *The Golden Hawk*. The 1952 western *The Redhead from Wyoming* (the original title was *Cattle Kate*) may have been better suited to Fleming, but she was otherwise engaged, so O'Hara stepped into the breach as high-spirited Kate Maxwell. When we first see her, she's alighting from a stagecoach to hook up with old flame Jim Averell (William Bishop). Her headgear could be mistaken for the Irish flag, except it's green, blue, and yellow instead of green, white, and orange. When she removes her cape with a sassy line to "the boys," we realize she's trying to pitch herself as a kind of Mae West character. That's the first problem with the film: miscasting. Alex Nicol isn't right as Sheriff Blaine, either (putting a splinter in one's mouth to look "cool" doesn't quite cut it). In addition, the chemistry between O'Hara and Nicol, a kind of low-rent Randolph Scott, is poor.

Averell gives Kate his saloon, which is actually a front for his cattle-rustling operation. He's hoping this will fund his seedy campaign to be governor of Wyoming. Kate is the patsy, signing the "maverick" cattle in, and it isn't long before she's gussied up like a madam and cutting cards for the boys. She advises Blaine to kick up his heels, but she doesn't even do that herself; instead, she spouts lines like "There's a fight comin' on" when a range war threatens. When Kate realizes what Averell is up to, she tries to derail him but ends up in jail, taking the rap for him. Now it's time for Blaine to stop chewing on that splinter, put Averell out of action, and live happily ever after with Cattle Kate.

Blaine thinks he has Kate summed up when he ventures, "You talk like you dress, but you don't feel that way." This line prefigures their eventual pairing, a prospect one greets with a mixture of dread and boredom. How does Kate really feel? We don't know because her character isn't buttoned down. She ranges indiscriminately from ideological speechifier to party gal, leaving one to conclude that her final choice of Blaine (a thoroughly unlikely "drifter") is predicated on his virtue quotient rather than any "man points."

We get flashes of vintage O'Hara in some of her lines: "I oughta kill you but I'd rather see you hang," she spits out at Bishop toward the end. But by and large, this is flat beer and not at all the "panorama of fast-paced excitement" promised by the trailer. The fault isn't really hers. Nicol seems to have had a personality bypass, while Bishop is a stock suave wheeler-dealer type. In such a context, O'Hara's misguided efforts to rebore her Mary Kate Danaher persona in sagebrush mode is doomed to failure. Her halfhearted blowsiness doesn't convince, and neither does her accent (which seems more Ena Burke School of Elocution than Wyoming drawl).

The film is only seventy-six minutes long. Such slightness, combined with its wafer-thin characterizations, slots it firmly in the "filler" bracket. O'Hara dubbed it a "stinkeroo." This was a term she frequently slapped on films that didn't do well for her.

As if to add to her woes, she was injured on the set. An extra fired a prop gun too close to her during a gunfight scene, causing powder burns on her neck and shoulders. She was rushed to the hospital to prevent any long-term effects on her skin. When she got home that day, she had an eerie feeling that something wasn't right. Female intuition made her check a closet where she kept her jewelry and important documents. When she opened it, she found, to her horror, a piece of paper covered with doodles of shamrocks—the same ones that adorned John Ford's love letters to her. But how had he gotten into her house? She could only put it down to his military connections. She was tempted to accuse Ford but felt that doing so would somehow play into his hands. She decided to say nothing, and the next time she saw him, he was as phlegmatic as ever. He was on the phone when she entered his office; he motioned her to sit down. As she looked around the room, she noticed that a picture of her on his wall had been turned back to front. Was this another ploy to humiliate her? (He was speaking to his wife about the forthcoming wedding of their daughter Barbara to Ken Curtis. O'Hara claims in her autobiography that Ford didn't approve of Curtis, but Harry Carey Jr. disputes this in his own memoirs.) Whatever Ford's motive, he said nothing to her about the break-in.

Things were going well between O'Hara and Parra at this point, but she was concerned that he might not be as estranged from his wife as he purported to be. She needed to be sure, so she employed a private detective. Here, we see O'Hara's pragmatism writ large: she was able to put her emotions in cold storage and do something sneaky. Others might say she had reason to be suspicious after what she'd been through with Price. The detective discovered that Parra's wife was dating a bullfighter, and this put her mind at ease. She then phoned Price and told him she was divorcing him. He was philosophical about the news. Now that she'd put the wheels in motion, she phoned her parents in Dublin and divulged how horrific the past few years had been—information she had carefully withheld from them up to this point. They were outraged, understandably, but happy that her psychological torture was about to end.

At the end of 1952 she sent a couple of trucks to her house to haul away most of her belongings—everything that wasn't nailed down. It wasn't easy for her to de-clutter this ruthlessly. "I'm a saver," she said, "a human squirrel. I had every letter Mommie and Daddy and my three sisters and my two brothers and my uncles and aunts ever wrote me, all labeled according to date, all neatly tied with ribbons." She'd also preserved everything from old theater programs to Bronwyn's first tooth wrapped in a Kleenex. She even had a piece of her wedding cake. But she'd made up her mind to start a new life, which meant emptying the house and putting it up for sale. The trucks stopped at her door, and "out of the house came my two brothers Charlie and Jimmy, my secretary, butler, my daughter Bronwyn's nurse, the gardener. They were staggering under boxes, crates and barrels which they dumped, like so much rubbish, onto the trucks. The trucks then drove off—with my past. I'd given it away."[17]

After Price moved out, O'Hara was free to spend a substantial amount of time with Parra in Mexico, without having to worry about a scandal brewing. She even enrolled Bronwyn in a Mexican school. She enjoyed doing the simple things with Parra—walking down the street holding hands, shopping, being taken care of in a way that Price could never understand.

She also started to learn Spanish. Eventually, she moved into one of Parra's homes with Bronwyn—but she kept one foot in Hollywood.

Once her marriage broke up, journalists felt emboldened to write more freely about her. Denny Shane was one of the first out of the traps. "For ten years," he expounded, "beautiful Maureen O'Hara managed to keep her private life mysteriously to herself." On movie sets, Shane continued, she was regarded as "cooperative but not particularly communicative." She commanded huge salaries on her seven-year contracts "and then proceeded to freelance at even more gigantic fees." But her expenses were also enormous. Now free of Price, she wanted to simplify her lifestyle: "When I was first married I was hopelessly, disgustingly efficient. I was the kind that overdid it—I even had labels neatly typed and pasted to every linen shelf. I made lists in duplicate for everything. Like an office manager."[18] That would all change now. She was looking forward to shedding the trappings of materialism: "I'm knee-deep in the process of reorganizing me. And to tell the truth, it's quite a job."[19] She made a brief reference to her trips to Mexico but didn't mention Parra by name. When in Mexico, she told Shane, she socialized with groups of interesting people. She was still playing her cards close to the vest. As for remarriage, that would be possible only if her marriage to Price was annulled, because her religion forbade it. For now, there were more movies to be negotiated to keep the wolf from the door.

John Ford continued to interfere in her life. He knew of her situation with Price and, more important, with Parra. When Price was in London, Ford met him for dinner and told him O'Hara was more or less living with Parra. Price called O'Hara after the meeting and said he intended to seek custody of Bronwyn because of her "immoral" double life. She knew he had no real interest in Bronwyn, that he was just looking for money, but she was deeply disturbed. Once again, Pappy had thrown a spanner in the works.

O'Hara filed for divorce from Price in July 1951 on the grounds of incompatibility, a euphemism that covered a multitude of situations in divorce suits; it was finalized a month later. The *Hartford Courant* reported that he was ordered to pay her $1 a year as token alimony, but she claimed she paid *him* alimony, as well as settling a $300,000 debt he owed. In a statement to the press, she described Price as an "excellent" director that she "wouldn't hesitate to work for" in the future.

It was difficult to keep her mind on her work while all this was going on. This may explain why she doesn't look quite right in *War Arrow*,
a western she made in 1953. Jeff Chandler plays Howell Brady, an army
major training a group of "good" Indians (the Seminoles) to help the army
defeat some "bad" ones (the Kiowas). His commanding officer, Colonel
Jackson (John McIntyre), opposes the idea of trusting any Indians at all.
O'Hara plays Elaine Corwin, a woman who spends much of her time
soul-searching about whether she's a widow (her husband may have been
killed in battle) and whether she really likes Brady, who may be attracted
to Avis (Suzan Ball), the fiery daughter of an Indian chief. She draws Brady
close and fends him off by turns (something O'Hara's film characters do
often with men). Such confusion accounts for some of O'Hara's fluctuating
attention.

This account makes the film sound much more interesting than it is.
O'Hara was bored with both the plot and her costar. She had lead billing over Chandler, whom she dubbed "a nice man but a bad actor."[20] In
her memoirs, she said acting with him was like acting with a broomstick.
This was cruel, as it would have been difficult for anyone to overcome the
moribund material. Maybe he was simply trying to dumb himself down to
its level.

Oscar nominations were due to be announced, and O'Hara's friend
Anne Baxter thought there was a good chance she'd get one for *The Quiet
Man*. Sadly, it never materialized. Once again, O'Hara felt Ford was
responsible. He had put out a rumor that she was having an affair with
Wayne to scupper her chances. To her face, he expressed sadness that she
wasn't nominated, even giving her a gold bracelet as a consolation, but deep
down she thought he was delighted.

She then went to Spain to film *Fire over Africa*, a film she would
remember for all the wrong reasons during her 1957 court case against
Confidential magazine. En route, she stopped in Dublin for an informal
visit and was snapped getting on the number 14 bus. "Could it be . . . ?" the
conductor wondered, mimicking the opening line from *The Quiet Man*.[21]

Fire over Africa has her as the Mata Hari–like Joanna Dane, a secret
agent trying to track down the leader of a gang of smugglers operating from
Tangiers. Macdonald Carey is Van Logan, another agent, although Dane
doesn't discover this until the film is almost over, and she suspects him

of being in league with the villains throughout. O'Hara's brother Jimmy, again using the surname Lilburn, has a cameo as one of her admirers. (He later changed his name to Jimmy O'Hara to capitalize on his sister's fame.) If one ever wondered why Jimmy's film career never took off, the answer lies in his thumbnail sketch here as Danny Boy. Binnie Barnes fares better as Frisco, the ice-cold nightclub madam who turns out to be the linchpin of the smuggling operation. The plot is so thin on drama that this revelation wakes the audience up.

The film is like the poor man's *Casablanca*, with Carey and O'Hara as second-string versions of Bogie and Bacall. They spar verbally. "See you tomorrow," Carey says to her at one point, getting the clichéd reply, "Not if I see you first." Elsewhere he warns, "Tangiers can be tough," eliciting the response, "So can I." They seem to speak in italics in their seriocomic exchanges. Things reach a head when she hisses at him (prior to pumping three bullets into his chest), "You're no good but I'd still hate to kill you." In the event, she doesn't—he's wearing a bulletproof vest—but not for lack of trying.

Matters aren't helped by Richard Sale's insipid direction. The *Monthly Film Bulletin* chided, "Maureen O'Hara looks very handsome in Technicolor but her expressions are limited—mostly to disgust at shooting smugglers or pulling knives from dying men."[22] By now, criticism from these self-styled arbiters of taste had developed a familiar pattern: the Technicolor sop, followed by a putdown based not so much on O'Hara's acting ability as on the scripts she was being offered. Why did she continue to take them? She may have been thinking of John Ford's dictum: "One doesn't become a better director by not directing." The secret was to keep going in the hope that something better would come along.

That something better was Ford's *The Long Gray Line*, which she made in 1955. John Wayne was supposed to be her costar, but when his schedule conflicted, she suggested Tyrone Power, with whom she'd worked well in *The Black Swan*. Ford was happy to go with that recommendation. She also secured a small role as a cadet for her brother Jimmy. Ward Bond plays the token hard-nosed superior, and Harry Carey Jr. has a cameo as a young President Eisenhower. Ford gave Carey the part after examining his head for signs of premature baldness. (This pretty much qualified as a screen test for a Ford movie—at least if he liked you.)

The Long Gray Line tells the story of Marty Maher (Power), an Irishman who becomes head physical instructor at West Point Military Academy. Maher is a raw recruit at the beginning of the film, but he eventually finds himself training cadets on the cusp of World War I. He marries Mary O'Donnell, a Donegal lass played by O'Hara. Their first child dies shortly after birth, and the cadets become like surrogate sons to Maher. In the scene in which she gives birth to their ill-fated son, Maher's father (played by Ford stalwart Donald Crisp) says to him: "We'll be needin' a rest after the great thing we've done this day." One wonders exactly how tongue-in-cheek Ford is being here, as the doctor reveals that the birth was rough on Mary (Ford could never have been accused of being a New Man). Tragically, the child dies. Worse, Mary is informed that she can't have any more children. Instead of Maher sympathizing with his wife, she finds herself imploring him to "forgive" her for this traumatic news. He then goes off on a bender, from which he's "rescued" by a group of cadets.

The film showcases Ford at his best and worst—best in his celebration of military life (his "masculine" side), and worst in his saccharine emotion (an excess of his "feminine" one). The accents of both O'Hara and Power are overdone, and O'Hara's carries no trace of Donegal in it. Power's brogue is, in Fred Lawrence Guiles's phrase, "as thick as Mulligan stew."[23] Nevertheless, O'Hara's performance is solid, from the silence of her first rendezvous with Power to the garrulousness of later ones, where her familiar headstrong persona comes to the fore. Power dominates the film, but O'Hara rides shotgun with both charm and feeling; she even manages to sound convincing while delivering lines like this: "Is it sorry you are already, Marty Maher?" (which sounds like something from a bad Sean O'Casey play). Critical views of the film differed radically. For one reviewer, it was little more than "sweetness and sunlight."[24] For another, the Irish emphasis wasn't true to the "ethnic balance" of real West Point history.[25]

In any case, O'Hara was proud of the way she died in the film. She decided to play it totally naturally "and simply let the audience put into the scene any sentiment or feeling they wanted to." She was in Ford's bad graces at the time, having been "in the barrel" for days, and couldn't wait to finish the picture. But if Ford saw that one of his stars had been pushed past the breaking point, that was when he became his most charming. And so it was here. After O'Hara "died," he called all the crew around and said,

"Ladies and gentlemen, if you want better acting than that, you'll never find it." But O'Hara knew what he was up to—using flattery to win her back.[26] "Periodically," she giggled, "he dropped you a little praise to keep you under control and you'd think, 'The old bastard.' He knew what he was doing and why he was doing it."[27]

The relationship between O'Hara and Ford reached a nadir on the set of *The Long Gray Line*. He made it his business to rob her of all dignity from day one of the shoot. Each day he greeted her with the words, "Well, did Herself have a good shit this morning?" Then he'd ask the crew what her mood was like. If they said it was good, he'd say, "Then we're going to have a horrible day," and vice versa.[28] Harry Carey Jr. was shocked when Ford reduced her to tears during a scene in which she had to shake a rug out a window.[29] Betsy Palmer, who also appeared in the film, viewed Ford's behavior toward O'Hara from a totally different perspective. "She needed some fire set under her at times," Palmer ventured, and to get that fire going, Ford had to make her angry: "He would refer to her 'fat ass' to get her kinda steaming. Then they'd shoot and she'd have the energy. I saw him tease her that way. He would say, 'Listen, Maureen, get your fat Irish ass over here.' The fire was there but it was banked down and he knew how to unlock it."[30] A more likely reason for Ford being so hard on O'Hara was that John Wayne wasn't there to protect her. (Wayne visited her one day on the set, but Ford refused to let them speak.)

Another day, O'Hara was in Ford's office and he started drawing penises on a piece of paper in front of her. Today, that would be regarded as sexual harassment. A few days later, she walked into his office without knocking and saw a sight that shook her to the core of her being: Ford had his arms around "one of the most famous leading men in the picture business" and was kissing him. She didn't know what to do, so she fumbled some papers to give them a chance to disentangle themselves.[31] She didn't say anything to Ford then or later, but the experience made her wonder whether he was a closet homosexual. That possibility made her reevaluate all the male bonding scenes he was famous for. Was there something deeper at work there? Instead of being awkward with her (or perhaps *because* of this awkwardness), he harassed her even more afterward. One day he accused her of having a crush on Wayne and then advised her not to think of him that way because he had a small penis.

O'Hara was aware that much of this nonsense came from resentment. Ford was jealous of her relationship with Parra and upset that she was finally crawling out from under Price's influence. In all the years she was with Parra, Ford never once invited Parra to his house.[32] Matters reached a head one day during an executive meeting concerning the promotion of *The Long Gray Line*. Ford snapped to O'Hara's brother Charles, "If that whore sister of yours can pull herself away from that Mexican long enough to do a little publicity for us, the film might have a chance at some decent returns."[33] Charles demanded an apology and got one, but it rang hollow; the damage had been done.

Maybe it was for the best that O'Hara's relationship with Ford deteriorated over the years. He gave her huge opportunities, to be sure, but he also limited her acting scope. Irish critic Philip Molloy wrote: "It is not something that she would accept herself, but Maureen O'Hara's career probably suffered from its long-time association with John Ford. Ford's view of Ireland, and things Irish, tended to be broad, sentimental and sociologically distorted, and his characters were often clichéd representatives of their nationality. They were played for their bigger, more overt qualities. The men were boisterous, gregarious and sometimes boozy. The women were betimes fiery and tender."[34] Molloy contended that she put herself out of the running for "Method-inspired" roles in the mid-1950s: "Because she was such an awed paragon of Ford's view of womanhood, it was unlikely the opportunities implicit in the evolving screen view of her sex would be available to O'Hara."[35]

The especial Method actor of the time was, of course, Marlon Brando. He was busily burning up 1950s film screens with a panoply of Oscar-nominated roles that had him in a multiplicity of foreign guises (Mexican, Polish, Roman), not to mention his role as a broken-down boxer from Hoboken with a one-way ticket to Palookaville in Elia Kazan's *On the Waterfront* (1954). The talk on the street was that he was a shoo-in for the Oscar that year, but O'Hara felt that because of his antiestablishment principles, the anal-retentive Academy "suits" would deny him that accolade. She emceed the Press Awards ceremony in 1955 and talked Brando up in her closing speech: "Ladies and gentlemen. . . . This year there is a young man up for the Best Actor Oscar and the vitriol against him is so horrible that he hasn't a chance of winning it if it is only about who likes whom best in this business."[36]

Whether O'Hara's speech had any effect, Brando won for *On the Waterfront*. He accepted the Oscar but later regretted it, saying he would "never again accept one of any kind" because he objected to the rationale behind such awards.[37] (He refused an Oscar for *The Godfather* in 1972.) Brando didn't believe he deserved to win; in fact, after he saw his performance for the first time, he got up and left the screening room: "I thought I was a huge failure and walked out."[38] Whatever his own feelings, O'Hara's speech on his behalf was rewarded with a bouquet of roses sent by Brando's minders. She affectionately called them her "Marlon Brando roses."[39]

Her next undertaking was *Lady Godiva*, the story of a woman who "put everything she had on a horse." It's difficult to appear unerotic dressed in only a wig and a body stocking, but O'Hara pulls it off here. She preserves her modesty, and audiences worldwide fell asleep. There's too much talk in the film, making it seem like a history lesson on camera, and too few battle sequences. How can people become excited by a plot based on a tax problem? We end up with a staid melodrama and wooden emotions. As for Lady Godiva's final ride through the deserted town, she remarks, "There will be no person in Coventry who will look upon my nakedness." Her flesh-colored outfit takes care of that. (The Rapunzel-like hairstyle also covers her "bare" back.) O'Hara's refusal to go au naturel means that Lady Godiva's protest against the crippling taxes imposed by her husband Lord Leofric (George Nader) is as flat as the town built on the grounds of Universal Studios. A minor item of interest is the blink-and-you-miss-him appearance of Clint Eastwood as "First Saxon." Even then, O'Hara professed that she sensed the potential of the rangy young man with the husky voice (probably an overstatement, as he had precious little to do in the film).

She gave an interview around this time to Mike Connolly of *Photoplay* magazine concerning the awkwardness of her marital situation. "Since you're a Catholic," Connolly inquired, "how can the stories be true that you will remarry after your divorce from Will Price is final. Doesn't the Church forbid that?" She replied that she hoped to secure a dispensation to marry again: "Any woman would be telling a lie if she said she didn't want to be married and have a man of her own—and children, lots of children." She conceded that love was important, but not, she suggested, as important as having children. The most important thing of all was God, but married love was godly because it was natural.[40] She seemed to be arguing herself into a position that would theologically justify remarriage if it resulted in a brood of "godly" children.

Another movie role beckoned, this one seemingly with more potential than *Lady Godiva*, at least on paper. *The Magnificent Matador* teamed O'Hara with her friend Anthony Quinn. "I felt Anthony and I would be thoroughly convincing lovers on the screen," she predicted, but sadly, they weren't.[41] Was this due to the wobbly direction or the fact that they were friends offscreen? Perhaps a combination of both.

The title of the film is ironic, as Quinn plays a matador who is long past his prime. As Luis Santos, he agonizes over his commitment to the (blood) sport while acting as mentor to his young protégé Rafael (Manuel Rojas). O'Hara is Karen Harrison, the love interest, but she becomes little more than a figure on a tepid landscape. Budd Boetticher, in the director's chair, seems more focused on showing us Mexico and the corrida than anything that might transpire between the characters.

The main surprise comes when Santos tells Karen that Rafael is actually his son, born to his young lover who died giving birth. This should have been the most dramatic scene in the film, but Quinn and Boetticher throw it away; he might as well be advising O'Hara what time he's having lunch. She encourages him to tell Rafael, and again, he relates the news nonchalantly. (Rafael already knows, as it transpires, but that's beside the point.) All that remains now is for Santos to show bravery in front of the bulls to impress Rafael and Karen.

Boetticher was a matador in real life, and he had a few close calls, so he knew what it meant to be on the receiving end of a bull's rage.[42] It's too bad he failed to transfer this authenticity to the screen. Describing himself as "the only gringo in Mexico," Boetticher regarded bullfighting as an art rather than a sport, but this doesn't come across in the film either. He claimed the word *macho* gave him a pain in the neck,[43] but unfortunately, his film is a hymn to such superficial definitions of masculinity.

The Magnificent Matador was Quinn's third bullfight movie and his fourth appearance with O'Hara. By now, they were almost like family. Quinn declared that at one time he thought O'Hara would be his "future." She was already an established star when they met on *Sinbad the Sailor*, whereas he was "bouncing from picture to picture." He fell hopelessly in love with her on the set of *Sinbad* and wrote in his autobiography: "She was dazzling, and the most understanding woman on this earth." At this point, Quinn was unhappily married to his wife Katherine. He intimated in his book that he and O'Hara had an affair, "but after a while we both tired of the deceit. It was one thing to bed around on our spouses but quite another to settle into a serious relationship."[44] Quinn claimed O'Hara brought out the Gaelic in him. (He was half Irish on his father's side.) "I cherished what I looked like through her eyes," he gushed, "the ways she made me feel, and she in turn could touch a part of me that no woman had ever known."[45] The writing here is like something out of a nickel-and-dime novel, and it gets even more rhapsodic: "She counted the days until her husband returned from overseas so she could divorce him and marry me and the thought gave me pause. I was already disentangled from Katherine in all but the material sense so it would have been nothing to pick up and start all over again. It would have been nothing and everything both."[46]

O'Hara didn't allude to any of this in her own autobiography. She told Larry King in 2000 that she'd never had a relationship with any of her leading men.[47] A few years later, Quinn told King that O'Hara's beauty made him forget his lines. King considered this a high compliment from someone "as particular as Tony Quinn."[48]

"Maureen and I were not meant to be married," Quinn concluded in his book:

> Something always came up to keep us apart—usually a picture, or another affair, or some problem in the timing—and yet there was a connection between us that even our indecision could not shake. We stayed together not knowing where our love would take us, not knowing that it mattered. Every once in a while we landed on the same picture—*Against All Flags, The Magnificent Matador*—and resumed our affair. It was a wonderfully uncertain relationship and in it we both found a lifelong friendship, but I was still left to search for the one woman who was meant for me.[49]

O'Hara never mentioned a romantic connection with Quinn. When a journalist asked her how she'd managed without a man in the "prime" years of her life, she replied, "There was one but I don't want to talk about it."[50] Was she referring to Quinn here? It's possible, but unlikely. Remember, this was a man who bragged, "Once you're a star you realize you can have any woman you want." He wouldn't have gotten far with O'Hara with that presumptuous attitude.

On the set of *The Magnificent Matador*, Quinn seated his girlfriend, a woman he described merely as "a society lady," in the front row as he prepared to fight the bulls. He then bowed in front of her. As for his feelings for O'Hara, "The time between us had passed and I was not prepared to re-ignite those embers."[51] Quinn then presented his mantilla to O'Hara. "There was still a closeness between us," he propounded, "and we were playing lovers in the picture so the meaningful glances we exchanged for the cameras were easy to come by."[52] To the audience, those glances look anything but meaningful.

In the final bullfight scene, the director has a tough job: he has to make it look authentic without spilling any blood, to satisfy the censors. Another problem was that Boetticher needed to fill the stands, but it would have been too expensive to employ so many extras. An elaborate advertising campaign was launched, and almost 25,000 bullfighting aficionados showed up—expecting to see a real bullfight. The trouble began when Quinn disappeared into a tunnel and was replaced by his stunt double. The people in the stands immediately knew they'd been duped and started to boo and throw fruit into the ring. Quinn's girlfriend led the chorus of disapproval. They were yelling in Spanish, "Tony Quinn's a whore. His mother should stuff him up her womb."[53] Boetticher started to panic as things spun out of control. The bull even got in on the act, refusing to charge Quinn's double. Famous matador Antonio Ordonez, who was on the set, told Quinn he'd have to fight the bull himself to restore his reputation. Quinn roared: "Are you out of your fucking mind? I'm an actor, not a bullfighter." He suggested Ordonez replace the bull with a cow to improve his chances of surviving. Ordonez tried to encourage him, telling Quinn he'd have to make only one or two passes and if anything went wrong, he'd be nearby. Quinn decided to give it a go. As he stepped out, his girlfriend was still shouting "Coward!"[54] It was decision time. He dropped to his knees to entice the bull to attack him, and it worked. To his relief, the second pass was even better than the first. The crowd erupted, throwing flowers at his feet in exultation. Ordonez then led the bull out of the ring. Quinn felt as if he'd won ten Academy Awards.[55]

His elation wasn't shared by many, as the press savaged the film. The New York Times critic sneered, "As near as you can make out from this picture, they kill the bulls by running them to death and, for that matter, Miss O'Hara nigh kills Mr. Quinn the same way."[56] This was a salad niçoise without the salad. The bulls didn't die, but the film surely did. O'Hara grew morose, as Lady Godiva hadn't been well received either. In that film, audiences had been promised nudity and felt swindled by the trick photography. Likewise, the promised violence in The Magnificent Matador fell short.

She was hit by another thunderbolt after the film was released as Price took her to court seeking custody of Bronwyn, as he'd threatened to do after his meeting with Ford in London. The newspapers picked up on the tug-of-love tussle, and the Irish Times quoted Price's allegation that O'Hara was an "unfit mother" by dint of her association with Parra. She filed a countersuit, charging him with contempt of court for failing to pay $50 a month child support and $7 a month alimony.[57] She also accused him of being so drunk in front of Bronwyn on certain occasions that he'd endangered her life.

One day, a stranger divulged something that almost knocked O'Hara off her feet: Will Price was gay. She found this revelation unfathomable, but the man said he was willing to testify in court. That might have been interesting, but as things worked out, he didn't have to. Price backed off (perhaps he heard about the gay allegation), and Bronwyn was entrusted to her mother.

The year 1956 was better forgotten for other reasons as well. It was a time of missed opportunities and poor career choices. She was rejected for the part of Anna in The King and I and also lost a starring role in the Gary Cooper film Friendly Persuasion, the latter due to John Ford's interference. Instead, she played a villain in the insipid Lisbon with Ray Milland, who also produced and directed. The outdoor scenes set in Portugal are attractive, but the human factor pales in comparison. Claude Rains is an international thief who hires Milland to rescue O'Hara's husband from his incarceration behind the Iron Curtain. At first, O'Hara genuinely wants her husband freed. It's only when she falls for Milland that she decides she wants the old man killed instead. O'Hara does her best to make the story credible, but Milland's direction isn't subtle enough to convince us of the sea change.

Rains and Milland spend most of their time trying to outsuave each other, with O'Hara caught uncomfortably between them. She makes a valiant attempt to appear villainous, even wearing her hair up to increase her aggressive edge, but she doesn't get enough scenes to drive it home. An interlude on a boat with Milland is inserted in a vague attempt to develop her character, but this is far too perfunctory: it acts as an isolated oasis in a plot geared toward a tepid resolution. She uses her stubborn persona effectively in her scenes with Milland, but unfortunately, this militates against their would-be burgeoning romance (a familiar O'Hara predicament). In the end, we're left with a too-neat finale: Rains is arrested, O'Hara is stuck with an old man she now despises, and Milland finds love with Rains's exotic secretary, Yvonne Furneaux. Despite the film's faults, it was an interesting change for O'Hara, and one she apparently enjoyed. "For the first time in my career," she chirped in her autobiography, "I got to play the villain, and Bette Davis was right—bitches *are* fun to play."[58]

She also made *Everything but the Truth* that year. Again, this was a mixed blessing. If she was trying to wean herself away from adventure films, she should have chosen a more cerebral alternative. She plays a teacher supporting an orphan (Tim Hovey) who joins a truth pledge crusade at school and ends up exposing details of a crooked real estate deal that stirs up a hornet's nest of trouble. The idea is interesting, but the film collapses under the weight of its pretensions. O'Hara struggles valiantly with the inchoate plot, and she exhibits something not normally associated with her: a gift for comedy. The pity is that director Jerry Hopper doesn't exploit this; nor does he develop the budding romance between O'Hara and an author (John Forsythe) she recruits to bolster Hovey's credibility. She hits him over the head with a doorknob to fend off his advances early on, in the great O'Hara tradition of fighting with her lovers or would-be lovers, but the romance is cut off at the knees. There's a token reconciliation at the end, but by then, it's too late to matter. The film tries to pass itself off as a kind of *Mr. Smith* (or, in this case, *Master Smith*) *Goes to Washington*, but the idea of an eight-year-old delivering a keynote address to high-ranking officials required the expertise of a Frank Capra or a Preston Sturges. O'Hara usually worked well with child stars, as she proved with Natalie Wood and Hayley Mills (if not Binkie Stuart), but she has too few scenes with Hovey to work up any energy here. O'Hara thought so little of the film that she didn't even go to see it.

The longtime collaboration of O'Hara, Wayne, and Ford came to an end the following year with the military-themed *The Wings of Eagles*, a biopic of famed World War I aviator Frank "Spig" Wead (Wayne). The first half of the film is adolescent. We get scenes of Wead flying planes into swimming pools and throwing pies in people's faces as a prelude to free-for-all fistfights. It's as if Ford is back in *Quiet Man* country. In one scene he even has O'Hara do the familiar routine in which she throws a punch, misses her target, and ends up spinning around in a circle. She plays Spig's wife, Min. "Spig just joined the Navy," she cribs, "I'm married to it." His obsession with things military makes it difficult for her to breathe. She wants to enjoy life, kick up her heels. When she tells Spig this, he drones, in classic MCP mode, "I think you're getting too big for your drawers." End of discussion.

Wayne and O'Hara interact well in these early scenes, giving effortless performances and exhibiting a strong chemistry. One can sense the off-screen friendship in little nuances between them. Ford probably had little direction to give them—not that he gave much anyway. Katherine Clifford claimed O'Hara fluffed her lines no fewer than fourteen times during one scene, but Ford was uncharacteristically patient with her, quietly commenting after each botched take, "We'll do it again, Maureen." Could he really have changed so much? And what had happened to the actress who set such store by mnemonics?

O'Hara understood what it was like to be married to an absent husband: in this regard, the film was close to her own experience. Min watches Spig drift away from her when the navy commissions him to set a new seaplane record. Their daughters know him more from newsreels than anything else. When he makes a surprise visit home, they don't even recognize him. "Don't you kids ever read the newspapers?" he wonders bemusedly. "Are you the funny man with the goggles?" one of them inquires.

Min takes the "star spangled" Spig back to her bosom with the words, "Let's grow up before our kids do." They're about to embark on a second honeymoon when Spig has a serious accident. Hearing one of the children crying in the middle of the night, he rushes down the stairs and falls, breaking his neck. His expression tells us he knows the injury is serious. So does Min's. At the hospital, the prognosis isn't good. He's paralyzed and is unlikely to regain feeling in most of his body. An operation saves his life, but his spirits are low when Min comes to see him. (This scene prefigures one years later in real life, when Wayne was dying of cancer and O'Hara visited him at his home.) Spig pushes her away, unable to let her see him in such a vulnerable condition. The most important relationship for Spig becomes his friendship with his navy buddy Dan Dailey, who keeps him in touch with the outside world and encourages him to move his limbs. He also encourages him to try his hand at screenwriting, and after a raft of rejections, Spig hits gold on Broadway.

A number of years later, Spig makes an overture to Min, hoping to reignite their relationship. Their children are grown, and she has a new life as a businesswoman, but she agrees to give the marriage another go. Just as she's about to move back in with him, Pearl Harbor is bombed. Spig is galvanized and goes back into action, this time in the Pacific. He performs heroically here, but it's all too much for his battered body, and he collapses. The film ends with him reminiscing about happier times with Min, tears in his eyes as he's airlifted to a ship. We don't know how much time he has left, and neither does he.

The Wings of Eagles is the story of a man who leaves his wife twice: first in health and then in ill health. Ford understood Wead because he resembled him in many ways. Neither of them was domestic, and both were rugged individualists and stubborn as mules. Min Wead, however, was no Mary Ford. If she had been, O'Hara's role could have been fleshed out significantly. As it stands, it's Wayne's film. O'Hara, as usual, is left to wring her hands on the sidelines as the demented spouse. Does Wead deserve to win her back? Within Ford's frame of reference, yes. But then, Ford was an incorrigible chauvinist.

It's a mixed blessing of a film, misfiring on a number of scores and causing the O'Hara-Wayne-Ford triumvirate to self-destruct before its time. A minor consolation is Ward Bond's cameo as John Dodge, a spoof of Ford himself performed with some gusto. Ford always enjoyed Bond's mischievousness, even though he might have bawled him out at the time. "Bond is a shit," he used to cajole playfully, "but he's my favorite shit!"[59] The film in general appealed to that part of Ford that fancied himself an army hero. Film scholars who see Wayne as the man Ford always wanted to be can justifiably cite *The Wings of Eagles* as a test case for that argument.

During that famous scene in *The Quiet Man* when Wayne and O'Hara engage in a passionate rain-soaked kiss, Ford insisted on multiple retakes, importuning his stars to kiss more passionately each time and to draw each other closer. Wayne's wife Pilar once asked him why Ford did that. Wayne guffawed, "Hell, honey, he just had me do all the things he wanted to do himself."[60] Sometimes this form of role-playing worked better than others. In *The Wings of Eagles*, Lindsay Anderson, among others, found the scenes of army-navy rivalry "charmlessly rowdy and full of liquored-up horseplay." Nor did he enjoy Ford's "heavy laughter."[61] (He meant this metaphorically.)

Joseph McBride felt the film's blend of tragedy and low comedy worked to its detriment.[62] Since most of the focus is on Wayne, all O'Hara can do is deliver squirm-inducing lines with as much conviction as she can muster: "All I know is I'm in the arms of a fellow, Spig, that I'm nuts about."

Wead is typical of the characters Wayne played, in the sense that they usually preferred to "nudge out alternative familial spaces away from the domestic." This is why Spig falls down the "unfamiliar" stairs of his own home when his daughter is crying.[63] What differentiates this film from other Ford films is his intense familiarity with the subject. In real life, Wead died in Ford's arms.[64] Ford was very close to the material—maybe too close. As with his Irish turns, this often led to bald sentimentality. Here, he just barely avoided it.

What might have been O'Hara's best scenes ended up on the cutting room floor. Min Wead became an alcoholic in later life, and O'Hara captured this in some steamy scenes, but the Weads' daughters wouldn't allow Ford to show her this way, so he had to sacrifice that footage. O'Hara believed this cheated her out of an Oscar nomination, and she had a point. Joseph McBride had commended O'Hara for her "shrewdly observed characterization of an acerbic modern woman forced to find her own identity while struggling with drink and loneliness." It had been years since she'd received such a ringing endorsement of her acting ability, and it felt good.

The irony of *The Wings of Eagles* is that the critics liked it more than the public did. As one writer remarked, "Ticket buyers expected to see John Wayne in aerial dogfights with Japanese Zeros." Instead, they got Wayne "*sans* toupee, fighting the war from a wheelchair and a desk."[65] Just as *The Wings of Eagles* was the end of the relationship among O'Hara, Wayne, and Ford, it also signaled the end of a genre that had once been popular with the public. The movie industry in general was changing too.

The studio system continued to wane in the late 1950s, as did stars' pulling power. Movies slowly began to be driven by content rather than form. No longer would they be cranked out on a conveyor belt of predictability with staple plots.

Glamour was dying, and in its place was kitchen sink realism. With the disappearance of censorship, directors were becoming bolder and more diverse. Taboos of style and substance were being broken. Topics that hadn't been discussed before, or even alluded to, were now common currency. Otto Preminger released *The Moon Is Blue* without a seal in 1953, and miraculously, his career survived the insolent move. Two years later, he had Frank Sinatra play a heroin addict in *The Man with the Golden Arm*. In such circumstances, films like *The Wings of Eagles* seemed strangely anachronistic, a jovial nod to a previous era.

Where would O'Hara turn, now that the hatch marked "Escapist Fantasy" seemed to be closing down on her? As it happened, the next phase of her life would be remembered because of an appearance not on celluloid but in court.

8

Keeping Things *Confidential*

O'Hara's brush with *Confidential* magazine in 1957 was one of the weirdest experiences of her life, but not because the story it printed about her was true (it wasn't) or even shocking (in fact, it was rather mild). What made the incident unusual was her excessive reaction to it, and then how that reaction seemed to mobilize others who'd been smeared by the scandal sheet in worse ways over the years, eventually resulting in its demise.

In many ways, *Confidential* was the *National Enquirer* of its day—not that this was necessarily a bad thing. Today we know much more about stars than we need to; every time they blow their noses it gets a headline somewhere. But in the 1950s they were protected by their press agents and the studios, so it was probably inevitable that a magazine like *Confidential* would come along as a kind of corrective. It let the greater public know that its idols had feet of clay.

Confidential first came out in late 1952 and caused an immediate sensation in an industry that had always airbrushed anything smacking of scandal. It was published every two months, and at a cost of a mere quarter an issue, it was highly affordable among those whose reading tastes didn't run to Dostoevsky or Sartre. Printed on red and yellow pulp paper, it left no doubt about its intention: to take down the high and mighty of Tinseltown's hallowed halls. *Confidential*'s founder was Robert Harrison, a Lithuanian Jew from New York's Lower East Side. He had a history of publishing girlie magazines with titles like *Titter* and *Wink*. He had, in one writer's view, "the face of a lordly asthmatic falcon."[1]

The first issue of *Confidential* sold a whopping 150,000 copies. It featured a story on a gay wedding, an article with the enticing title "I Was Tortured on a Chain Gang," and an array of photographs culled from Harrison's pornographic magazines. The chain-gang story was false, and the gay wedding, allegedly set in Paris, was actually filmed in Harrison's own apartment. (Many of his "exclusives" were anything but, and the accompanying photographs often featured Harrison in disguise, to save money on models.) Harrison upped the ante in August 1953 with a story that claimed Joe Schenck, then chairman of Twentieth Century–Fox, had tried to block Marilyn Monroe's wedding to Joe DiMaggio. The magazine flew off the shelves, selling a record 800,000 copies.

Harrison made it his ambition to bring Hollywood's dream factory to its knees. He had a lot of material to work with in an industry notorious for its deceptions. He knew that once stars came to prominence, they often had their biographies modified to look exotic and their eight-by-ten glossies touched up. Interviews consisted of prearranged questions that studiously avoided any whiff of past misbehavior. Being asked to name their favorite color was about as invasive as the questions got.

In many ways, the stars were prisoners of self-imposed gilded cages. Ava Gardner liked to say, "We were the only pieces of merchandise allowed to leave the factory." O'Hara admitted, "If I was told to go somewhere, I went. Even parties were business. You have to dress for business, make yourself up for business." Show business was the business of show.[2]

With O'Hara, the spin doctors pumped the Irish angle. There had been a special relationship between the United States and the Emerald Isle ever since the famine of the late 1840s resulted in large numbers of Irish immigrants, and a pretty continuous flow thereafter. Female Irish stars were thin on the ground (Maureen O'Sullivan, Greer Garson), but there were many male A-listers with Irish blood, including James Cagney, Gregory Peck, Spencer Tracy, and Gene Kelly.

O'Hara's theatrical past was often alluded to as well. Dublin's Abbey Theater was world famous, and her association with it, however brief, didn't do her any harm. She also had "pedigree" in her family tree: her mother had been an operatic contralto, and her father was a successful businessman who owned a share of a football team. Such credentials weren't to be sneezed at, but she was still vulnerable. She'd led a double life with George Brown—her secret husband. Now she was leading one with Enrique Parra as well, and coming to the end of one with the secretly alcoholic Will Price. *Confidential* could have had a field day with such stories.

The fanzines turned a blind eye to anything unsavory about movie stars. As one writer put it: "Theirs was supposed to be a life of sunshine, pleasure and endless lovemaking, where the living was easy amid orange blossoms and sea breezes, and everyone stayed eternally young and devastatingly beautiful."[3] Nobody needed a picture in the attic, like Dorian Gray—just the phone number of their local plastic surgeon.

O'Hara sidestepped the surgeon's scalpel. That's not to say her appearance was perfect. She always thought her face was too square and her jawline too narrow, and she had a crooked tooth. The studio wanted to remove it and replace it with a false one, but she refused. When she was informed her nose was too big, she also refused to have anything done with that. Sophia Loren had the same problem. Hollywood liked retroussé noses, but neither of these women wished to indulge such a silly whim. O'Hara told the moguls in no uncertain terms, "My nose comes with me. I've got a big square face and I need my big nose. If you don't like it I'll go back where it came from." The ploy worked, and the nose stayed. On issues like this, she wasn't to be tampered with. It was only when it came to choosing films—and husbands—that she faltered.[4]

She fell afoul of *Confidential* in March 1957 when it carried a story headlined "It Was the Hottest Show in Town When Maureen O'Hara Cuddled in Row 35." The gist of it was that she'd been in the balcony of Grauman's Chinese Theater with a "south-of-the-border sweetie," but not to watch *The Robe*, which was playing at the time. The incident had supposedly occurred the previous November and been witnessed by the assistant manager at Grauman's. (In fact, two Grauman employees, assistant managers James Craig and Michael Patrick Casey, claimed they saw the erotic grope, although they gave different dates for it. Craig sold the story to Michael Mordaunt-Smith, a London-based representative of *Confidential*.) O'Hara had entered the theater, the article stated, "wearing a white silk blouse neatly buttoned. Now it wasn't." Her date's "spruce blue suit" had also been removed. Further, she had taken "the darnedest position to watch a movie in the whole history of the theater. She was spread across three seats—with the happy Latin American in the middle seat."[5]

O'Hara was probably targeted because she hadn't been stung before. With this magazine, content had little to do with evidence and everything to do with naming names. Even Harrison admitted, "We were running out of people."[6] It was simply O'Hara's turn. Up until now she'd been a protected species—possibly because, being such a homebody, she wasn't

featured in the "Out and About" columns of the tabloid papers that fed
the industry and therefore wasn't seen as hot copy. But that was about to
change.

According to the article, the manager coughed repeatedly as a gentle
hint to the woosome twosome to stop their canoodling, but "for all the
reaction he got from Maureen and her rumpled boyfriend, he could have
had double pneumonia." What they were doing "threatened to short-
circuit the air-conditioning system." Eventually, he had to issue the ad-
monition, "It might be better if you left the theater."[7] Row 35 had never
felt hotter.

The story was obviously concocted to exploit O'Hara's relationship
with Parra, which was well known to Hollywood insiders. Its source is
widely believed to have been gossip columnist Mike Connolly, who wrote
elsewhere: "Word wafts up from Mexico City that Maureen O'Hara is having a whirl." He added that if she had her heart set on "that Mexican," she
should bear three things in mind: "(1) He's married and has a 17 year-old
daughter, (2) Mexicans don't divorce easily in Mexico, and (3) He doesn't
own that hotel or that bank but merely works for the people who own
them."[8] The implication was obvious: she was after his money.

One of the reasons O'Hara was so shocked by the allegations was that
she'd been treated so well by the press up to this time. Almost every article
printed about her extolled her beauty, her charm, the fact that she wasn't
a diva and didn't go gallivanting around Bel Air to wild parties. She was,
if you like, the full package: an actress who didn't throw tantrums yet was
forthright, who stood up for her rights yet "knew her place," who didn't
threaten the established order yet wasn't intimidated by it, who was neither
prudish nor outré—at least until Robert Harrison came along.

She was understandably furious about the article and immediately filed
a $5 million suit against the magazine. Soon afterward, two FBI agents
were sent to stay in her house because they'd heard through the grapevine
that *Confidential* intended to send a naked man into her boudoir and photograph them together to bolster the earlier story. That fortified her resolve
more than ever.

By this point, a number of other lawsuits were pending, most notably
one from Lizabeth Scott, based on the allegation that she was a lesbian, and
one from Robert Mitchum, who'd been the subject of an almost Python-

The young Maureen FitzSimons on the cusp of stardom.

An early studio still shows her in "sultry siren" mode. This image wouldn't last long.

A dramatic scene from *The Hunchback of Notre Dame*.

A hirsute Tyrone Power looks somewhat like Rhett Butler as he cradles "Scarlet" O'Hara in his arms in a posed publicity still from *The Black Swan*. (Courtesy Sales Production)

She appeared opposite a rougher-than-usual Tyrone Power in *The Black Swan*.

Staving off Power's romantic advances in *The Black Swan*.

Looking every inch the happily married woman—though this was far from the case.

O'Hara groomed to perfection against a luxurious backdrop.

She may not have done "leg art," but this shot of her plunging neckline more than satisfied hot-blooded males.

At home with her beloved dogs.

Posed studio still with Joel McCrea from *Buffalo Bill* in 1944.

A smoldering O'Hara shows off those famous green eyes, with her hair uncharacteristically parted in the middle.

A relaxed pose that didn't match her fiery screen persona.

Another stunning mid-1940s portrait.

O'Hara gazes adoringly at Henry Fonda, one of her favorite costars, in *The Immortal Sergeant*. (Courtesy Sales Production)

A fairly typical 1940s pose emphasizing her stubborn demeanor and strong character. (Courtesy Sales Production)

(Below) In heated discussion with Anthony Quinn and Douglas Fairbanks Jr. in *Sinbad the Sailor* in 1947.

Displaying a more triumphant mood with Fairbanks.

In *Miracle on 34th Street* (1947) O'Hara starred opposite the young Natalie Wood.

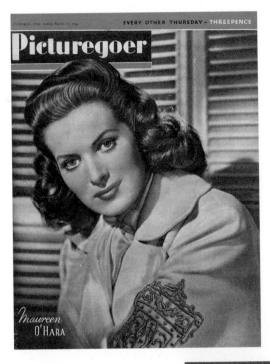

O'Hara's Celtic mood on a 1949 magazine cover. (Courtesy Sales Production)

The "come hither" look usually promised more than it delivered. (Courtesy Sales Production)

Poster from *Flame of Araby*, one of her "Maureen Sahara" outings. (Courtesy Sales Production)

Poster from *Kangaroo*, one of her less felicitous assignments. (Courtesy Sales Production)

The scowling firebrand.

(Above) With John Wayne in her favorite and most famous movie, *The Quiet Man*. *(Below)* The wedding scene from *The Quiet Man*.

O'Hara's classic "don't mess with me" expression that became her trademark.

She could also show great charm.

Distaff knight-errant opposite Errol Flynn in *Against All Flags* in 1952.

Squaring up to Flynn
with typical arrogance
in *Against All Flags*.
(Courtesy Sales
Production)

Although she seems to
be feeling the heat of Jeff
Chandler's ardor, in reality
she likened the experience to
"acting with a broomstick."
(Courtesy Sales Production)

The (anti)climactic would-be nude scene from the ill-fated *Lady Godiva*.

An earlier shot from *Lady Godiva*.

Wrapping up for the Irish weather in the late 1950s.

O'Hara made a transition from comely maiden to trendy mother for *The Parent Trap*.

With her good friend Brian Keith in *The Parent Trap*.

In a dramatic scene with Keith from *The Parent Trap*.

Sparring with the Duke in one of their late "spoof" westerns, *McLintock!*

O'Hara made a controversial return to movies in 1991 to star in *Only the Lonely* after a twenty-year hiatus.

esque smear in a 1955 story with the appetizing header: "Robert Mitchum . . . The Nude Who Came to Dinner!" At a wrap party for the Charles Laughton movie *The Night of the Hunter*, hosted by the director, Mitchum had allegedly stripped down to his socks, sprinkled his whole body with catsup, and proclaimed to the assembled gathering, "This is a masquerade party, isn't it? Well I'm a hamburger."[9]

O'Hara was confident she'd win her case, as she'd been out of the country at the time of the alleged incident. (A stamp on her passport testified to that fact.) She was also aware that *Confidential* was suffering under the weight of the other suits. After nearly five years of taking sucker punches from the scandal sheet, Hollywood was finally starting to fight back. O'Hara had always been somewhat litigious, and she probably would have sued even in the absence of a profusion of other angry stars. But the timing of the story, printed when the hunted were poised to become the hunters (including *Tab* Hunter), made it even more likely that she'd sue.

On March 27 Los Angeles district attorney William McKesson launched a general action against the scandal magazines on the grounds that they flagrantly conspired to libel people. Shortly afterward, California governor Goodwin Knight called for such magazines to be banned outright. O'Hara welcomed these developments and offered to testify on any related matter that concerned her. So did others who felt they'd been besmirched by *Confidential* and other rags. O'Hara's alleged cuddle with her "south-of-the-border sweetie" was the first case on the roster. One filed by Dorothy Dandridge was scheduled to follow it, as were other cases involving Mitchum, Gary Cooper, Mae West, Liberace, and June Allyson.

O'Hara's case began on August 7. Assistant district attorney Clarence Linn gave his opening statement to a jury of five women and seven men in the Los Angeles Hall of Justice. He described Harrison as the "Mr. Big" of an operation that used prostitutes to lure celebrities into compromising positions; Harrison then followed such "stings" by recklessly publishing falsehoods about the stars. Art Crowley, for the defense, responded by telling the jurors that *Confidential*'s reports were published without malice and were true in all important particulars.

The first witness for the state was Howard Rushmore, a leading anticommunist columnist for William Randolph Hearst's *New York Journal-American*. Rushmore had worked for *Confidential* but left after

Harrison suggested his writing was too right wing and would have to be toned down. (Rushmore, a former member of the Communist Party, had turned against anyone with "red" affiliations after he became friendly with J. Edgar Hoover. In time, he became one of Senator Joseph McCarthy's key witnesses at the House Committee on Un-American Activities hearings.) Rushmore testified that Harrison urged his staff to resort to any means necessary to dig up juicy tidbits on Hollywood celebrities, including paying prostitutes and known homosexuals to put stars in compromising positions. His testimony, though convincing, didn't sit well with the jurors. They probably saw him as a turncoat as well as an ex-member of the operation he was now impugning.

The day before O'Hara testified, prosecution witness Polly Gould was found dead in her apartment from an overdose of sleeping pills. Was it suicide? Murder? Gould was an interesting figure who had been playing both ends against the middle. She'd been on Harrison's payroll, keeping him informed of impending legal moves against him, while simultaneously liaising with the district attorney and acting as a "stoolie" for him.[10] The plot thickened.

The O'Hara case became more like slapstick than sleaze when James Craig was called to testify. He said O'Hara appeared to be drunk on the night in question and was sitting across the lap of a short, dark man. When the jurors were unable to form a mental picture of the scenario, one of them, LaGuerre Drouet, asked Judge Walker if they could visit Grauman's and act out the grope. Astonishingly, Walker went for the idea, so the entire courtroom—bailiffs, lawyers, judge, and jurors—boarded a bus and headed for Hollywood. The spectacle drew a crowd, and reporter Theo Wilson wrote that the highlight of the event was watching a bailiff try to free the seriously overweight Drouet from a seat in row 35, where he'd become lodged. He had to be prized out in the end. It was arguably funnier (and more dramatic) than any of O'Hara's recent movies. Harrison must have been delighted at the publicity.

The slapstick-style developments gave O'Hara pause, and she considered dropping her case. She wasn't sure what to do until George Murphy, president of the Screen Actors Guild, expressed his belief in her innocence and urged her to press ahead. "I saw myself as Joan of Arc," she blared afterward. But then Murphy dropped a bombshell: the film industry wasn't going to back her. She was shocked but thought: "To hell with them, I'll go by myself. And I did."[11] Well, not quite. Her two brothers flanked her each day as she walked to and from the court. So did her sister Peggy, the nun, whom she'd flown from the convent to vouch for O'Hara's "spotless character."[12]

As she took the stand, O'Hara chirped "Up the Irish!" to nobody in particular. This was a Macdonald Carey line from *Fire over Africa*, the film that was her alibi. She informed the defense attorney that the article had devastated her as well as Bronwyn, who cried herself to sleep at night "because children at school were talking about the scandal."[13] That personal detail seemed to get the spectators on her side. She spoke confidently throughout her testimony, admitting that she had a Mexican boyfriend in 1954, but when asked whether the two of them had gone to Grauman's, she replied defiantly, "Never!" Several defense witnesses contradicted her on this, including one who testified she had practically had sexual intercourse in her lover's lap. A clerk who worked at Grauman's candy counter disputed her testimony that she'd been to the theater only twice, both times with her brother. The clerk stated that after one of O'Hara's visits to the theater, the ushers were all abuzz about what had happened in row 35.

In her autobiography, O'Hara chronicles the moment she debunked such piffle:

> The dramatic courtroom climax came when *Confidential* testified, on the record, and gave the precise date and time the incident in the theater supposedly occurred. That proved fatal for them and we were ready for it. In a moment of great drama, I promptly whipped out my passport and showed it to the judge. The official dated stamps proved that I wasn't in the United States of America then. I was in Spain making *Fire over Africa* for Columbia pictures. (No one connected with the picture ever came forward in my defense.) The courtroom broke into applause and the judge had to quiet it. My passport proved my innocence. *Confidential* was found guilty of conspiring to publish obscenity and libel. My victory was the first time a movie star had won against an industry tabloid. *Confidential* magazine would never survive the loss in court and shortly thereafter passed into history.[14]

This is stirring stuff, but there are a few problems with her interpretation of events. First of all, the magazine wasn't found "guilty," and she didn't gain a "victory." She also neglects to mention that the so-called witnesses to her indiscretion dug in their heels, even after she produced the "irrefutable" passport evidence. Although the assistant manager backtracked, admitting it might have been more of an "affectionate embrace" than an orgiastic display, he otherwise stood by his version of events.[15] A subsequent lie detector test also proved inconclusive.[16] Matters dragged on long after this, both in and out of court.

The incident allegedly occurred on November 9, 1953, but O'Hara's passport proved she had left the United States a month earlier and didn't return until January of the following year. According to an August 1957 article in the *Irish Times*, the manager of the Dorchester Hotel in London claimed O'Hara had stayed there from November 20 to December 22, 1953, but these dates are largely irrelevant.[17]

Things started to go wrong for O'Hara when both Liberace and Dandridge decided to settle their claims out of court. It's unknown why they chose this course of action, as they both had strong cases. Was it fear of the unknown? A reluctance to take on Harrison, who could seemingly concoct a scandal if somebody upset him? Or was there a tacit acceptance in the industry that scandal sheets were a fact of life, so it was better not to tussle with them?

O'Hara's lawsuit, along with the others, was referred to as "Hollywood vs. *Confidential*." In a general defense of himself, Harrison dictated this message from his New York office: "California has accused us of a crime, the crime of telling the truth. Hollywood is in the business of lying. Falsehood is a stock in trade. They use vast press-agent organizations and advertising expenditures to build up their stars. They glamorize and distribute detailed—and often deliberately false—information about them. . . . They have the cooperation of practically every medium except *Confidential*. They can't influence us. So they want to 'get' us."[18]

Fred Meade, the husband of Harrison's niece, took the stand for the defense. He argued that many of the litigants couldn't reasonably complain because the stories about them hadn't negatively impacted their careers. "Take Robert Mitchum," he began. "He's a convicted narcotics user, has served time on a Georgia chain gang, and was tossed out of his last picture for being obnoxious." Notwithstanding these facts, "his income continues to increase since the *Confidential* story."[19] As for O'Hara, Meade charged that her husband had accused her of "openly consorting with a married man, while she herself was married and [had] her own child with her. She has not been hurt."[20]

These arguments were clever and, to a large extent, true. As a result, the prosecution decided not to call most of its celebrity witnesses to testify. But in the third week of the trial, a group of organizations including the Writers Guild, the Screen Actors Guild, the Society of Cinema Photographers, and the Association of Motion Picture Producers joined forces to put their side of the story across.

The trial dragged on for six weeks, after which the jury deliberated for another fortnight. The result was a deadlock, with only seven jurors favoring conviction, so the judge declared a mistrial. Both sides claimed victory, but the state attorney general recommended a retrial, which would be funded by the taxpayers on the state's side, but not on Harrison's. It was a deliberate ploy to rattle the publisher, and it worked. He was loath to fund another trial, so he compromised. He agreed to pay a fine of $10,000 and to back off celebrity scandalmongering in the future, concentrating instead on more general issues such as consumer fraud and insurance scams. This was a bitter pill for him to swallow, but he knew he had no choice. Harrison's legal fees alone had cost him $500,000. He later settled out of court with O'Hara, Liberace, and Dandridge to avoid the expense of another protracted hearing.

O'Hara liked to think she put *Confidential* out of business. Tab Hunter agreed. In his view, she turned out to be "the crucial witness for the prosecution," the one that caused the pillars of the *Confidential* empire to crumble. "Leave it to a fiery Irish redhead," he exulted in the trial's aftermath.[21] O'Hara's case finally ended in July 1958 when she settled out of court for an undisclosed sum. A caption in the *Irish Press* simply stated that she'd "dropped" her million-dollar suit, but the terms of "any settlement O'Hara might have received remained secret."[22]

A more worrying upshot of the case was that O'Hara became persona non grata with the studio chiefs, for some reason. The fact that she underwent an operation for a slipped disk didn't help her chances of landing plum roles either. For four months after the operation she had to wear a neck-to-ankle brace.[23] Action movies would be out of the question for her now. She used the time off to take voice lessons (she would eventually release two musical CDs) and to move her parents to California, where she'd bought a house for them. She wouldn't get another film offer until *Our Man in Havana* came up in 1959. Was there a connection between this dry spell and her court case? Nobody knew for sure. She wasn't blacklisted because of it, but one could say she was "graylisted," having suffered negative personal publicity for the first time in her career.

Robert Harrison surveyed other publishing options after *Confidential* closed down, but none of them came to anything. He spent his last days in a Manhattan hotel under an assumed name. Howard Rushmore suffered a much more horrific fate, as did his wife, Frances. After the trial she experienced problems with drink and depression, at one point throwing herself into Manhattan's East River in an unsuccessful attempt to drown herself. In December 1957 her husband chased her from their New York home with a shotgun, and her psychiatrist advised her to leave him. She did, but in January 1958 Howard asked her to meet him for lunch, and she agreed. After lunch an argument broke out between them and continued when they got into a cab. A few minutes later, Rushmore drilled two bullets into Frances's head and then turned the gun on himself. The news broke on the radio while Harrison was in another cab at the other end of town. The misinformed driver said to him, "Did you hear that? The publisher of *Confidential* just shot himself in a cab." Harrison experienced a weird sensation: *he* was the publisher of *Confidential*, and *he* was in a cab—it was as if the driver was talking about *him*. He outlived Rushmore by twenty years, but O'Hara's case had caused his empire of sleaze to come tumbling down around them all like a house of cards.

9

Reality Bites

There are no second acts, they say, in American lives. Are there in Irish American ones? The penchant for escapism that had gripped Hollywood immediately after World War II had more or less abated. This meant that O'Hara's decorative, exotic roles were largely a thing of the past. Angry young men—and women—were fashionable now, along with gritty urban dramas dealing with issues of the day. You couldn't really "do" neorealism in a flouncy skirt and a bonnet.

The *Confidential* imbroglio didn't help. Sometimes it seemed that even winning a legal case had undesirable undertones, or even overtones. It was one thing to bite the hand that feeds, but O'Hara had bitten the one that *poisons*. (Unfortunately, in Hollywood's murky underbelly, sometimes the two were well-nigh indistinguishable.) The fact that the case had wider ripples than she anticipated was evident in certain small but significant details. For instance, the poster for *Everything but the Truth* was altered so that its tagline read: "They Were Caught with Their Scandals Showing"— the only concrete indication that O'Hara's lawsuit had some connection to the lack of work coming her way.

But she didn't let the hiatus get her down; nor did she sit waiting for the phone to ring. "The Irish," she announced ambivalently, "although they sink into the depths very easily, are basically happy people. Very few Irish people go to psychiatrists because whatever happens to them, they accept it."[1] (Is this true? Hardly then, and certainly not now.) To fill the gap, she embraced the world of television, where she got to show off her singing ability. (She often said she regretted not singing professionally for a living. She sang briefly in *The Quiet Man*, *Bagdad*, *The Foxes of Harrow*, and *How Green Was My Valley*.) In 1958 she appeared on *The Dinah Shore Show* and later with Ernie Ford. Other engagements followed, and her affable Irish charm was a hit with people like Perry Como, Bob Hope, and

Andy Williams. At one point there was even talk that she might host her own show, but that didn't happen.

RCA invited her to join its record label later that year, and she released an album called *Love Letters from Maureen O'Hara*. "Hollywood would not trust me with a musical," she complained, "so this is my revenge. I've paid for all my own singing lessons so it's gratifying to feel I haven't been wasting my time." The album performed moderately well, but the genre (pop music) didn't appeal to her as much as opera or folk music. Her choice of pop standards wasn't going to set any rivers on fire, but she managed to win the Music Critics of California Award for the album. More surprisingly, the National Hosiery Manufacturers presented her with the "Most Beautiful Legs in America" award that year. (She never thought her legs were particularly great.)

She also appeared on a quiz show in 1959 called *What's My Line?* The premise was that a quartet of blindfolded interrogators threw questions at a secret celebrity and tried to guess who he or she was, based on the answers they received. O'Hara put on a Deep South accent to confuse them, and when asked if she was American, she replied that she was.[2] This didn't sit well with those who recalled her groundbreaking 1946 crusade, when she'd flown the Irish flag so convincingly on the "subjugation to Britain" issue.

After a lengthy hiatus, at least by her standards, O'Hara was offered *Our Man in Havana*, a spy spoof with a quality cast: Alec Guinness, Burl Ives, Ernie Kovacs, Noel Coward, and Ralph Richardson—a veritable shopping list of cinema and theater legends. The film was based on a book written by Graham Greene, who had been a spy in real life, working for MI6 in his youth. (His uncle, also called Graham, had been one of the founders of Naval Intelligence during World War I and continued in that capacity as an old man when World War II broke out.) When Greene was serving in Portugal near the end of the war, he met some German spies who were sending fabricated reports back to Germany. As a result, he developed a screenplay about an Englishman who does the same thing in prewar Estonia. The British film censors rejected it because it showed the British Secret Service in such a poor light, so he relocated the story to Havana (and changed the wife into a daughter). This eventually became the novel *Our Man in Havana*.

Guinness plays Jim Wormold, a vacuum cleaner distributor who is recruited by the British Secret Intelligence Service. He takes the job mainly because he needs the money, as his daughter is something of a spendthrift. What the BSIS doesn't know is that Wormold is just pretending to recruit new agents, thereby earning more money for himself. He also tricks British Intelligence by drawing up plans for a new military weapon, but these are just elaborate variations on his trusty vacuum cleaner. When one of his fake recruits is killed by a real agent, Wormold's life is in danger, and he has to become a genuine spy.

Guinness was looking forward to appearing in the film. He was an avid reader of Greene's work and also admired director Carol Reed, with whom he'd worked on *The Third Man*. (Greene himself had somewhat less respect for the book, referring to it as a minor entertainment.) Reed decided to play the story mainly for laughs, apparently not unduly concerned about the possibility of losing the effects of a dark thriller.

Coward plays Hawthorne, the agent who recruits Wormold. Kovacs is a corrupt police chief, and Burl Ives is the enigmatic Mr. Hasselbacher. O'Hara is the secretary sent over from London to find out what Wormold is really up to. She knew she was in sterling company. She also knew she was lucky to be in the film at all (Lauren Bacall had been first choice, but she was unavailable).

O'Hara arrived in Havana on April 15, 1959. Six months earlier, Greene and Reed had gone to Cuba for preproduction. At the time, Fulgencio Batista was barely hanging on, and the United States had withdrawn military aid to him. After he fled the country in January, the way was clear for Fidel Castro and his "Fidelistas" to take control. Castro was reveling in his newfound glory as the crew prepared to start shooting. His army was everywhere. Guinness was perturbed because his wife couldn't get her hair done in the hotel salon, "as it was always crowded with Castro's officers having their shoulder-length hair permed and their beards curled while they sat with sub-machine guns across their knees, being flattered and cossetted by adoring Cuban hand-maidens."[3]

Reed had a more serious problem. Although the film poked fun at British Intelligence, its satirical nature could have been interpreted as being aimed at Cuba as well. It was a delicate balancing act, particularly because Castro's new regime was so sensitive. The Cuban authorities were persnickety about some of the details they wanted changed. A shoeshine boy, for example, wasn't allowed to be seen in ragged clothes. Kovacs also got a shock when he heard he would have to shave off his beard (Cubans associated facial hair with the present Cuban leaders rather than the overthrown government). For the scenes in the Tropicana, Cuba's famous strip club, there was a censor among the extras who jumped up to protest whenever he thought one of the strippers was revealing too much flesh. One scene shot in the Tropicana featured a riotous floor show that annoyed the censor so much he ordered filming to stop immediately. Afterward, Reed had to hand over all of that day's footage so the censor could vet it.[4] Greene was well aware of the awkwardness of the situation. "Those who had suffered during the years of dictatorship," he reasoned, "could hardly be expected to appreciate that my real subject was the absurdity of the British agent, and not the justice of a revolution."[5]

Guinness couldn't do much with the part of Wormold, as Reed had exhorted him to play it straight. "We don't want any of your character acting," he scolded.[6] This caused Guinness to go to the other extreme, underacting to the point of flatness. Anthony Carthew later reproached: "He glides through the picture colorless, ordinary, negative—a ghost of the Guinness of previous films."[7] O'Hara enjoyed working with him, though, and the feeling was mutual. He admired her as an actress and complimented her on her English accent. (Wormold's daughter was played by an American actress, Jo Morrow, so her accent seemed out of place.)

Castro visited the set one day and talked to O'Hara in such a whisper that she couldn't make out a word he said. The press reported that he had asked her out on a date, but she denied this. She also met Che Guevara during filming and was astounded to learn that his grandmother was from Galway.[8]

The final cut of the film ran almost three hours. This was obviously unsustainable, but when it was edited, O'Hara felt her part suffered. Nonetheless, she won guarded praise for her performance in the trades. Our Man in Havana wasn't cutting edge, but at least it was work. "You're only as good as your last movie," is the classic Hollywood saw.

In the absence of other film offers, O'Hara appeared in a CBS version of Mrs. Miniver in 1960. She received positive notices for her performance, but the general view was that the project was mistimed. It was a wartime drama, but there was no current war that would allow the audience to relate to the sentiments it espoused. And no matter how impressive O'Hara was, Greer Garson seemed to be on everyone's mind. As one critic wrote, "Maureen O'Hara was wholly convincing in the title role but Mrs. Miniver is still Greer Garson, and vice versa."[9]

O'Hara considered acting on the stage to fill in the gap in her career. Interesting things were happening on Broadway at the time. She'd been considered for *Fanny* in 1954, but that didn't take off. Now she had a project called *Christine* that seemed to have potential: it was based on a book by Pearl Buck and had songs by Oscar winners Sammy Fain and Paul Francis: "Welcome Song," "My Indian Family," "A Doctor's Soliloquy," "I Never Meant to Fall in Love," and "Ireland Was Never Like This." She played an Irish lady, the widow of a baronet, who falls in love with her dead daughter's Hindu husband in India—an unlikely plot. What concerned O'Hara more was that her voice was deemed "reedy," especially on the high notes.

Broadway was a new experience for her, and perhaps she didn't factor in how different it was from Hollywood. Whatever went wrong, the show didn't grip the public's imagination. *Christine* was fraught with problems, receiving derisory reviews when it went on the road for a dummy run. It was restructured as a result, but this worked to its detriment, and two of the writers had a public spat about it afterward. Jerome Chodorov, the director, even asked that his name be removed from the program. It played to modest houses but shut down after a week. O'Hara was bewildered and broken. For many years she had wanted to do stage work, and now that dream lay in tatters.

It was time to take stock again and try to reinvent herself, even though screen beauties generally weren't renowned for doing this. Many actresses felt that once they reached a certain age, that was it. Their faces were their fortunes, and once they began to show signs of wear and tear, depression set in.

O'Hara's next role came from an unlikely source: Walt Disney. Disney had adapted a 1953 comedy called *Twice upon a Time* from Emeric Pressburger: in short, a pair of twin girls meet up at summer camp and hatch an elaborate scheme to get their estranged parents back together. David Swift, who also wrote the screenplay, was directing. O'Hara's excitement about the project was clear from this outpouring: "My love for David Swift started the day I read his script."[10] Swift, a former animator's assistant, had a keen cinematic sense and liked working for Disney for the same reason O'Hara did: he was reminded of the "old days" in the movies, when a single vision prevailed, in contrast to the new breed of executives who presided over the film business by committee. Disney wanted O'Hara for $25,000, a mere third of her usual asking price, but she dug in her heels and demanded "$75,000 or nothing." Disney gave in—a tribute to both O'Hara's gumption and the respect she had earned in the industry. The fact that she was a household name also helped.

The main roles of the twin sisters (Sharon and Susan) are played by Hayley Mills, the teenage sensation who'd come to prominence in *Pollyanna* (also directed by Swift) the previous year. O'Hara is their "trendy" mother Maggie McKendrick—more like an older sister than a matriarch (her secret is not to present herself as the "opposition" to the young girls). Here O'Hara rejects the frumpy, middle-aged types that some starlets turned into when they stopped playing sirens. Brian Keith plays her ex-husband Mitch. Keith, who was more accustomed to playing heavies than cuddly fathers, rises to the challenge. The scene in which he finds Maggie's bra and thinks it's Susan's is the first time a bra is seen in a Disney movie. Swift was surprised when it somehow escaped the censor's scissors. (We're not exactly talking *Deep Throat* here, but it was still a development.)

The film is credible, if one overlooks Mills's mid-Atlantic accent.[11] The "family values" theme was just what Middle America wanted after the frenzied decade of teenage-rebel movies that had just passed, with its wicked, wicked ways. The idea of Mills playing a dual role was also a big selling point. Trick photography wasn't as sophisticated back then (no computer-generated special effects), so it was quite an achievement to pull it off.

For its time, the story line was as original as the camera work. Mills claimed young people wrote to her for years, telling her they loved the film because it empowered them.[12] In contrast to most films of the time, children were in control of the situation, instead of adults. Less distinctive was the frequently road-tested theme at its core—that the alienated couple care for each other more than they realize. The new woman in the ex-husband's life has to be portrayed as thoroughly unlikeable to torpedo that point home, and Joanna Barnes plays her with a commendable degree of bitchiness.

Swift berated himself for not being more daring with O'Hara's wardrobe in the scene toward the end when Keith finally realizes he still loves her. Even though she's wearing a low-cut blouse, her skirt looks too "house-wifely," in his view. He wanted her to appear sexier to convey Keith's desire, but O'Hara disagreed, arguing that it was precisely the homemaker aspect of his ex-wife that he missed. Both made valid points, but the scene would have worked better if O'Hara had been facing Keith at the time (she has her back to him and is standing on a stool).[13]

The film cost only $2 million to make and recouped nearly five times that amount at the box office. It made a star of Mills and became the third most profitable film of 1961. It also revived O'Hara's flagging career. "My Irish luck is holding out," she told reporters.[14] If Natalie Wood had rescued her career back in 1947 with *Miracle on 34th Street*, another child star was doing the same thing fourteen years later. Because O'Hara liked children, she was more natural in their presence. (In her teens, she'd taught children with cleft palates to talk properly.) Being a mother helped too. She remembered Bronwyn playing a game of "Let's Pretend" with a doll and convincing herself it was a real baby. Acting began early, she realized. We're all actors, in a way. The trick is to harness it.

O'Hara was on a high after making the movie. Never slow to ring the bell on her bike when she believed she'd done a creditable job, she told Roddy McDowall, "I thought I was wonderful in it. In fact one critic said it was the first time somebody had come along who could do the same kind of sophisticated comedy as Irene Dunne. I consider that a great compliment."[15]

When the movie was released, though, she was shocked to discover that Mills's name preceded hers in the credits. She was outraged with Disney, as her contract clearly stipulated that she was to receive top billing. She approached MCA with her gripe. Disney was contacted, but he was obdurate and refused to budge. The Screen Actors Guild then got involved and was prepared to back her claim against the studio. The day before she was due to file court papers, she got a message from Disney: "Sue me and I'll destroy you." Her first instinct was to contest it, but her advisers told her that even though she might win the case, she'd probably never work again: it would be a Pyrrhic victory.

O'Hara had always been particular about her billing, and she often appeared before the male lead, a courtesy accorded to few actresses of the time. As early as 1951, her contract for *The Quiet Man* specified: "Costar preceded only by Wayne in type of same size and prominence used for Wayne. If name of any member of cast displayed above title, her name to appear above title. If her name displayed below title, lines upon which her name and Wayne's name appear to be immediately preceded by 'starring.'"[16] She backed off in this instance, though. She'd outmaneuvered Disney on the salary issue, and he wasn't the type of man to roll over a second time.

The story has an interesting coda. After the hullabaloo about *The Parent Trap* died down, O'Hara and her brother Charles approached Disney with an idea for a film based on *Mary Poppins*, Bronwyn's favorite book. Disney's reaction to her proposal was a blunt "Rubbish."[17] As we all know, he eventually made the movie, and it was an enormous hit, but O'Hara had effectively committed career suicide with him.

Some years later, the famous producer lay seriously ill in the hospital and O'Hara's agent, Helen Morgan, stopped by to visit him (her brother was his doctor). When she introduced herself as O'Hara's agent, Disney hissed, "That bitch."[18] Quizzed about the insult, O'Hara reacted in fighting mode: "I don't mind what Walt Disney said. He didn't like me because I wouldn't let him get out of a contract. Not many people had the guts to stand up to him. At least he didn't say 'That wimp.'"[19] Notwithstanding her row with Disney, the film remained one of her favorites. It still turns up on television frequently and has aged well.

O'Hara also appeared with Brian Keith in her next movie, a western called *The Deadly Companions*. It was Sam Peckinpah's directorial debut, but not an auspicious one. As the shooting progressed—or, more appropriately, deteriorated—the film's title became more applicable to the relationship between Peckinpah and O'Hara than to anything in the plot.

Peckinpah was chosen to helm the film based on his success with TV's *The Westerner*. When the show was canceled due to poor ratings, Peckinpah reacted with bemused derision. "It was too good for television," he concluded scornfully.[20] His marriage was breaking up at that point, due to his heavy drinking and his immersion in his work. This left him little time for his wife or daughter, whom he refused to visit even when she was in the hospital. He readily admitted being "married to a camera."[21]

The script of *The Deadly Companions*, written by A. S. Fleischman, had been in dry dock in Hollywood for more than three years. Nobody showed much interest in it until Fleischman novelized it, at which point people started to sit up and take note. O'Hara formed a production company with her brother Charles (FitzSimons) to help finance the film. Her stock was high after the success of *The Parent Trap* so it wasn't too difficult to raise money on the property. Pathé-America eventually came through. It was Keith who suggested Peckinpah as director; the two had been friends since *The Westerner*. But FitzSimons didn't like the director from the moment they met, and the feeling was apparently mutual. O'Hara didn't like him either, finding him oblique and somewhat creepy.

Keith plays a character called Yellowleg, a former Union soldier who has a grudge against a former Confederate, Turk (Chill Wills), because he tried to scalp him during the Civil War. (Yellowleg's head is scarred as a result, which is why he rarely removes his hat.) Yellowleg persuades Turk to rob a bank along with a third party, Billy (Steve Cochran). Yellowleg intends to kill Turk after the robbery, but the plan goes awry when another gang of robbers gets to the bank before them. Yellowleg shoots at one of the robbers, but the bullet kills a young boy instead—the son of saloon dancer Kit Tilden (O'Hara). Kit wants to take her son's body to a town far away so he can be buried beside his father, and Yellowleg is so remorseful that he offers to accompany her. She berates him for trying to salve his conscience by riding shotgun, but reluctantly agrees. Billy and Turk go along on the journey, but after Billy tries to rape Kit, Yellowleg beats him and forces him to leave. Turk goes with him. Yellowleg and Kit are now alone with the body. They're beset by various misfortunes, including snakes and Indians, but somehow they manage to reach their destination. When they get to the town, they find that Turk and Billy have already arrived.

Peckinpah didn't like the screenplay from the outset and set about rewriting it, but he met stiff opposition from FitzSimons, who distrusted his judgment and was protective of the property he'd been nurturing for so long. Whenever Peckinpah suggested a change, FitzSimons shot him down, creating tension on the set that impeded progress. The film's budget was low—a mere $500,000—which meant it had to be shot quickly. Peckinpah, who was used to fast-paced work in television, was given twenty days to bring the project to fruition.

Keith also made many suggestions to improve the script, which helped Peckinpah get a decent performance from him. But FitzSimons forbade Peckinpah to speak to O'Hara (perhaps a first in Hollywood history), which meant he couldn't offer suggestions about her interpretation. Because he wasn't allowed to speak to O'Hara, Peckinpah said in a *Playboy* interview, "all of [her scenes] were dead."[22]

O'Hara was ill advised to go along with her brother. If she'd liked Peckinpah, she probably wouldn't have, but she didn't. Neither of them believed Peckinpah knew what he was doing. When he called "Cut," O'Hara stayed in the shot for a few extra seconds, on her brother's advice. FitzSimons didn't think Peckinpah understood editing, and he intended to paper over the cracks and splice the scenes together himself.

As things panned out, there were effectively two directors on the film. There were also two distinct camps. O'Hara was obviously going to align with her brother, but Keith liked both Peckinpah and O'Hara and tried to placate them both. In so doing, he succeeded in keeping at least a semblance of civility on the set.

Today, *The Deadly Companions* has acquired something of a cult following (like *Ride the High Country*, another early Peckinpah film that was virtually ignored when it was made but has earned many plaudits since). It's not a great film; in fact, it's sometimes an exceedingly poor one. Its greatest interest lies in the clues it provides to Peckinpah's later style—to the extent FitzSimons allowed it to seep through.

Peckinpah and FitzSimons had their most abrasive argument about the film's ending. Yellowleg shoots Billy when he gets in the way as Yellowleg is about to kill Turk. FitzSimons didn't like this idea, so he recut the scene to make it look like Turk shoots Billy. But why would Turk try to kill his friend? It doesn't make sense. Peckinpah wanted to convey the fact that Yellowleg is so focused on killing Turk that shooting Billy means nothing to him. FitzSimons couldn't accept that a man could be this brutal, particularly when he refuses to kill his archenemy (Turk) a few seconds later. Peckinpah was indignant, protesting, "At the end of the picture, Mr. FitzSimons took over the editing, scrapping my original cut. He then got in such a mess that he had to return to my original pattern, although I defy anyone to make sense of it."[23]

What was intended to be an experimental western ends up being a traditional one—without any of the traditional *données* of the genre. In such circumstances, O'Hara's character is radically underdeveloped. There's some muttering about her being a lady of low virtue in an early scene, and this raises her hackles. Periodically, in later scenes, she becomes defiant about her integrity. Most of Kit's anger seems to focus on the question of whether she was married to the father of her son. She's adamant that she was. She's equally adamant that the boy be buried beside him, which seems to weigh more heavily on her mind than his death. At one point, she even threatens to kill Yellowleg if he buries her son anywhere but beside his father. These are unusual priorities.

O'Hara begrudged Peckinpah his subsequent fame, railing, "I didn't enjoy Sam at all. I have to be honest—I didn't think he was a very good director. I think he was lucky that whatever happened in his career happened. I think it was luck, not talent. I'm sorry. You have to forgive me. He was not a good director. . . . Different people protecting him made him *look* good."[24]

After finishing the film, O'Hara went to visit John Ford at his office. She was dismayed to discover that he was more depressed than ever. One day he said to her, out of the blue, "I have over a million dollars stashed away in France. Why don't the three of us just run away and escape all this?" (His wife, Mary, with whom he was growing increasingly tetchy, was the third member of the proposed party.) O'Hara felt more sad than shocked by his offer. He then started to visit her at all hours of the night, usually drunk. When she let him in, he'd roar something like, "Bring me coffee!" When she did, he'd often spill it on the carpet deliberately, just to annoy her.[25] At other times, he'd rant in a quasi-sentimental mode, indulging his fantasies about the Celtic Twilight. He did this with O'Hara's parents, too, but her father had less patience than she did. One night when Ford was going on about the IRA's armed struggle, he barked, "Why the hell don't you stop talking about things you know nothing about?" O'Hara thought Ford was going to explode. "I was ready to run," she said, "but he clammed up immediately and was quiet as a church mouse the rest of the night."[26]

She was back to routine situation comedy again with *Mr. Hobbs Takes a Vacation*, starring as James Stewart's wife in a film about a family's holiday along the California coast. It was directed by Henry Koster. After the first day of filming, Jack Bolton from MCA told O'Hara that Stewart wanted her off the picture. His fear, apparently, was that she would exert too much control over the production. She put two and two together and concluded that Ford had planted the idea in Stewart's head (they'd just finished making *The Man Who Shot Liberty Valance* together). Stewart was eventually convinced this wouldn't happen, so everything went ahead as planned, but the experience shook O'Hara. She became subdued on set, which seemed to please Stewart. Maybe that was his plan. Was it possible Ford hadn't spoken to Stewart at all, that Stewart had pulled rank on her simply to, as it were, put her in her place? Possibly.

The fact that the film's title refers to "Mr." Hobbs rather than "Mrs." didn't bode well for O'Hara. Mrs. Hobbs has few opportunities to relate to her children, spending most of her time trying to allay her husband's fear about their welfare. The turmoils about their upbringing are his, not hers. She exists as a pacifying force, cuddling up to him at nightfall for their daily kiss, appearing at doorways as he discusses literature with a sexy beach babe, carrying towels and doing other wifely things as he stutters and stumbles in that very Jimmy Stewart way. She's just there to hold down the fort.

The film deals with the generation gap in a contrived manner that is condescending to young people. In one exchange, we're proffered the observation that there are no juvenile delinquents, only parents with guilt complexes. Elsewhere, Benjamin Spock gets a mention. Wherever one looks there are pampered children and overfussy parents.

Everything is related in flashback, with an occasional voice-over from Stewart that overdramatizes what happens—he even jokes about speaking from the grave about his tragic vacation. One chuckles mildly as the plumbing goes crazy, as Hobbs's out-of-work son-in-law leaves the house, as the beach babe talks about *War and Peace* as if it's the latest blockbuster from Harold Robbins. It ends on a whimper, with Mr. Hobbs back in the city smog and contemplating another summer in the House of Horrors. How does O'Hara manage to look so cheery throughout it all? Maybe she sensed it was going to do well at the box office.

It was, as she forecast, a moneymaker. Coming on the heels of *The Parent Trap*, it seemed to suggest that O'Hara was back on the winning trail. She also received the Exhibitors Award for best performance by an actress in a comedy role, an attribution that was doubly sweet, as it confirmed the notion that she could do herself justice outside her preferred genres.

But there were some negative noises. "I received more criticism than you could ever imagine," she complained, "for playing a grandmother."

This despite the fact that she'd been a mother to some thirty-six children onscreen to date, "and that's not even counting the grandchildren. But then I was born and raised in Europe, where a woman isn't considered really attractive until she's past 35."[27]

In the 1960s many of her contemporaries were contemplating retirement or appearing in second-string roles as a new breed of stars leapfrogged over them. Not O'Hara. As determined as ever to preserve her perch in the middle of the Hollywood road, she felt she was good for another decade. At least, if they'd have her.

10

Love in the Air

After the box-office success of *The Parent Trap* and *Mr. Hobbs*, O'Hara felt she was back on the winning trail, but then she received the worst news possible: her mother had cancer, and the doctors didn't hold out much hope. She contacted Father Aloysius, a Spanish priest living in Los Angeles who'd been credited with giving sight to a little boy who'd been blind from birth. After her mother went to the priest, her tumor shrank to the size of a pea. O'Hara saw this as nothing short of a miracle. Her spirits buoyed, she returned to work, appearing on two TV shows, *Spellbound* and *Ed Sullivan*. But her mother's cancer soon returned, and she eventually died from the disease. O'Hara found John Ford to be an unlikely comforter at this time.

In 1962 she made *Spencer's Mountain*, a family drama costarring Henry Fonda and directed by Delmer Daves. Shortly after filming began, Daves came to her trailer with the news that Will Price had died of a heart attack. (She would later learn he'd committed suicide.) She experienced little sorrow at the revelation, particularly so soon after her mother's death. In fact, all she felt was relief. "This is the happiest day of my life," she gushed to Daves.[1] Bronwyn was safe now. O'Hara had always feared he might harm her in some way, either during a drink-fueled attack or in some more insidious manner.[2]

Later that year, Bronwyn went to court to have her name changed from Price to FitzSimons. O'Hara gave her written permission for the change.[3] Bronwyn also had a small part in *Spencer's Mountain*, playing a college secretary.

The film was shot at Jackson Hole, Wyoming, the location for the majestic *Shane*. Sadly, that's the only thing that reminds one of George Stevens's classic western. Fonda and O'Hara are Clay and Olivia Spencer, the parents of nine children. The eldest, Clayboy (James McArthur), wants to attend college, but they question whether they can afford it. Clay is gifted at odd jobs, but he only earns peanuts. He wants to build a new house for himself and his family. Can he use Clayboy as collateral if the boy lands a scholarship? This is one of the unexciting central themes of this eminently unexciting film.

Like Clayboy, Clay is from a family of nine, so Clayboy and his siblings have eight tall uncles. The Spencer family is so big, in fact, it has a mountain named after it (hence the title of the movie). Clayboy dallies with Cloris (Mimsy Farmer), a spirited lass who wants him to get physical, but this terrifies him. Or is it just that he would prefer to be studying his textbooks? Cloris specializes in looking up "dirty" words in unexpurgated dictionaries. (That's as outrageous as things get in Jackson Hole.) She tells Clayboy she used to think "friction" was a dirty word. Clayboy says he did too. "Will you friction me?" she asks him. He looks too frightened to refuse.

O'Hara, using her usual part–*Quiet Man*, part–Noo Yawk accent, is an unlikely mother of nine with that fabulous face and figure. She doesn't mind Clayboy having a kiss and a cuddle with Cloris, as long as he doesn't go any further. She's whipped all her kids into shape with old-fashioned family values. The only person in the house who seems to be stepping out of line is Clay, who likes to cuss and drink. "I learned to swear before I learned to walk," he informs us. Clay doesn't go to church. His idea of heaven, we learn, is "a fish pole and a riverbank." One day while out fishing with the new pastor, he gets drunk. More to the point, he gets the pastor drunk as well. This is a very inauspicious start for the latter's ministry, and nobody turns up for his first service. This angers Clay, so he tells everyone that if they don't attend the pastor's next service, he'll charge them all the "back money" for the plethora of odd jobs he's done for free over the years. (This is rich, coming from a nonchurchgoer.)

Spencer's Mountain was written for the screen by Earl Hamner Jr. and became the template for the long-running TV series *The Waltons*, featuring another close-knit rural family. It presents us with a world in which God's in his heaven and all's right with the world.

Fonda makes a valiant effort to create an "aw shucks" onscreen relationship with O'Hara, but for some reason, they don't look right together. O'Hara wrote in her autobiography, "Just knowing they had nine children together provided all the sex appeal the film needed."[4] Still, we don't get any sense of long-term familiarity. She gives a commendable performance but loses her naturalism when the film opts for a lachrymose finale. The Spencers' money problems threaten Clayboy's odyssey toward the groves of academe, but all ends happily when Clay torches the fancy new house he's been building and decides to fix up the old one instead. Olivia is delighted. She was never in favor of going posh anyway. "Remember how much you're loved," she tells Clayboy as he leaves for college in the final scene.

Fonda wasn't in a happy place when he made the movie. His third marriage had just hit the rocks, and he was also annoyed that he wasn't on Broadway starring in *Who's Afraid of Virginia Woolf?* Its author Edward Albee had wanted him for the lead role, but Fonda's agent, imagining that America wouldn't want to see its beloved hero as a "neurotic cuckold," didn't even show him the script.[5] Fonda knew *Spencer's Mountain* was emotion-by-numbers pap. He told James Stewart before shooting began that he thought he'd reached the end of the road in his career. Stewart rejoined ruefully, "You too?"[6] The aging cowpokes seemed to be heading for the same barn on very tame steeds.

Donald Crisp plays O'Hara's father-in-law. They also appeared together in *How Green Was My Valley* and *The Long Gray Line*. She remembered him fondly as "a stingy old Scotsman." He used to take her out to dinner with other cast members and buy them just one drink, because two were bad for you, he claimed. O'Hara didn't swallow this: "We used to say it was because he didn't want to pay for a second one," she teased.[7]

Fonda conducted what he called an "orgy" of interviews about the film, but the same question kept recurring: "Is this a movie about a boy who wants to go to college?" In truth, there isn't much more to it. Tired of this line of questioning, one enterprising interviewer broke new ground by asking Fonda what size shoe he wore—a much more interesting topic. "Ten!" the actor responded delightedly.[8]

The critics slaughtered it, but it was another box-office hit for O'Hara. She also got to sing in the film, which was probably why she decided the time was ripe to bring out another record album. This one was simply called *Maureen O'Hara Sings Her Favorite Irish Songs*. It sold moderately well for Columbia, and the company sent her a case of the records for her personal use. Bizarrely, John Ford came to her house one day and took them away with him. She never knew why, and she never saw them again.

She was feeling optimistic about herself at this point in her career and advertised that fact by observing, breezily, "There's no one in Hollywood quite like me. The actresses are either youngsters coming up the ladder or established dramatic stars. I can sing, dance a little, play comedy and dramatic scenes as well. No-one is in competition for my type of role. Someone said I fit into the old Myrna Loy category and I think that's about right."[9]

Toward the end of the year Charles Laughton died of cancer. O'Hara wasn't surprised, as she'd been in touch with her old booster periodically since he'd contracted the disease. She wanted him to see a priest before he died but he refused. (Elsa Lanchester pretended he did to make O'Hara feel better.)

Her next film, *McLintock!*, was released in 1963. Films with exclamation points in their titles are usually strident, and this is no exception. Costar John Wayne treats O'Hara more aggressively than usual, even using a wooden shovel to spank her bottom toward the end of the sprawling Andrew V. McLaglen western. Those who perceived O'Hara as a female role model by dint of her spirited turns in the male-dominated genre of the adventure saga were surprised. He thrashes her with great gusto and even receives some encouragement from his victim. "You can't cheat on a scene like that," she remarked rather oddly. "I was black and blue for weeks afterwards."[10] The poster for the film features the spanking image, conjuring up memories of the famous *Quiet Man* poster that has Wayne pulling at her. Henry Fonda had also put her over his knee in the just-completed *Spencer's Mountain*. This was a curiously masochistic aspect of O'Hara's persona. She didn't view these scenes as demeaning, just good fun. In fact, she wished she had a dollar for every time she had her bottom smacked in a movie. If she did, she would have "a healthy bank balance."[11] She even featured photographs of both spankings in her autobiography.

The tagline of the movie describes Wayne's character, George Washington McLintock, in no uncertain terms: "He likes his whiskey hard, his women soft, and his West all to himself." He owns the Arizona town that's named after him and almost everything in it as well. O'Hara is Katherine, his estranged wife (similar to her roles in both *Rio Grande* and *The Wings of Eagles*). The film begins with Katherine demanding a divorce and custody of their seventeen-year-old daughter, Becky (Stefanie Powers), who's at college in the East. She's afraid that continued exposure to her father might divert Becky from her studies. George has a new woman in his life (Yvonne De Carlo) who cooks for him, among other things. The plot proper kicks off with Becky's appearance at her father's ranch house and her subsequent love trysts with characters played by Jerry Van Dyke and Wayne's real-life son Patrick, as a cowhand. There's also a congregation of Indians present, one of whom almost meets a premature end on the gallows. Marital felicities are ushered in during the last reel when Becky and the young cowhand announce they're tying the knot. George and Katherine also reconcile.

Wayne and O'Hara enjoyed themselves immensely during the film and exhibited a healthy rivalry. "Half the people in the world are women," Wayne (as George) drawls, "why does it have to be you that stirs me?" And elsewhere, "Who put that burr under your saddle?" During one altercation, Wayne encouraged O'Hara to take more control. "Come on Maureen," he urged, "get going. This is your scene." She demurred, telling him she wanted to go "fifty-fifty" with him. "Fifty-fifty?" Wayne pondered. "It's your scene, so take it." Then he muttered under his breath, "If you can."[12] Such amiable tussling continued throughout the shoot.

The highlight of the film is a mud fight. The mud was made of a substance called bentonite, which, O'Hara informed a reporter, is "used as an additive in chocolate syrup. It was sticky, and I wouldn't like to tell you how it tasted."[13] When she told Wayne she thought it was like "birdshit," he replied, "Ya mean snot!"[14]

O'Hara performed a number of stunts in the film. In one, she had to fall backward from a ladder into a trough. All Wayne said to her afterward was, "You didn't get your hair wet."[15] There was another stunt she wasn't allowed to do: a leap through a plate-glass window. O'Hara revealed, "That was done by the great Olympic runner Dean Smith, in my clothes. The studios and insurance companies wouldn't permit a woman to do that, not even a stuntwoman. It had to be a man."[16] He was the only person thin enough to fit into her corset and petticoat. "He was teased about that for weeks," she recalled. In another scene she wanted to wear her petticoat shorter to show off her "good legs," but Wayne prohibited her. "This is a family picture," he growled.[17]

Everything Wayne ever did in a comic western is done in *McLintock!* and then some. It succeeds admirably in what it set out to do, even if that goal wasn't particularly admirable. The film wouldn't rate very high on the totem pole of O'Hara's screen highlights but it turned in a handsome box-office profit. It was a kind of second-rate John Ford film. In fact, Ford directed some scenes when McLaglen fell sick. Stefanie Powers said he arrived on the set in an aggressive mood (nothing new) and pushed both Wayne and O'Hara aside, something O'Hara didn't mention in her memoirs.[18]

She also neglected to mention a 1965 film called *The Ravagers* in which Bronwyn, billed as Bronwyn FitzSimons (reversing her mother's FitzSimons-to-O'Hara trajectory), plays the female lead. It is set in the Philippines during World War II and demonizes a Japanese army terrorizing a convent of nuns. John Saxon plays the leader of a group of Filipino guerrillas that defeats the Japanese in a blood-soaked climax. Bronwyn is the token eye candy sandwiched between the warring factions and the nuns, wearing a worried look throughout. She's sexually assaulted by one of the guerrillas before being rescued by another. Apart from this brief scene, she has little to do except deliver melodramatic lines while frowning. She does look beautiful, though. But one must question whether someone holed up in a rundown convent being terrorized by a marauding army should appear so attractive. A bit less eyeliner might have been a good idea, or more rips on the pretty dress she wears.

There are a few scenes in which Bronwyn threatens to act, but the contributions of her costars are of such poor quality that it probably would have looked incongruous. Instead, she contents herself with thrusting her bosom at the camera. A romance with her rescuer (Fernando Poe Jr.) is hinted at, but it comes to nothing except for a lingering look at the end. The last half of the film is almost constant bang-bang, like a deranged video game. Daughters of famous actresses rarely become stars themselves, but if this was Bronwyn's attempt to do so, somebody should have advised her to take a closer look at the script before committing to it. More promising careers have been killed off by less pathetic movies than *The Ravagers*.

Later that year O'Hara made *The Battle of the Villa Fiorita*, again directed by Delmer Daves. She passed through London on her way to Italy, where it was being shot, and took a bus from the airport to her hotel. Eyebrows were raised by many onlookers who weren't accustomed to seeing famous people on buses. A reporter quizzed her on the matter, and O'Hara explained, "Unless the studio pays for a fancy car I always take the bus. I would never dream of taking a taxi. I save my money. I intend to

be a rich old lady."[19] One thing was sure: with such spartan budgeting, she
could never be accused of "going Hollywood." She didn't bring Bronwyn
with her, feeling that her daughter's career prospects would be better in the
States.

She defended the plot of the movie—about a married woman who
takes a lover—and fended off taunts that it could be perceived as squalid:
"I don't like those off-color films that a few people in Hollywood seem to
make now. There were parts of La Dolce Vita I didn't like."[20] It's a pity she
picked Federico Fellini's masterpiece to make her point about the salacious
turn the industry had taken. O'Hara derided the preponderance of "filth"
that was currently on view. "Don't call them adult pictures," she railed.
"They're not grown up." She called for a boycott on them, thanking her
lucky stars she had the financial freedom to turn down a script the previous
summer that featured nudity and perversion. "But what about the young
actors and actresses who have to take any work they can get to pay the
rent and the grocery bills. What can they do?"[21] A film didn't have to be
unseemly to be a hit, she reminded people, mentioning The Parent Trap as
a case in point. Geoffrey Shurlock, vice president of the Production Code
Association, actually had some concerns about the script of Villa Fiorita,
which contained the expression "sleep together," spoken by a child. Later
on, there was this line of dialogue: "Saint Agatha had her breasts cut off.
You can see pictures of her with them on a plate."[22]

As well as denouncing the pervasiveness of sex in modern films ("The
greatest love stories in the world were made without that, and something
was left to the imagination"), O'Hara took a sideswipe at the "sinful"
amounts of money being spent on contemporary movies, "money which
only goes to the taxman when it could be used to make better films."[23] Her
own financial arrangement was interesting: she turned down a percentage
deal, asking instead that her fee be paid over a ten-year period.

The Battle of the Villa Fiorita is a lightweight story about a British
woman, Moira (O'Hara), who leaves her British diplomat husband Darrell
(Richard Todd) for Italian pianist and recent widower Lorenzo (Rossano
Brazzi). Her son and daughter travel to Italy and try to persuade her to come
home with them. They're joined in their mission by Lorenzo's daughter.
Brazzi gets lines like this: "Do your children perpetually have to vomit?"
delivered to Moira when her children go on a hunger strike to ensure she

will leave him. Lorenzo doesn't understand children, referring to them as "brats" in his near-apoplectic rages.

O'Hara veers uneasily between a British accent and her Irish one, which she was always reluctant to discard. Once again, her costume changes are the most interesting thing about her in the film. It tries to be a weepie but is frustrated by a jaunty musical score that's totally at odds with the events being portrayed, making it seem more like a comedy at times. The relationship between Moira and Lorenzo peters out like a slow puncture. The film's main message, hardly earth-shattering, is that children are what marriage is all about—which of course had special significance for O'Hara.

It's the children's film, really. *Villa Fiorita* is like a sudsy rehash of *The Parent Trap*, centering on the child-power theme. As the marquee poster advertised: "Two Blue-Eyed Brats Stormed the Villa Fiorita to Rescue Mother from Her Italian Love Affair."

There was more drama off set than in the film. One day when O'Hara was in Milan with Daves and her father, the three of them entered a store to buy some gifts and heard gunfire. A store three doors away was being robbed. She saw the robbers dash into the getaway car and later learned that they'd made off with half a million dollars worth of jewelry. The police asked her if she could identify the thieves, but she declined. She later remarked ruefully, "We were so frozen with terror we couldn't even have identified one another."[24]

O'Hara was bored to tears making the film. She had to endure Brazzi's interminable boasting about all his female conquests—always a turnoff to a woman. She also had a falling out with one of the cameramen after she supported Italy in a soccer game she played for charity. He was British and took offense, exacting his revenge by shooting her in the worst possible light thereafter. She cried when she saw the finished print—not from emotion but frustration. She also complained that some of her love scenes were excised from the final cut.

Villa Fiorita didn't fare well at the box office. It probably would have been more successful if it had been called *The Affair of the Villa Fiorita*, Daves's preferred title. This would have been more appealing to women, who wouldn't have thought they were going to see a war movie. The publishers of Rumer Godden's novel of the same title advised her that she could have sold twice as many copies if she'd done this.

O'Hara was happy to shake the dust of Italy off her heels when the last frame was shot. Afterward she set off for Mexico, where more problems awaited her. First, Parra accused her of making derogatory comments about his son Quico, which she hadn't. Soon afterward she realized that her business manager, Bill Duce, was still siphoning money from her bank account—a practice he'd started when Price was alive, the pair of them colluding to purloin her assets. His latest exploit was to drain money from a company she'd set up with him called Cal Cuba Enterprises. It explored for oil and gas sources in Cuba and would have been a lucrative investment over the years if not for Duce. It was her vigilant brother Charles who alerted her to Duce's machinations. She took him to court and was awarded a settlement of $160,000 and a share of the proceeds from the sale of the company's stock, but this was a mere fraction of what she could have earned if Duce had been honest.

She was now offered another collaboration with James Stewart—this time a western, *The Rare Breed*. She plays a widow, Martha Price, who travels to Texas with her daughter Hilary (Juliet Mills) and a Hereford bull she's hoping to mate with some American longhorns. Andrew McLaglen directed, and her costars included Don Galloway and her old friend Brian Keith as Alexander Bowen, an explosive Scottish widower with flaming red hair and a grizzly beard. The film is largely played for laughs, like most of O'Hara's later westerns, but they don't come off. Keith tries his best with a guttural Scottish accent, but he looks like a reject from a Rob Roy audition. The sight of him in a red tunic and tartan trousers, playing the bagpipes to try to win O'Hara's heart, does little for him or the film.

O'Hara seems to have modeled her performance on Julie Andrews, adopting a schoolmarmish voice and demeanor that ill befit her. She also comes out with pronouncements like "Cleanliness is next to godliness" that are both boring and irrelevant to the (very flimsy) plot. The appearance of Jack Elam as a villain doing the kinds of things he has done in fifty other westerns is equally tiresome.

O'Hara's private life wasn't going well at this time. The luster had disappeared from her relationship with Parra, and they were seeing less and less of each other. She claimed she still loved him but felt he was too quick to believe rumors about her, like the accusation that she'd been speaking badly about Quico. In February 1967 she flew from Mexico to Los Angeles without him. In March 1968 she returned to Mexico, not having seen him in the meantime. She wrote a note asking if he wanted to meet her, but he didn't reply to it. She was almost relieved. Parra had once threatened to kill her if she left him, and she had taken the threat seriously at the time.[25] But she wasn't fearful of his possessiveness now. She felt grateful to him for rescuing her from Price, but their relationship couldn't advance for a number of reasons, not least because of his complicated family situation. She never spoke to him again.

One door was closing, but another one opened. O'Hara was about to begin the happiest phase of her life with a chivalrous man she'd known platonically since the 1940s: aviator Charles Blair. Blair was eleven years older than O'Hara. He had flown her back to Ireland after World War II, and the relationship began from there. She remembered the sequence of events vividly: "We became good, good friends and so did our families, including Charlie's wife at the time. Then they divorced and she married someone else. But we were still good friends until he came to town one day and my brother couldn't go out to dinner with him. I took his place and soon discovered I was mad about him, and he about me."[26]

O'Hara's marriage to Brown was over before it began, and her marriage to Price self-destructed. Charles Blair was different. He was serene and watchful, a slow-burning fuse. This was the way to enthrall O'Hara, not with sweet little nothings and alcohol-engendered promises but with solidity—the importance of being earnest. Blair appealed to her because he was a straight-arrow guy who called things as he saw them. "I like decisiveness," she said. "I'm August, Leo the Lion. I like men who possess that quality too, people with the courage to make decisions and stick by them."[27] After so many wasted years with Price—and even Parra—she was entitled to such probity.

Blair was born in New York. He studied aeronautical engineering at the University of Michigan and mechanical engineering at Vermont University. After flight training in Florida and a tour of duty as a naval aviator, he joined the air force. He made the first nonstop commercial flight across the Atlantic in a Sikorsky VS-44 flying boat. During World War II he flew the first nonstop winter flight over the North Atlantic between the United States and Britain. In 1951 he made the first solo flight over the North Pole, where he dropped something from the cockpit window—a letter to Santa Claus from his young son Chris.

Blair wrote his autobiography, *Red Ball in the Sky*, in 1951. It's engagingly transcribed but of interest only to students of aviation, as there's nothing of a personal element in it. (The "cast of characters" he lists is actually six planes. This sets the tone for what follows.) He resigned his naval commission in 1952 and was later commissioned a colonel in the U.S. Air Force Reserves while still flying for Pan Am. After retiring from Pan Am he founded Antilles Air Boats, with the idea of providing a flying boat service from New York to the Caribbean. In 1974 he purchased two Sandringham flying boats from Ansett Airlines, which had serviced the Sydney-to-Lord Howe Island route. In 1967 he also acquired the last Sikorsky VS-44 Excambian, which Antilles operated until it was damaged in 1969.

Blair proposed marriage to O'Hara in an almost by-the-way manner. She accepted in a similar vein—surprised, but not unduly so. After twenty years of unofficial dating, maybe it could have been called an "Irish proposal." They married in March 1968. He sold his Connecticut home, and she sold hers in California; they went to live in St. Croix.

With Blair, she had everything missing from her previous marriages. He was up with the larks and retired early, and so did she. Suddenly she didn't feel like a movie star anymore; she felt like a real housewife—a bona fide "Mrs." to Charlie Blair. Being married to him, she learned about aviation and met "crazy people doing pioneering things."[28] Blair himself was that kind of person. He referred to himself as King of the Skies and to O'Hara as Queen of the Earth. "The whole world respected him," she said. "I don't know a woman walking who didn't love Charlie Blair." With him, she got to "live the adventures I'd only acted out on the Fox and Universal lots."[29]

Antilles Air Boats was based in St. Croix in the Virgin Islands, but in 1968 the couple also put down roots on a lavish twenty-five-acre estate in Glengariff, County Cork. "Within minutes of visiting Glengariff," Bronwyn revealed, "they decided they'd like to live there. Dad wanted to bring in the Sandringham seaplanes he was manufacturing. He could even see where he'd land them in the lake."[30] In subsequent years the couple commuted between the two bases. O'Hara played a large role in running Antilles Air Boats, which eventually had twenty-six planes and employed twenty-three pilots. This kept her in touch with the public; she was well aware one couldn't sell tickets in any business without being hands-on. Blair wanted her to retire from the movies, but she liked to keep her options open. She assured him she'd think about it, but she was nervous about leaving the profession entirely.

In 1970 O'Hara returned to the screen after a four-year break to do a wacky comedy with Jackie Gleason. It wasn't a wise decision. In *How Do I Love Thee?* she plays Elsie Waltz, the bewildered wife of Stanley (Gleason). Stanley is determined that their son will have a prestigious academic career. Tapping into the boy's early love of books, Stanley promises to get him into college, even if he has to "mortgage my kidneys." Thankfully, that eventuality is averted, but we're still vouchsafed much nonsense about the Second Coming, the imminent end of the world, and lines like "God can move mountains, but can He move a piano?"

It's Gleason's film, with O'Hara malingering on the sidelines as his befuddled wife. When their grown-up son, played by Rick Lenz, decides to leave his post as a philosophy lecturer, Gleason makes a pact with God: Let him stay at the university, and in payment for this divine favor, Stanley won't ever speak to him again. The son decides to stay when the head of the department dies and he's offered the vacant spot. Stanley, keeping his end of the bargain, doesn't speak. He is eventually brought to Lourdes to see if he can be cured of his muteness. The son visits him in the hospital, where he's all but given up for dead, suffering from an ailment that turns out to be nothing more than the result of gluing his dentures together.

By now, it should be clear that this is comedy on the epic-kitsch scale. O'Hara makes a gallant effort to be credible, but it's a difficult task in a farce as bloated as this one. The *Guardian* dismissed it as "the most mawkish film of the year/decade/era. You name it."[31]

O'Hara's old friend Duke Wayne was faring somewhat better, pocketing an Oscar for playing the eye-patched Rooster Cogburn in *True Grit*, a largely ordinary western with an elegiac edge that Wayne exploited to his advantage. He beat off a strong field that year, including two "bridesmaids" at the annual Oscar fest, Peter O'Toole and Richard Burton. (They notched up a total of fourteen nominations in their respective careers but never won.) He also prevailed over Dustin Hoffman and Jon Voight, whose twin nominations for *Midnight Cowboy* (the first X-rated film to win a Best Picture award) probably canceled each other out. It proved to be the harbinger of a new era that Wayne would despise, but he was elated at his win—even if, deep down, he knew it was more a life achievement testimonial than anything specific to this movie. (He had been better in many others—including *The Quiet Man*.)

After all the excitement died down, he asked O'Hara if she'd be interested in making another western with him. She said yes. The film was *Big Jake*. He told her she wouldn't have too much to do in it, which was fine with her: age was gaining on her. It would be a relief not to have to fall off a ladder into a trough to get a laugh. Blair was all in favor of his wife making another film with Wayne. He and Wayne were friends, and Blair knew Duke would never make a pass at his wife. He couldn't say the same for many of her other costars over the years. How did he feel about his wife doing a passionate love scene onscreen? "I'm very conservative and I wouldn't like that," he admitted.[32] But he would make an exception for Wayne.

There was another reason for Wayne's call: to congratulate O'Hara on becoming a grandmother—at age fifty. (She shared the title of "Hollywood's Most Glamorous Granny" with Elizabeth Taylor.) Bronwyn had married in 1968, a mere six months after her mother, and now she had a baby, Conor Beau. Bronwyn's marriage didn't last, however. O'Hara had disapproved of it from the beginning, but she couldn't talk her daughter out of it (any more than her own mother could have talked her out of marrying George Brown). It was the cycle of history.

Big Jake has her—again—as Wayne's estranged wife, Martha. (At this point, it almost could have been a passport description.) It was exactly twenty years since the glory days of *The Quiet Man*, and the fire of their relationship in that film is replaced by ice here. He's Jacob McCandles, an aging cattle baron trying to find his grandson, who's been kidnapped by his ruthless near-namesake John Fain (Richard Boone). Wayne's real-life grandson Ethan plays the kidnapped child, and his actual son Patrick plays his screen son (not for the first time). The film was directed by O'Hara's old colleague George Sherman (she hadn't worked with him since *War Arrow*, way back in 1953).

It opens with a bloodbath, as Fain and his gang mercilessly wipe out most of Martha's ranch staff before kidnapping the boy. Wayne claimed he was still making "family pictures" (as he told O'Hara during *McLintock!*), but he was making them for a generation raised on violence. Wayne calls the shots here—literally. He shoots more people than usual and delivers more tongue-in-cheek one-liners. This was perhaps expected, given the "spaghetti" westerns of Sergio Leone and others. A standing joke in the movie is people saying to Jacob, "I thought you were dead"—including the dying Fain.

O'Hara first appears with a beehive hairdo that looks like it could have had a career of its own. Her involvement in the action ends after the first quarter; she doesn't even make a token reappearance in the last scene to telegraph her reconciliation with Jacob. His son closes the movie by saying, "Let's go home," and Jacob replies, "Good idea," suggesting such a reconciliation. The few scenes they do have together are convincing. They knew each other so well by now that they could almost finish each other's sentences. But for O'Hara, this was a very trivial role in a very trivial picture. It's a pity her joined-at-the-hip collaboration with Wayne ended so tamely.

Director Budd Boetticher believed Wayne's chemistry with O'Hara was "head and shoulders" over that with any other leading ladies. She was also his own "big, big favorite."[33] O'Hara herself described Wayne "as gruff as a bear, soft as a marshmallow, steady and reliable as a rock."[34] "There's never any change of wind," she said of him: "He plays it as it lays." She revered Wayne's discipline, in contrast to the young "slobs" he sometimes acted with, who "slumped" around sets "leaning on anything that was convenient at the time."[35]

Wayne didn't think O'Hara was like other women. "She didn't mind you using four-letter words around her, which I tend to do often, and she didn't get all girly and dainty. And yet she's still totally feminine. She's like a guy almost. She's a woman who speaks her mind and that impressed me, despite my old-fashioned chauvinistic ways. She's feminine and beautiful but there's something about her that makes her more like a man. It's her stubbornness and her willingness to stand up to anyone."[36]

Something else Wayne shared with her was his eminent common sense. When he appeared with Laurence Harvey in *The Alamo*, he said to Harvey, "We'll get along fine just as long as you don't give me any of that Method crap." His own self-estimation was, "I stick to simple themes. Love. Hate. No nuances. I stay away from psychoanalysts' couch scenes. Couches are good for one thing (only)."[37]

Wayne's fondness for O'Hara as a friend was equaled by his respect for her as a performer. When another actress tried to advise him about a scene in a movie, he put her in her place by asking, "Who in the hell do you think you are—O'Hara?"[38] Wayne praised her ability to "ride with a scene" if something happened between script and take: "She was always quick enough to grasp the change . . . you just couldn't rattle her."[39] George Sherman also recognized this. She'd learned the importance of spontaneity from her time with John Ford.

O'Hara's feelings about Wayne were equally uncompromising. "I have never been in trouble," she praised, "or needed help at any time in my life that I didn't pick up the phone and call Duke, and within five minutes I had what I wanted or needed. He never asked for a thank you. He wouldn't think of that. He has a soft heart and if you make a mistake he'll bend those rules he lives by—not for himself but to forgive you. And that is friendship and love."

Speculation was rife about whether they were an "item" offscreen. Pat Stacy, Wayne's partner in his final years, remembered getting a letter one day from a woman claiming to be Wayne and O'Hara's love child. John Ford tapped into this rumormongering to boost ticket sales for movies featuring the two stars.[40] O'Hara herself heard a rumor that she'd had an illegitimate daughter with Wayne who was living in an "undisclosed location" in California's San Fernando Valley. "I sure would like to meet her one day," she wrote in her autobiography.[41]

Many people mistook O'Hara for Wayne's wife over the years. On the set of *How Do I Love Thee?* Jackie Gleason had her chair labeled "Mrs. John Wayne" as a joke. At airports all over the world, she met people who asked her if John Wayne was coming too. "I usually hold up the lines at all these places," she confessed.[42] One time when she was waiting in line to see Wayne's film *Cahill*, a woman came up to her and said, "Oh, Mrs. Wayne, your son just went in." She was referring to Wayne's son Michael. O'Hara's actual husband was with her at the time, and he could only laugh. "Honey," he chuckled, "you can do a movie with that Wayne fella any time you want to."[43]

Michael Wayne believed O'Hara was a woman who could match his father "kiss for kiss, punch for punch, stride for stride." Something happened between them on the screen: "There was an electricity there."[44] (Their kissing in *The Quiet Man* was alleged to have given rise to an electrical storm.) He commended her for being the only woman who could go "toe to toe" with his father, and that touched her. "To have his kids feel like that was kinda nice."[45] Hitting Wayne in a movie was like striking a blow for embattled women everywhere. O'Hara told Steve Jacques about one woman who wrote to her, "saying she was angry enough to divorce her husband after seeing me belt John Wayne. It made her feel much better."[46]

Having said that, the kind of films Wayne and O'Hara most enjoyed making were fast becoming a thing of the past. To the young generation that both ran the movie industry and made up its core audience, the right-wing Wayne was a dinosaur. His friendship with O'Hara would continue to the end of his life, but their glory days onscreen together had ended almost a decade before with the adolescent antics of *McLintock!*

11

A Streetcar Named Retire

O'Hara's father died in 1972. He and her mother were now together in heaven, which was a consolation to her.[1] But she felt as if her past was being eroded; the last links to her childhood were disappearing one by one—a counterpoint to her waning film career.

She decided to concentrate on television. Shortly after her father died, she made a TV movie to get her mind off herself.[2] It was called *The Red Pony,* based on John Steinbeck's novella of the same name. It was a gentle film that wasn't seen by too many people but was true to itself. She was proud of her work in it and gratified to share scenes with Henry Fonda again. Shirley Booth went into ecstasies about her performance.[3]

It would be her last movie for twenty years, but after finishing it, she seemed to be energized with a new vigor. "When I have a project I attack it like a tiger," she declared with that fighting Irish spirit. Asked if she was worried about the passage of time, she replied, "If you're just a glamour girl it could be very hard on you but I'm an actress who enjoys her work so there's no problem. I can't wait to grow old. I'm going to be the nastiest old lady you ever saw." Pressed as to whether she had any regrets about her life thus far, she revealed, "My one real tragedy isn't the parts I missed but the children I didn't have."[4]

Nonetheless, time was gaining on her. This was illustrated one day when someone called Twentieth Century–Fox with an inquiry about O'Hara. The young girl who answered the phone asked, "Who's that? Did she ever work at Fox?" (O'Hara had been employed by the studio from 1941 to 1962.) "You have to look at the funny side," she said when she heard the story. But it was still a "Norma Desmond" moment for her.

Her decision to quit acting, though in the cards for some time, came without warning. One day when Wayne was visiting her in St. Croix, he and Blair said almost in unison, "Don't you think it's about time you stayed home?" They were expecting a fight, but she just muttered, "Okay, I quit," and that was that.[5] Afterward she claimed they "ganged up" on her to force her hand.[6] Whether they did or not, she was ready to retire; otherwise, she wouldn't have done so.

Scripts continued to pour in, but she ignored them. Having just appeared with Fonda and Wayne—"the two top men in Hollywood," as she saw it—meant she was going out on a high.[7] She also felt that the new male leads lacked charisma, especially in period pieces. "They don't know how to take off plumed hats any more," she anguished, "or make their eyes twinkle. It's the twinkle I miss most."[8]

Some stars looked on retirement as an end, others as a beginning. Joan Crawford became a virtual recluse when she stopped making films. "I don't want to meet the press anymore," was her valediction, "because the interesting part of me is over."[9] O'Hara was different. She didn't want to sit at home reliving past glories. Instead, she chose to fly around the world with Blair: "I went to Australia with Charlie when he was buying big old four engine seaplanes. I was on the planes when they flew back to the United States and then into Washington D.C. on the Potomac and into the Battery in New York and down to Miami and the Virgin Islands. So it was very exciting."[10] She also spent time fishing and hiking with him.[11]

She disparaged many of the new movies being made. "I will not do dirty pictures," she protested in 1972, "and Hollywood is making so many of them now."[12] (Bernardo Bertolucci's *Last Tango in Paris* had just been released, to some fanfare.) She considered the idea of directing films herself, to stem the tide of angst-ridden liberalism. "I seem to have a facility for telling other people what to do," she speculated, "even things I can't do myself. It's one of my three ambitions. The other two are to have a smash musical on Broadway and to write a best seller." (At age fifty-two, she wasn't asking for much.) She concluded effusively, "I firmly believe I'm the happiest person alive."[13]

She'd had a good run of it by now—more than thirty years at or near the top. This was a special achievement for a woman, especially a beautiful woman, in an era when one's face was one's fortune and any imminent lessening of that beauty was like a red light to directors. She had been induced to retire for another reason as well: the family atmosphere of the studios was gone as they were taken over by oil conglomerates and whatnot. By now, cinema audiences were a "mere" 820 million per year in the United States, as opposed to 4 billion in 1946. Crippling overhead costs meant that many studios had to sell off assets to stay afloat. One by one, they fell into the hands of corporate America. In 1969 MGM's lion gave his famous roar for the last time as the studio was bought by Kirk Kerkorian. Other entrepreneurs took over elsewhere. Warner fell to Seven Arts, United Artists to Trans-America Corporation, and Paramount to Gulf and Western: often stars weren't sure who they were working for. They also started to "freelance" as they moved from studio to studio. The seven-year contracts O'Hara swore by were now largely things of the past.

The Harry Cohns and Jack Warners and Darryl F. Zanucks were gone. O'Hara's old friend Lew Wasserman left MCA to run Universal. This represented a different kind of climate change, as Wasserman's background was in agenting rather than film production. She pined for the old warlords, seeing them not so much as moneymen but as larger-than-life figures like the stars themselves, who were also becoming an extinct species. She saw grass growing wild over the old lots, watched the luminaries of yore being put out to pasture, and was determined that wouldn't happen to her. It was better to jump before you were pushed; that way, at least you had some dignity.

In 1972 she was asked to give a speech at a Lifetime Achievement Award ceremony in honor of John Ford—the first of its kind. (By now, he had been adopted by the auteurist movement as a kind of guru, a testimonial he greeted with typical disdain.) It was the last time she saw him. The common thinking in Hollywood was that such awards were given only when the recipient was in very poor health, and that seemed to be the case here. She knew Pappy wasn't long for this world as soon as she saw him. Nonetheless, he threw himself into the evening. Stars such as Charlton Heston and Jack Lemmon were also in attendance. The award was presented to him by President Richard Nixon. Ford pretended to gab to O'Hara in Gaelic to impress him.

Ford chose *How Green Was My Valley* as the film to be screened that night. Philip Dunne was surprised; he had expected *Stagecoach* or *The Informer*. But *Valley* got the sentimental vote, which was appropriate to the occasion. Dunne likened it to an Irish wake—"which in a way is just what it was."[14] O'Hara sang a medley of old faithfuls to round off the evening.

Ford died later that year. He was barely cold in his grave before the tributes were trotted out. O'Hara was saddened by his passing and shed a tear or two for the "old bastard." He'd been both blessing and curse to her, just as she had been to him. What were his true feelings? Who knew? He once called her "the best fucking actress in Hollywood" but told a film student on another occasion: "That bitch couldn't act her way out of a brick shithouse."[15] Many of his feelings about her talent morphed into a personal attraction to her. As these ebbed and flowed, so did his estimation of her dramatic sense. Maybe he was tortured by both her unavailability and her fairly constant presence.

Ford once commented in a letter that O'Hara was the best actress in Hollywood, which caused her to quip, "I'm sure he would have wanted it back so he could tear it up and I couldn't tell people about it. But I kept it so he couldn't."[16] He praised her only once in a blue moon, but this time it was on paper, so it could be preserved. According to Joseph McBride, Ford spoke disparagingly of O'Hara when he was considering casting her in his 1957 film *The Rising of the Moon*, telling Michael Killanin, "She's a greedy bitch and I wonder if she'll accept our terms. Of course her name on an Irish film has value."[17] He went even further in a 1966 interview in France with Bernard Tavernier, asserting, "Maureen O'Hara is one of the actresses I most detest. Everybody believed I was her lover. In fact I hated her and she hated me. But she suited her roles very well."[18] Here, as in the previous quote, he softens the abuse with a banal general comment. "Hate" is a strong word. Did he mean it? It's hard to know. He might have been under the influence of alcohol. In her autobiography, O'Hara wrote that "when Pappy was drunk he made Will's episodes look like serene moments at a Transcendental Meditation seminar."[19]

O'Hara's overall estimation of Ford was simple: "He wanted to be born in Ireland and he wanted to be an Irish rebel. The fact that he wasn't left him very bitter."[20] In another context she dubbed him an "instant conman" who would "deliberately say the opposite of what he meant." She spoke these words with tears in her eyes, though, and ended by saying that all you could really do with Pappy was love him.[21] This was easier said than done, especially when his comments could range from flattery to damnation in an eyeblink. It's possible that he lavished praise on her to her face because of his physical desire for her; then, when that wasn't reciprocated, he gave her the full lash of his Celtic tongue.

Ford's death closed a huge chapter in O'Hara's life. Her attention now shifted to more pressing matters. In 1976 Blair bought her a travel magazine, the *Virgin Islander*, which he thought might help ease her into retirement. She edited it and also wrote columns on anything that struck her fancy. The "black art" took her mind off any regrets she might have had about quitting Hollywood. She enjoyed meeting deadlines and getting others to do so. She spent most of her time in St. Croix. Wayne visited occasionally and went flying with Blair. The two of them also had a passion for chess.

But Wayne's batteries were running down too, just as Ford's had. On November 6, 1976, O'Hara attended a tribute to him hosted by Frank Sinatra. It was one of the last functions he attended where his health wasn't an issue. At the end of the evening he stood up and told the gathering of stars, "Tonight you made an old man very happy." He then looked over at Sinatra and joked, "You *are* happy, aren't you, Frank?"[22] The following month he had prostate surgery. In March 1977 an angiogram detected a defective mitral valve in his heart.

O'Hara had her own health issues. She was diagnosed with uterine cancer in 1978, which necessitated major surgery. Wayne called her after her operation. They talked shop for a while and then Wayne started to cry. This threw her, as it wasn't in his nature to be so emotional. Then out of the blue he said, "Why you? Why me?" It was the last two words that shook her. Was he unwell? Had his own cancer returned?[23]

Wayne had just made a movie called *The Shootist*, about a cowboy with cancer who wants to shoot his way to Boot Hill. The film was framed as a kind of coda to Wayne's whole career, with clips from some of his earlier westerns emblazoned over the opening credits. His character says at one point, "I'm a dying man, scared of the dark," a rare admission for the erstwhile bulwark of virility. In real life he said, "I know the Man Upstairs will pull the plug when he wants to but I don't want to end my life being sick. I want to go out on two feet, in action."[24]

Wayne's illness upset O'Hara greatly, but a much worse tragedy was about to unfold closer to home. Blair died in 1978 when the engine of a Grauman Goose he was flying from St. Croix to St. Thomas exploded, killing himself and the three other people on board. According to witnesses, the craft struck the water, flipped over, and sank within minutes. O'Hara was hysterical upon hearing the news: all of a sudden, her guiding light was gone, absurdly and without warning.

She called Blair's mother, expecting her to be equally distraught. Instead, she found her remarkably cool. As O'Hara wept into the phone, the older woman barked sternly, "Stop that nonsense. He died the way he would have wanted to." O'Hara was amazed she could be so philosophical, but in time, this attitude rubbed off on her, and she focused on more pragmatic concerns.[25] Running Antilles Air Boats in the following months was therapeutic for her; it gave her something to do other than contemplate her tragedy. Asked by a journalist how long it took her to get her life back together after Blair's death, she deadpanned, "About five minutes. People depended on me."[26] Going into more specific detail, she explained bluntly, "I don't have time to sit in a corner and cry. I had 165 employees to be paid every week and 125 scheduled flights a day." Asked how she managed to concentrate on running a business after what had happened to her, she answered simply, "By being a tough Irish woman."[27]

Various questions were asked about why the accident happened. Was Blair partly to blame? Was sabotage involved? Many theories were presented to O'Hara in the months and years that followed, and she always suspected there was something sinister about the crash. Shortly after it happened, her phone rang three times, and three different voices spoke. Each said, "Will you please give us the true story of the assassination of General Charles Blair."[28] She wondered whether it had something to do with his connections in the Pentagon, or the fact that some Antilles pilots might have flown reconnaissance missions for the CIA, reporting on who was going in and out of Cuba. She called somebody "important" in the government to satisfy her curiosity, but no answers were forthcoming. The "important" person warned: "Maureen, don't ask. Keep your mouth shut. It won't do you any good and it won't bring Charlie back."[29] A few days later she was at the airport in St. Croix when a man behind her ventured, "I know who killed General Blair." The words stunned her, but she was too frightened to turn around and identify who had uttered them.[30]

For Blair's funeral, O'Hara petitioned Jimmy Carter, no less, to make sure he was buried with full military honors at Arlington cemetery—the place she herself asked to be interred when she died. John Wayne importuned Barry Goldwater to expedite this. Afterward, she was elected president of Antilles Air Boats, thereby becoming the first female president of a commercial airline. She also became a steadfast supporter of the Flying Boat Museum in Foynes, County Limerick.

Wayne's health had deteriorated by now. In March 1978 he was admitted to Massachusetts General Hospital, where the doctors intended to replace his failing mitral valve with a valve from a pig's heart. He joked that after it was over he'd probably be able to "oink" with the best of them.[31] Everything appeared to go well, but six months later he developed agonizing stomach cramps and his weight started to plummet, so he knew something was wrong. By Christmas Day he was too weak to even dress. He rallied somewhat in the early days of the New Year, but on January 10, feeling poorly again, he checked himself into UCLA Medical Center and learned he had stomach cancer. Wayne had already "licked the Big C," as he put it, in 1965. Joan Didion commended him for "reducing those outlaw cells to the level of any other outlaws," but she sensed that "this would be the one shoot-out Wayne could lose."[32] Time proved her right. The tumor was the size of a golf ball. Could he cheat death again? After a nine-hour operation, tests revealed that the cancer had spread.

Wayne appeared at the Oscar ceremonies in March looking like a shadow of his former self. Before he went onstage, he asked his makeup man to use light powder because, he quipped, "I'd rather not look as if I'd been embalmed just yet." The gallows humor was alive and well.[33] He wore a thick wetsuit under his tuxedo to make him look heavier, but nobody was fooled.[34] He looked like a dead man walking. His speech, given as he presented the Oscar to the producers of *The Deer Hunter* (the kind of antiwar film he would have detested in the old days), was sentimental. "Believe me when I tell you I'm mighty pleased that I can amble down here tonight," he smirked. "Oscar and I have something in common. Oscar came to the Hollywood scene in 1928. So did I. We're both a little weatherbeaten but we're still here, and plan to be around a whole lot longer."[35] It was a touching piece of wish fulfillment, of whistling in the graveyard. He knew the prognosis was bad, and so did everyone else.

Nine days later he was rushed to Hoag Hospital with pneumonia. He was so depressed that he asked his partner, Pat Stacy, to bring him his Smith and Wesson .38 because, he said, "I want to blow my brains out."[36]

Life was imitating fiction: he was starting to speak like his character from *The Shootist*.

O'Hara paid an emotional visit to Wayne not long before he died. She was determined not to be downbeat, for fear it would rub off on him. She lost her way en route to his house and ended up getting a police escort to the door. She related the story to Stacy with her customary enthusiasm: "The policeman recognized me and wanted to know if I was in Newport to visit John Wayne. I told him I didn't see how that was any of his concern. But before I could put my foot on the brakes he whipped out his traffic book, handed me a pen and asked for my autograph. The nerve of that lad!"[37]

It wasn't so easy to be jaunty when she saw Wayne. She was shocked by his skeletal appearance and started to cry. "Is that for Charlie?" he asked. She lied and said that it was. He probably saw through this. Then he said, "Maureen, why did you and I have such lousy luck?"[38] There was no answer to that. There had been too many tragedies in both their lives—his broken marriages, her broken marriages, cancer on the double, deaths and suicides of loved ones, the works. The Man Upstairs had a wicked sense of humor. But one couldn't complain. That wasn't Duke's style. And it certainly wasn't O'Hara's.

The atmosphere lightened afterward as they chatted about everyday matters. He asked her to stay over, and she did. The next day he was back to his old self, discussing the happy times, the wild times, a drunken escapade with John Ford (knocking on the door of a total stranger because he needed another drink and, amazingly, being invited in for a nightcap). Wayne appeared to be depressed about the fact that he was going to turn seventy-two the following month. "So what?" O'Hara countered, "I'll be 58 in August. Mileage never hurt a Rolls Royce. We're a couple of Rolls Royces!"[39] Wayne guffawed at that.

She stayed for three days even though she had only the clothes on her back. Stacy was too short to loan her anything, but she had the maid launder O'Hara's clothing each night. She put on a "cheerful Irish act" with Wayne, according to Stacy: "At no time did she let on how seriously worried she was about him. I never met a gal who could talk as much as Maureen." Wayne told Stacy that his recollection of some of the anecdotes they exchanged differed from O'Hara's, "But what the hell, she makes them sound better."[40] As was the case with John Ford, when facts conflicted with the legend, it was better to print the legend. At one point during their reminiscences, Wayne's grandchild turned to him and asked, "Grandpa, did you really do that?" Wayne replied, "Well, if your Auntie Maureen says so, then I guess I did."[41]

Such anecdotes blotted out the trauma of what was happening, but only for a while. Soon it was time to go. O'Hara had to catch a flight to St. Croix. She put on her coat and went over to Wayne to say good-bye. "That's a gorgeous coat," he said. "It looks beautiful on you."[42] Those were the last words she ever heard him speak. After she left, Stacy pondered who was worse off, her or O'Hara? Blair had been killed instantly, "with no fear or suffering," while she was living "day after agonizing day" with Wayne, holding on to the slim hope that some miracle might happen.[43] The following day he was taken to the hospital again, and that tiny glimmer of hope was gone.

On May 21, 1979, Congress held hearings on the minting of a special medal to honor Wayne. The bill had been introduced by his old friend Barry Goldwater. Goldwater chose O'Hara to speak to his colleagues, believing she had the best chance of ensuring the bill would pass. As she flew to Washington, she fretted about what inscription she would suggest for the medal. Finally it came to her; it should be engraved with just three words: "John Wayne, American." She made a poignant request to the congressional subcommittee. "To the people of America," she pleaded, tears in her eyes, "John Wayne is not just an actor. . . . John Wayne *is* the United States of America." Some people found this excessive, but Congress agreed with her, and the bill was passed. Wayne watched the event on TV from his hospital bed. On his seventy-second birthday he received a letter verifying that the medal had been approved. It bore a landscape of Monument Valley. Wayne's portrait on the front had been chosen by O'Hara.

Three weeks later, John Wayne, American, died. To everyone's surprise, he was buried in an unmarked grave. One of his neighbors remarked, "It seems to be a special bit of irony that this most visible of men in his lifetime is anonymous in death."[44] Wayne had converted to Catholicism on his deathbed, so O'Hara got further with him than she had with the more doggedly atheistic Charles Laughton.

She remembered Wayne lighting cigarettes in every other scene of *The Quiet Man*. "That's what did him in," she concluded. "If we knew then what we know now about cancer maybe we'd have done something about it."[45]

Looked at from a distance, Wayne was more figurehead than man, a paradigmatic archetype that brooked little resistance. In future westerns and future civilian dramas, the issues wouldn't be as clear-cut as he made them, nor would the solutions be so readily accessible, both in political contexts and in fictional ones. As long as Wayne was in charge, audiences knew he'd figure a way out of a tight fix on the prairie or be able to out-gun the villains on Main Street. Later heroes and antiheroes wouldn't be blessed with his luck or self-belief. They would investigate the gray areas of moral and military scenarios and sometimes end their deliberations with a question mark.

Wayne had famously decried the film *High Noon* because Gary Cooper showed fear, because he threw his sheriff's badge away at the end, because he needed the help of a "mere" woman to defeat the bad guys (and a peace-embracing Quaker woman at that). On another occasion he remonstrated with Kirk Douglas for playing the "weak" Vincent van Gogh in *Lust for Life*. With O'Hara, he negotiated various perils with an arrogance match-ing her own, but in the future, the definition of what constituted right and wrong would be more malleable and less attainable. A later generation of macho men would bring doubt into the locker room.

12

Ready for Her Close-ups

With Blair and Wayne both gone, life was especially lonely for O'Hara. But she was, in her own estimation, a tough Irishwoman. She also had Bronwyn and a steel-strong network of siblings and friends. She spent nine months of the year in the Virgin Islands and the rest split between Ireland and the United States. "The weather is excellent in St. Croix," she enthused. "Sure we get the hurricanes and the storms in September, October and the beginning of November but when they come you go down into your storm cellar. Otherwise it's beautiful—a gorgeous sky and aquamarine sea—and you can see all the way to the sea bed."[1] In addition to the landscape and the weather, she liked the people.

She sold the *Virgin Islander* to USA Today in 1980, giving up journalism so she could spend more time with Bronwyn and Conor Beau. She was also close to Blair's children and visited them often. The following year she sold Antilles Air Boats, off-loading the controlling stock to Resorts International. With 120 flights a day and a 27-plane commercial fleet ranging the upper Caribbean, it was getting to be too much for her. She loved running the company but found that dealing with men all the time made her prone to expletives, comments that she considered unladylike, and shows of temper that she didn't like in herself.

As the years went on, she was honored in many capacities outside the film world, perhaps compensating for Hollywood's failure to recognize her talents. In 1982 she became the first recipient of the American Ireland Fund Lifetime Achievement Award in Los Angeles. That year she also became the first woman to win the John F. Kennedy Memorial Award as "Outstanding American of Irish Descent for Service to God and Country." The following year she received the Ireland Fund Peace, Culture and Charity Award. Such honors disguised (or perhaps emphasized) the fact that she was relatively inactive.

For the first time in her life, she had time on her hands and wasn't totally sure how to occupy her days. As time passed, she felt more drawn to her homeland and cut back on her nomadic lifestyle. She'd put down many roots in America over the decades, but they were very much tied to her career. Now that it was over, she returned to the girl she'd always been—the girl who failed to share Charles Laughton's enthusiasm over the Statue of Liberty in 1939 because she was so homesick.

She continued her thriftiness as a retired diva. One day at Shannon Airport, Conor Beau put twenty pence into a gaming machine and nothing happened. Another grandmother might have advised him to try another machine, but not Maureen O'Hara. She called for the officer on duty and got a refund, telling him plump and plain: "I worked hard for my money. These machines should work."[2] The officer was probably amused—and impressed.

In 1984 she set up an annual golf tournament in Glengariff to honor her late husband's memory and encourage tourism in the area. There were two trophies for the winners: the General Charles F. Blair for men and the Maureen O'Hara Blair for women. She became a familiar figure around Glengariff and made it her main home. The locals were momentarily awed, but once they got to know her better, it was as if she'd never been Maureen O'Hara the movie star.

She gave interviews at irregular intervals. A frequent inquiry was whether she would ever remarry. Her answer was always the same: it was unlikely. "I don't even date anybody. Who would put up with a woman who's constantly talking about Charlie Blair."[3] It seemed that Blair was too hard an act to follow.

The social life of Glengariff offered some relief from the enforced isolation of widowhood. There were also occasional invitations to return to the glitter of Tinseltown. She usually greeted these with a mixture of mild curiosity and vague boredom, but when Roddy McDowall called in 1985 to tell her he was being given a Career Achievement Award by the American Cinema Foundation, she pricked up her ears in deference to their strong bond. He asked her to present the award to him, and she agreed. She flew to the States and even prepared a speech, but when the night came, Elizabeth Taylor was asked to make the presentation instead. O'Hara could have made a fuss over the snub, but out of respect for McDowall, she didn't. Maybe her day was over, she thought.

She didn't disappear from public view; she just became more measured. She commuted between her homes in St. Croix, New York, and Ireland, keeping in close contact with family members and some old friends from her schooldays. Occasionally she spoke to the press about her life both on and off the screen, preserving the spiky, up-and-at-it quality that had always defined her. One day a reporter asked her how she'd dealt with cancer. The answer she gave was vintage O'Hara: "The same way I dealt with everything—fists up and fighting. That's the only way to approach cancer or any other problem."[4] John Wayne's can-do attitude had rubbed off on her. Like him, she'd licked the "Big C."

She considered returning to the screen, but if she did, it would have to be for something special. Her brother Charles kept on the lookout for potential projects, but as time passed, these became thinner. By now, most people thought they'd seen the last of Maureen O'Hara on the big screen.

In 1989 there were rumors of a sequel to *The Quiet Man*. Charles had commissioned a screenplay in which Sean Thornton's son, also a boxer, is pitted against the son of the man his father killed in the ring all those years ago. It was an interesting concept, and both of them were excited about it. "It's a great script," Charles beamed. "It's packed with action and I reckon it will do well. It's set against the ethnic background of the Irish-Americans and Italian-Americans in the U.S."[5] Alas, it came to nothing.

Later that year O'Hara's home in St. Croix was hit by a hurricane. The house that she and Blair had built together, the site of her happiest memories, had nearly been reduced to rubble. In the aftermath of the devastation, she went to survey the damage with Blair's son Chris. It would have been more practical to write the house off, but she couldn't do that. She insisted on rebuilding. In addition to the obvious damage, she was heartbroken over the loss of personal effects such as Blair's chess set, John Wayne's hats, and a set of ceramic dolls the young Natalie Wood had made for "Mama Maureen" on the set of *Miracle on 34th Street*.[6] "The chess set is somewhere whirling around the earth right now," she bemoaned.[7] The two men who'd sat around it so often had long since played their endgames.

It was when O'Hara went to New York to sort out the financial costs of the hurricane that she first started getting chest pains and feelings of paralysis. A few days later she was hallucinating, imagining that a cab driver was trying to kill her and that two men with knives were approaching her threateningly. At the hospital, the doctors diagnosed multiple heart attacks. To avoid open-heart surgery, she underwent an angioplasty. But as she was recovering from that, she had additional heart attacks, necessitating a second angioplasty.

Undeterred by a mere half dozen coronaries ("I have no intention of dying young," she joked), she decided to return to the screen the following year. Charles had received a script he thought would be suitable for her. The film was called *Only the Lonely*, and it was going to be shot in Chicago and directed by Christopher Columbus (who would become famous in years to come for his work on the Harry Potter movies). O'Hara would be playing Rose Muldoon, a possessive Irish American mother who stands in the way of her son's happiness when he becomes romantically involved with a woman with a decidedly unusual job. "This you do," Charles prompted.

As soon as she expressed an interest in the project, the publicity machine cranked into overdrive. "When Maureen O'Hara left the green hills of Ireland for the klieg light heat of Hollywood some fifty years ago," one journalist wrote, "she haughtily stooped to conquer castle and sea in a low cut bodice. Flashing a pair of stormy green eyes, a bounding mane of auburn hair and a dagger edge brogue, she charmed a generation by playing to sword's hilt the high-spirited lass who made pirates rue the day they abducted her."[8]

She saw the departure from her roles of yore as a challenge. "I didn't want to do the same thing I'd always done. It had to have another dimension. That other dimension was meanness."[9] At last she was getting to play one of those "fun bitches" she used to envy Bette Davis for.

The original script was Italian, but Columbus adapted it. Why had he thought of O'Hara for the role? "[She's] one of the strongest women in film history. There's not a weak bone about her. I had no idea what happened to her. She was just a springboard for me to write the character."[10] But then he found it all but impossible to contact her. It was a bit like trying to locate Greta Garbo. "I'd completely dropped out," she admitted. "I didn't even have an agent."[11] He eventually tracked her down through an Irish American newspaper, and this in turn led to Charles.

John Ford wouldn't have liked Rose Muldoon. She represented the ugly face of diaspora, the bitter immigrant Irishwoman trying to convince her vulnerable son that because she needed him, he should need her. From this point of view, Rose was light years away from Mary Kate Danaher's bucolic charm. All they shared in common was a hair-trigger temper. There was racism in Muldoon's character in the Italian draft, and Columbus preserved this. "I'm Italian but my wife is Irish," he explained. "The bigotry and racism that's apparent in Rose Muldoon was a big part of Italians I had known, and also in the generation of Irish people that I'd met. Back when Rose was Italian in the first draft, she was still prejudiced against Sicilians. Italians break up people into sectors of Italy where they were raised. These people actually think there's a difference between the Milanese, the Calabrese and the Sicilians."[12]

O'Hara was relieved to be back in movies. No matter how long she'd been away, the hunger was still there—maybe more so. Everything was more or less the same since she had bid adieu to all the hoopla after *Big Jake*. "Twenty years is a long time," she allowed, "but it was surprising how little has changed. The equipment is lighter now, and they work a bit faster, but I hardly felt I'd been away."[13] Nonetheless, there were some obvious differences. For one thing, audiences had become more sophisticated. The explosion of sex and violence that had contributed to her departure from the screen in the early 1970s had plateaued, but were films any better as a result? Were they worse?

Columbus had to "sell" O'Hara to the studio because most of the executives in the industry barely knew her. "Is she too old to act?" they asked. Columbus showed them *How Green Was My Valley* to sway them. It was as if she had to do another screen test a half century after her first one for Charles Laughton. They were impressed but wondered whether she still had what it took, after such a long time away. O'Hara, too, wondered about her decision to return to the screen. Few stars make comebacks without good reason. Was this film reason enough? The last thing she wanted was for her former fans to ask why she'd bothered. For the first time in her life, she was short on confidence. Life, she reflected, had a habit of draining that out of people: "When you're very young you're very assured and you have total knowledge of what you're going to do. As we get older, life knocks all that confidence out of us. We think, 'How'd we do that?'"[14] The old defenses were crumbling—refreshingly.

She saw Rose as a multifaceted creature: "bad-tempered, possessive, prejudiced, domineering, very funny—but in the end you love me." Was she like that herself? "I don't think I'm strong. I'm bossy and I do like my own way, but don't think I'm not acting when I'm up there, and don't think I always get my own way. There have been crushing disappointments. But when that happens I say, 'Find another hill to climb.' Perhaps I'm doing that now."[15]

Once they met, Columbus was delighted to see that O'Hara was so young at heart. He knew this would make the lusty attraction of Nick the gardener (Anthony Quinn) more believable. (Columbus wrote the part of Nick with Quinn in mind. If O'Hara was an elderly Danaher, he could be Zorba the Greek a few decades on.) Rose has two sons: Patrick (Kevin Dunn) and Danny (John Candy). Patrick is a lawyer, and Danny a policeman who specializes in removing corpses from crime scenes. Rose's relationship with Danny is more like "smother love" than mother love. No woman is good enough for him, in her eyes. When he falls in love with Theresa (Ally Sheedy), an undertaker's daughter who is a makeup artist for corpses, she faces the prospect of losing him. As she sits down to a meal with Sheedy, she says to her, apropos her lack of décolletage, "You're built like a thirteen-year-old boy." One doubts Mary Kate Danaher would have uttered such a comment—at any age.

Columbus found the script easy to write because he could relate to Candy's character. "I was a real heavy kid," he confessed, "and I didn't go out on a lot of dates. Saturday nights I stayed home and watched Carol Burnett with my parents."[16] But the "mother fixation" theme came not from his own life but from his father-in-law's: "He had a group of five friends he grew up with on the south side of Chicago and he was the only one who got married. The other guys all lived with their mothers till they died and then they went off to the YMCA or got a single apartment. One of the guys was engaged to a woman for 17 years and finally got married when his mother died. He was 58 years old."[17]

O'Hara refused to soft-center Rose: "I thought if I played her absolutely straight and didn't ask for any forgiveness or sympathy, audiences would still understand her."[18] It was a clever strategy, and it worked. "Mothers with sons will identify with Rose," she supposed. "Boys who live at home will root for Candy, their girlfriends for Ally." This didn't bother her. How did she feel about herself? "Me? All I want is to live to be a hundred."[19] But she was sensitive about her age. When one newspaper reported that she was seventy-one, she protested: "I don't want to be robbed of one precious year of my life. I'm 70."[20] She clung to the extra year with limpet-like tenacity.

Candy was thrilled to be working with a movie legend. As for O'Hara, "Kids in the family are so impressed with the fact that I'm working with Uncle Buck I've now taken on a whole new stature."[21] O'Hara got on excellently with Candy. She rated him on a par with Charles Laughton—an extravagant claim for the former standup comic.[22] He was so taken with her that when he learned the producers hadn't provided her with a trailer, he gave her his.[23] (She was shocked when Candy died a few years after making the film. Although many believe he was a victim of obesity, O'Hara felt his untimely demise was due to a congenital heart problem.)

Only the Lonely grossed $35 million. An Oscar nomination for O'Hara was rumored, but she thought this was unlikely. Hollywood hadn't seen fit to award her one for close to half a century. Why would that change now? (It didn't.) But she was learning not to care so much about such things. Personal concerns were closer to her heart.

A private screening was held before the commercial release and she was anxious to see the reaction. "A small portion of the family went to see the movie the other night," she beamed, "twenty people."[24] Sometimes 20 people can mean more to a person than 200 or 2,000—if they're the right people. She was garlanded with wreaths from friends and family and considered this the true barometer of success.

O'Hara toyed with the idea of a full-scale comeback after the movie was released. "Find me another script and another character like this one," she teased, "and we could be talking."[25] But she would only consider a leading role. "No cameo appearances or bit parts, thank you very much."[26]

In July 1991 she attended a reception in Galway to commemorate the fortieth anniversary of *The Quiet Man*. When a journalist had the temerity to suggest the possibility of a remake, O'Hara turned on him. "I couldn't play Mary Kate now," she snarled, "but I'd kill anyone else who tried."[27]

Many awards came her way in subsequent years. In 1993 she was inducted into the Western Performers Hall of Fame at the National Cowboy and Western Heritage Museum in Oklahoma City. That year she also began a new venture: selling quality Irish goods on the Home Shopping Network (HSN), which reached more than 60 million U.S. households. She didn't see this as any different from trying to sell tickets to movies or for Antilles Air Boats. "My life has been sales of one kind or another—including movies." Her parents had a drapery shop, Ernest Blythe's, on Kildare Street when she was growing up, so selling was in her blood.[28]

Only the Lonely hadn't made her an A-lister again, but at least it showed people she was still around, and it reawakened the acting bug. Movies might not have been a viable option, but television was. O'Hara wasn't ashamed to gravitate to the "small screen" and made the TV movie *The Christmas Box* in 1995.

Richard Thomas and Annette O'Toole are Richard and Keri Evans; they have a young daughter, Jenna, played by Kelsey Mulrooney. They're having problems paying the rent on their apartment, so they answer an ad placed by wealthy widow Mary Parkin (O'Hara). The arrangement is that they live rent free in her mansion in return for cooking and gardening and generally taking care of Mary, who lives alone. The relationship between Richard and Mary is tense. She picks on him for any minor infraction of her iron-clad routines and fixes him with a gimlet-eyed stare. He wants to leave but is curious about her past. Why are there no photographs of her husband on display? Did she have children? "Nobody ever visits," Keri remarks. "I can't imagine why," Richard snaps back. After a time, Mary thaws out, even becoming possessive of Richard. One day she asks him, "What's the first gift of Christmas?" Obviously, she's trying to tell him to spend more time with his daughter. (Her secret is that she had a child that died.)

The film's message would have worked better if Richard was a less likeable character or less of a family man. As things stand, it's superfluous and overly didactic. O'Hara gives a decent performance, though. She looks matronly, but the old sparkle in her eye shines through as the film goes on. She has a Rose Muldoon moment when the subject of nursing homes comes up. "I don't like old ladies and bingo!" she roars. But for the most part, the movie is a failed Capraesque affair that barely steers clear of mawkishness.

O'Hara found herself in demand for interviews after it aired. "The acting muscles never get out of shape," she advised one reporter. "Actors are born. Throughout life you hone the gifts that God gave you but you don't lose them."[29] Had anything changed about the business since she'd last "trodden the boards"? "I'll tell you what *hasn't* changed. You're still waiting for the gift of a great writer giving you a great script. And I think *The Christmas Box* is a wonderful gift."[30] She was still the public relations lady, still "selling" a basically formulaic exercise, almost willing it to be better than it was.

Pressed about her motivation for doing the TV movie, she placed it in high company by likening it to *Miracle on 34th Street.* "So few films with sentiment and heart get made today, when one this good comes along, you do it. I don't know if we have a classic on our hands but the chemistry is right and you have to start with that. That's why *Miracle* is still the favorite. It hasn't been replaced by the remakes. You can't recapture magic."[31] Asked whether she liked the new movies, none sprang to mind. "It's all sex and violence and car chases and explosions today, isn't it?" she ventured.[32] It was hard to disagree with her: in many ways, it seemed as if the industry had dumbed down into a kind of cultural apartheid. (She didn't get small; the films got small.)

O'Hara was rocked by another tragedy the following year when she heard that her friend Brian Keith had shot himself. He'd been suffering from lung cancer and emphysema and was brokenhearted by his daughter Daisy's suicide just ten weeks before, but O'Hara refused to believe he'd done it deliberately. She preferred to think the gun had gone off during "a spasm of agony."[33] She refused to countenance the suicide allegations and appeared to be in denial about his depression. The more she was criticized for this, the angrier she became.

John Sessions witnessed her famous temper firsthand in 1998 when he got her name wrong at a function. She'd been regaling guests at Roddy McDowall's house with anecdotes about James Stewart and Henry Fonda, when Sessions said he wished his parents were there, as they really would have enjoyed meeting "Maureen O'Sullivan." The mix-up in names was like a red rag to a bull, Sessions revealed: "Eyes blackening to full Norma Desmond, her head tipped back like that of the Tyrannosaurus Rex in *Jurassic Park* just before it eats the bloke who's sitting on the can. Suddenly I wished that I too was in the can, in Mongolia perhaps. Maureen O'Hara eventually brought herself to say the words, 'I did not swing in the trees with fucking Tarzan!'"[34]

She made another TV movie, *Cab to Canada*, later that year. Based on

a real event, it tells the story of a septuagenarian (O'Hara) who decides that
life is too short for tears after attending the funeral of a friend. She asks her
cab driver to take her on an extended ride, and they wind up in Canada,
having adventures all the while. It's a sweet little film, replete with knowing
touches, and it stays on the right side of soggy emotion. She enjoyed making
it but didn't expect it to pull in huge audiences. It was difficult to attract
viewers to new work when there were so many classics being aired on TV.
She was still well represented in these classics, as well as at film festivals.
The ever-growing video market also helped. To cap the year, she won the
Helen Hayes Lifetime Achievement Award.

In March 1999 O'Hara was selected to be the grand marshal of the
New York City St. Patrick's Day Parade (she had previously been rejected
owing to her status as a divorcée). Four months later she attended the sixti-
eth anniversary celebration of Pan American Airways' first scheduled flight
across the North Atlantic at the Foynes Flying Boat Museum. The museum
had had more than 160,000 visitors since opening. From 1939 to 1945,
Foynes had been a transportation center, boasting a commercial harbor,
an international airport, a passenger train service, a passenger bus service,
and hackneys. Passengers on the flying boats included such personages as
Humphrey Bogart, Ernest Hemingway, Gracie Fields, John F. Kennedy,
and Douglas Fairbanks. O'Hara was in her element, recalling trips to and
from Foynes over the years. Blair had taken his last flying boat out of the
Foynes airport in 1945.

It was easy to live on such memories now. Her time with Blair had
been short but precious. She didn't want to forget any part of it or the
importance of his achievements and his brave dignity. His life was more
significant than a life in movies, she held, and she had become part of that
significance. Movie people, however, were less keen to hear her views on
Blair than on movies. So no matter how many times she was interviewed,
the conversation tended to drift back to the old chestnuts of how she felt
about Hollywood, John Wayne, John Ford, and all the others. She generally
gave good copy, even if her answers sometimes seemed like movie scripts
she'd learned by heart, to be regurgitated with minor adjustments for each
visiting journalist.

Toward the end of the century she was asked to document her feelings
about John Ford. She obliged with this *aperçu*:

He let me use the talent I was born with. I was never happy with the things Hollywood made me do. I felt there were chains around me but the first time I worked with Ford the chains were gone. I could do any damn thing I wanted and it was all right. He gave me freedom. Some of the directors used to direct every little movement of your hand. It was like being in a prison. Ford put you in a situation and let you fight your way out of it. Yes he was tough, very tough. You could get mad at him off the set, but in the time between "Roll it" and "Cut" he was a pleasure to work with.[35]

In August 2000 she hit the eighty mark but could have passed for at least ten years younger. Clean living obviously had its benefits. She traveled to Ireland for a party held in the Dunraven Arms Hotel in Adare, staying up until the wee hours when people half her age had turned in for the night—despite an injury to her arm, which was bandaged and strapped. She had been standing on a sofa cushion, trying to see if there was some Irish money from a previous trip in an overhead cupboard, when the cushion slipped and she came tumbling down. She made light of her injuries, preferring to look on the positives of her life, as always. "I don't feel much different than I did when I was at school in Milltown," she announced to the packed gathering.[36] She went on to say she had no plans to retire, having just completed a TV movie for CBS: "Working keeps the mind and body active. If people have to retire because the industry they work in insists on it they should get involved in voluntary work."[37] It was stirring stuff from an octogenarian.

Her last TV movie was *The Last Dance*, in which she plays a retired teacher who has a heart attack. When she gets to the hospital, she discovers that her nurse is one of her former students. The film explores her relationship with him and his wife and children. Asked if her character was loving or cantankerous, she answered bluntly, "For me she has to be a little cantankerous. If she was too bland it would be terrible. I've always done spicy women." Had Hollywood changed since she was in her prime? "No. The actor has to act. The writer has to write. The director has to direct and the producer has to put the whole thing together. But the technical things have changed—film cameras, computers and computer images."[38] It was refreshing to hear such common sense.

She appeared on *Larry King* later that month and was a big hit with him, despite indexing most of her costars with references to their Irish ancestry. When King mentioned Charles Laughton, she said he was "half Irish so he had to be wonderful." Anthony Quinn was "super handsome, and Irish too." Errol Flynn was "Irish too, you know—Australian Irish." When they got to Jackie Gleason she piped up, "Did you know his father was from Ireland?" King blurted out, "Everything comes back to the Irish with you. By the end of the show *I'm* going to be Irish!"[39]

Did she feel eighty? "Not for one second. I think my mother gave me the wrong birth date." She expressed a desire to live to be 102, the age Charlie Blair's mother had attained. "She was the oldest scout mistress in the United States," she told King. "She was a tough old gal and she was terrific. I thought: By God, I'd like to be a tough old gal and carry a stick and thump it on the ground at all the kids."[40]

The Last Dance was being shown in conjunction with the interview, and King alluded to its tearjerker quality by advising the audience to "bring your handkerchiefs." O'Hara wasn't put out by the implied slight. She countered, "To hell with the handkerchief, bring a box of Kleenex!" To her, the film's value lay in its homage to schoolteachers, "because schoolteachers have raised half the children of the world. The parents raise the other half."[41]

O'Hara's brother Charles died in 2001. As well as being an actor and producer, he'd served as executive director of the Producers Guild from 1981 to 1999. He was the most successful of her siblings, but like the others, he lived largely in her shadow.

That year also saw the publication of a biography of Tina Brown, the daughter of George Brown, O'Hara's first husband. Written by former *Washington Post* journalist Judy Bachrach, the book is of interest to students of O'Hara because of the light it throws on George Brown. O'Hara never liked to speak about him, and her memoirs tell us nothing beyond the fact that he lured her into marriage against her wishes. Bachrach, however, goes into some detail about his life.

George Brown was born in 1913 and raised by relatives in Barcelona after his father, a pilot in the Royal Flying Air Corps, was shot down and taken prisoner by the Germans during World War I. His mother was an actress and singer with the D'Oyly Carte Company. This probably accounts for his early interest in show business. He was a production assistant on two Pommer-Laughton productions before *Jamaica Inn* (where he met O'Hara): *Vessel of Wrath* and *St. Martin's Lane*, both made in 1938. Bachrach recounts that before Brown met O'Hara, he had also been a film stuntman. His colorful résumé includes an early role in which he rode a horse bareback, wearing just a pink jockstrap.[42]

After O'Hara left him, he started dating Bettina Kohr, who, like O'Hara, had an Irish heritage and a film background. She had been a secretary to the famous film director Alexander Korda and had also done publicity work for Laurence Olivier. They originally met at Denham Studios, outside London, when Brown was still a casting director. In contrast to O'Hara, Kohr was smitten with him.

Brown was associate producer of the propaganda thriller *The 49th Parallel* in 1941. He then became a member of the RAF film unit in the North African desert. Brown and Kohr were married in 1948, when Brown was thirty-five and Kohr just twenty-five. The couple threw dinner parties for the rich and famous; guests included Sophia Loren, Sean Connery, and Peter Sellers.

Brown formed a partnership with Peter Ustinov and coproduced the film *School for Secrets* with him in 1946. He produced a number of diverse films in the 1950s: the comedy *Made in Heaven* in 1952, a thriller called *Desperate Moment* the next year, and an antipodean western called *The Seekers* in 1954. He ended the decade with a Tommy Steele film, *Tommy the Toreador*. One of Brown's major coups was casting Margaret Rutherford as Miss Marple in *Murder, She Said*, which spawned three sequels. His output was patchy in the 1960s. He made the army movie *Guns at Batasi* in 1964 and *The Trap* two years later. In 1971 he persuaded Joan Collins to strip down to her bra and panties for a scene in the B movie *Terror under the House*. That year he also produced the spy thriller *Innocent Bystanders* with Oliver Reed.

Brown and Kohr moved to Spain in the early 1970s and lived there happily until his health began to deteriorate. He died in 2001 at the ripe old age of eighty-seven.

Tina Brown became infinitely more famous than her father. She was a wild child, managing to get herself expelled from no fewer than three boarding schools. At one, she explained, she was expelled after protesting that she wasn't allowed to change her underpants, and another threw her out because she referred to the headmistress as an unidentified flying object. After finally graduating from college, she became a playwright and a journalist. She dated Auberon Waugh and Dudley Moore, both of whom she interviewed, as well as Martin Amis. In 1974 she met Harold Evans, editor of the *Sunday Times*, and began working for him. They also began dating, but he was married and twenty-five years her senior.

She became editor of *Tatler* magazine in 1979 and quadrupled its circulation. She married Evans two years later, after he divorced his wife. They moved to New York, where she became editor of *Vanity Fair* in 1984, eventually increasing sales of the magazine to a record million copies per issue. She had two children with Evans—George born in 1986, and Izzy in 1990. In 1992 she became editor of the *New Yorker,* restructuring the magazine considerably and bringing in many new writers. She became chairperson of a new Miramax company in 1998, and the Hearst Company came on board to take it in a multimedia direction. Tina's next venture was *Talk* magazine, a show-business glossy, but sales plummeted after the terrorist attacks on the Twin Towers in 2001. She subsequently produced a number of CNBC specials. "Everything she set her mind to," her father said in his old age, "she did with intense application. She was extraordinarily resolute."[43] This was one of the qualities that had attracted him to O'Hara.

In 2002 Brown brought her daughter to a Manhattan screening of *Miracle on 34th Street* at which O'Hara was present. After the film was over, Brown and her daughter stood before O'Hara, waiting for an autograph. Tina grabbed the bull by the horns and blurted out: "I'm the daughter of your first husband, George Brown." O'Hara looked stunned as Brown repeated, "You were married to him." O'Hara then answered waspishly, "For five minutes." When Brown asked O'Hara why the marriage had been annulled, an enraged O'Hara roared, "It was the lies on the marriage certificate. His age and so many of the other details were untrue. He should have sought parental consent." Brown wasn't convinced, describing her father as "the most unduplicitous gent in the world."[44] She was so flummoxed by O'Hara's anger that she forgot to ask her why George would have lied about his age (he was only twenty-six at the time). The incident brought back unpleasant memories for O'Hara and obviously put a damper on an evening she'd been looking forward to for some time. *Miracle* was one of her favorite films and George Brown a part of her past that she desperately wanted to forget.

O'Hara was presented with a lifetime achievement gong at the Irish Film and Television Awards in 2004, a long overdue accolade. Everybody who was anybody was there. Even Steven Spielberg sent a message, commending her for being "a role model for all women" and for bringing strength to the types of roles women typically played in the 1940s.[45]

She was now, at long last, getting around to working on her long-awaited autobiography. It was Conor Beau, her grandson, who prevailed on her to put pen to paper. "He kept nagging me to do it so eventually I gave in," she admitted. She called it *'Tis Herself.*[46]

The reading public didn't expect any tawdry revelations, considering she was eighty-four years old and had lived a life free of the whiff of scandal. The thinking was that if she had any secrets to tell, she would have done so by now. The book became a best seller. It contained a rash of effectively narrated anecdotes about her life and career. She went into great detail about her various bouquets and brickbats, both onscreen and off. The book also had its fair share of melodrama and conspiracy theories: she believed Charlie Blair had been murdered, that there had been a plan to kidnap "herself" in Dublin, and that Hollywood had plotted to deny her Oscars for both *The Quiet Man* and *Only the Lonely.*

When she wrote about domestic events, she used loaded language, as when she blamed family and friends for breaking up her relationship with Enrique Parra: "They had conspired behind the scenes and fired at us from the grassy knoll."[47] At times like this she definitely exhibited signs of a persecution complex, but despite such tabloid elements, the book was a fiercely entertaining read. The fact that John Nicoletti, her coauthor, was a screenwriter may have been significant. As with any autobiography, there were omissions and embellishments in *'Tis Herself.*

One of its main selling points was the amount of ink she spilled on John Ford—his tantrums, his genius, his obsession with her, and his almost constant abuse both during and between films. She also wrote about the day she saw him kissing another man on the lips, even if she didn't identify him. (Many believe it was Tyrone Power.) Some readers of the book imagined it to be a "belated revenge" on Ford.[48] It could also be seen as revenge on her first two husbands and other safely dead Hollywood celebrities, such as James Stewart, whom she accused of upstaging her; Sam Peckinpah, her ultimate bête noire; and Jeff Chandler, whom she once compared to a broomstick. In fact, she had outlived nearly all her contemporaries.

O'Hara was apprehensive about "dishing the dirt" on anyone. Such fears were eschatological: "I'm terrified about the day that I enter the gates of heaven and God says to me, 'Where did you get permission to tell that story?' What am I going to say to God?"[49] She apparently overcame her scruples in this regard once she got cracking, as she launched a full-frontal attack, guns blazing, on everyone who had ever crossed her. Having said that, it isn't a bitter book. It also contains large slices of warmth, most of it directed toward Blair and her family.

She was coy about her sex life, so the revelation that she lost her virginity on her wedding night made one sit up—not so much because it was unusual (and it was—the only thing new to most Hollywood brides was the wedding cake) but because she addressed the subject at all. Her attitude toward sex bordered on the puritanical at times, which wasn't what one expected from a sex symbol. But this, after all, was a woman who resolutely refused to do swimsuit shots in her heyday because, as Johnny Grant put it, she was "an actress."[50]

She promoted the book with her inimitable enthusiasm, giving interviews to all and sundry on both sides of the Atlantic. She even had a signing at Macy's (featured so prominently in *Miracle on 34th Street*). Had Hollywood been fair to her over the years? She expressed this view to Thomas Myler: "Much of my life is part of a public persona that was carefully sewn together, like a magnificent quilt, by the powerful Hollywood studio system. An entire publicity team had to see to it that at least one item about me was published every day. Many were total lies or studio publicity department inventions. . . . Of course my loved ones know me in a far different way. To them I'm just Mammy, Gran or Auntie Maureen—a terrible cook but one helluva cleaning lady!"[51]

She expressed pride over the fact that nobody had ever turned her down as a costar. No one ever said, "God, not that woman again." It made her feel good to be able to say that she had appeared more than once with people like Charles Laughton, Henry Fonda, John Payne, Tyrone Power, Anthony Quinn, John Wayne, and James Stewart and that she'd worked so much with John Ford. What were her feelings about Ford now? "When he got tough and nasty we forgave him. At times we wanted to punch him in the nose. He treated Duke the same way he treated me, Ward Bond and Jimmy Stewart, but when you'd think about it going home at night you were proud of your day's work."[52]

O'Hara also revealed how horribly Ford had treated her brothers. She was especially bitter about what he did to Jimmy after he failed to turn up at a casting meeting. Ford's "punishment" was to arrange to have Jimmy arrested on a charge of draft dodging. O'Hara asserted that Ford had also tried to get *her* arrested, on a trumped-up charge of smuggling jewelry from Mexico.[53] Were these allegations true? Either O'Hara had a very active imagination or Ford was a seriously disturbed individual.

Los Angeles Times journalist Merle Rubin wrote one of the most corrosive reviews of the book, damning it as "harsh, unpleasant and unforgiving" and criticizing the use of a cowriter as a shield, so readers wouldn't know which author to blame. "No slight seems too trivial to be irrigated," Rubin continued, "and if possible avenged, from the nastiness of the nuns who taught her in Ireland to unwanted passes from (among others) the husband of that other Maureen, John Farrow." (O'Hara certainly didn't hold back in her account of Farrow's stalking her on the set of *A Bill of Divorcement*.) Rubin inveighed against the general tone of the book, finding it self-congratulatory: "Modesty is not a concept with which she seems familiar (she likes to brag), and self-righteousness is often to the fore." Rubin also accused O'Hara of lacking a sense of humor, such as when she took umbrage at Franklin D. Roosevelt's teasing remark that Ireland was a communist country, calling O'Hara "clueless." Rubin took particular exception to the allegation that John Ford was gay: "It is O'Hara's propensity for ascribing homosexual tendencies to people she really dislikes that is most disturbing. This outmoded attitude, which was so much a part of the bad old days in Hollywood, reminds one that not everything about them is to be missed." Rubin even abjured O'Hara's high-profile fight for her national pride in 1948, seeing it as a self-important exercise in grandstanding.[54]

Perhaps the main talking point of *'Tis Herself* is the revelation that Ford sent O'Hara so many billets-doux over the years. These are reproduced in full in the book. They certainly seem to suggest that Ford was obsessed with her. They also seem blatantly at odds with the man who was so irascible with her on set. But O'Hara didn't believe Ford's letters meant he was pining for *herself*; rather, he was in love with her screen character from *The Quiet Man*: "He wrote them to me but you realize when reading them that he was writing the letters from Sean Thornton to Mary Kate Danaher."[55] He wanted O'Hara to be Danaher in real life, and he regarded any deviation from that ideal as an imperfection and an excuse, even a license, to mistreat her and her family. It seemed to be a case of "Hell hath no fury like a director scorned." This is possible, but it's equally likely he was writing those letters to Maureen O'Hara—a woman he lusted after but knew he could never possess.

13

Grande Dame

When O'Hara was in her late eighties, a journalist asked her the secret of her longevity. She replied, "Say your 'Hail Mary' every night when you go to bed."[1] Such a devotion seems to sum her up. No matter who she kissed or killed onscreen, no matter how many convolutions attended her lengthy life, she hung on to the simple "Ave Maria" for direction. Once a Catholic, always a Catholic. She often made statements that affirmed her faith. "How could you have had such a wonderful life as me," she asked, "if there wasn't a God directing?"[2] Even in matters of religion she used a cinematic metaphor. The fact that many people *didn't* have wonderful lives didn't seem to enter her quasi-theological equation. Was God directing them, too?

She often promised (threatened?) to become frumpish in later life and to wave her walking stick at people she disagreed with, but this didn't happen. Instead, she preserved her serenity and sense of self, slipping into her golden years like a comfortable old shoe.

When asked in January 2010 about the special highlights of her career, she gave an interesting answer: "When I look back at the movies I've made, the honors and awards I've received, the people I've met in the industry and loved, it all seems to blend into one big highlight." It was a gracious paean to her near half century of screen time.[3] But had she achieved all her ambitions? "I've never lost the desire to be an opera singer. It was always a passion with me but a passion that did not come to pass."[4] It was one of the few unfulfilled ambitions of this indomitable lady.

As her ninetieth birthday was approaching, she was as busy as ever. A journalist described her roster of activities: "She's caught up in meetings, suppers, a backlog of fan letters and she's the honorary president of the Glengariff Golf Club. She also attends film festivals and fashion shows. She goes to Mass and she watches soccer and Gaelic football."[5] Very little had changed since her youth.

Glengariff was buzzing with excitement over the upcoming milestone. She confided to Conor Power that she planned to mark the occasion with a "quiet party comprising 55 to 70 people."[6] By Irish standards, that was very quiet indeed.

She was uncharacteristically humble in some of the interviews she gave as her birthday approached. Maggie Armstrong wrote: "These days she has a certain punchy, streetwise self-mockery when reflecting on her talent and the astral beauty that propelled her to fame." O'Hara confided to Dublin broadcaster Ryan Tubridy that she was a "ham" of an actress.[7] Asked to sum up her career, she said simply, "I worked hard and knew my lines."[8]

Mary Kennedy interviewed O'Hara in her home on the day before her birthday. "You have some nice awards," Kennedy observed, gazing around the living room. "Well I never won the Academy Award," O'Hara replied grumpily, "and I think I should have for *The Quiet Man*." She would never stop chewing on that particular bone. She went on to say that many of her period costumes had been very hard to wear, necessitating what she referred to as a "BICO" resolve. When Kennedy expressed puzzlement at the term, the grand lady explained, "Belly in, chest out." "The wonderful thing," she ended elegiacally, "is to have gone out in the world and to have been a success and then to have been accepted again by the country of your birth."[9] But why shouldn't she be? Hadn't she been Ireland's prime cinematic ambassadress for the past six decades?

She entered into the spirit of her birthday celebration in the buzzy manner people had come to expect of her. Greeting cards and goodwill messages flooded through her door. She spent the day with Bronwyn, Conor Beau, and other family members and friends in Blair's Cove, Durrus, where she was greeted by St. Michael's Bandon Pipe Band. A dinner hosted by the Glengariff Golf Club followed in Casey's Hotel.

In September she traveled to Dublin to celebrate Ireland's Culture Night and to launch a local arts festival in Ranelagh, the suburb where she grew up. "Be proud of where you came from," she exhorted the crowd, insisting on delivering her words from a standing position. "They told me I could sit down if I wanted but you don't like someone saying that to you so I'll stand." The fiery spirit that had been her trademark in her prime was still present. She finished by saying she hoped God gave her "enough years to come back many times to visit 'dear old dirty Dublin,' as we used to call it when we were kids."[10]

On November 11 she unveiled the Princess Grace collection of jewelry at the Newbridge Silverware Museum of Style Icons, wearing a triple-strand pearl necklace priced at 150 euro. "It's very fabulous," she allowed, "but by the time you pay taxes, bills and mortgages, what is there left for fancy stuff?"[11] Her austere mind-set and down-to-earth attitude were appreciated by the populace, reeling from the collapse of the national banking system—the last nail in the coffin of the famed "Celtic Tiger" that had raged across the world as an example of a buoyant economy before crashing like 1929 Wall Street. O'Hara had seen poverty growing up, even if her own family had been well-to-do. She now watched her country returning to those dark fiscal days as the International Monetary Fund took control of the nation's financial structures.

A few days later she was asked—again—about the secret of her longevity. This time she gave a different answer: "Be born to the right mother and father."[12] Another familiar question followed: Had she any regrets about her career? Yes, she regretted her lack of control over it. "I used to think: I wish I was in this or that movie. Or: why did she get it instead of me? The studios notified you that you were cast by them because they felt you'd earn more money for them in a particular role." Did she feel "gorgeous" when she looked at her old posters, with her perfect posture and not a hair out of place? "I didn't do it. The director told the makeup man or makeup woman how he wanted me to look and it was up to them. If they didn't get what he wanted they lost their jobs."[13] It was gratifying to hear her play down her beauty. (Sometimes she claimed she wasn't even the best-looking girl in her own family and that Peggy was.)

She "took the fifth" when asked if there were any stars she didn't enjoy acting with, despite the interviewer's insistence that it would be "fun" to unleash some venom. "Fun for you, maybe," O'Hara replied, "but one of these days I'm gonna kick the bucket and I don't want them to be up there waitin' for me."[14] But surely she'd already covered this in her autobiography.

Later in the month she appeared at the Cork Film Festival to see the premiere of a documentary directed by Sé Merry Doyle, *Dreaming* The Quiet Man. In it she recalls doing fight scenes with Wayne: "When you had to sock Duke you always wondered whether he was going to accept it or was he going to strangle you for trying." Martin Scorsese praises the film in the documentary, calling it a "work of art, a work of poetry, very unique and beautiful."[15] Scorsese goes so far as to cite *The Quiet Man* as an influence on *Raging Bull* (the greatest movie of the 1980s, in many people's view). The flashback sequence in which Wayne realizes he's actually killed a man (many viewers wondered how he could have known this so soon) left an indelible mark on the famous director. It was a huge honor for O'Hara to hear such a giant of the modern screen tipping his hat to a film that many intellectual snobs saw as little more than popcorn whimsy. "I'll never forget the vibrance of [John Wayne's] emerald green trunks," Scorsese said. (In fact, they were red, not green.)

In December 2010 O'Hara launched the Maureen O'Hara Foundation, an organization set up to fund a legacy center in Glengariff to house Hollywood memorabilia and train budding film stars and movie directors. It was originally scheduled to be completed in 2013 but has been delayed. The Cork County Council handed over a one-and-a-half-acre site for the center, which is expected to cost more than $10 million to build.

Frank McCarthy, head of the foundation, announced: "Maureen had a brainchild about six years ago to give something back to the people of Ireland. This center will be the only film school of its type here. It will house a 120-seat auditorium and we'll hope to attract international students as well as providing workshops given by leading Hollywood actors. Maureen will be very involved in the management side of things and will oversee all the classes. In her acting career she was famous for only needing one take when filming. She'll demand the same standards from the students here."[16] (Needless to say, it would be a pity if all aspiring actors were judged on their first take. Perfection is more often attained only by trying different ways.)

O'Hara's longtime assistant Carolyn Murphy did much to spearhead funding for the center. O'Hara first met Murphy in 1978, when both moved to Ireland. Twenty years O'Hara's junior, Murphy was originally from Michigan, but her husband, Bill, had Irish roots. Her original function was to catalog O'Hara's memorabilia, with a view to one day donating the collection to a museum, but as time went on, the idea of the foundation was born. Said Murphy of the proposed center: "Maureen is still very friendly with the Wayne family and as we speak we have a package of memorabilia on the way to us from Gretchen Wayne, John Wayne's daughter-in-law. There will also be a *Miracle on 34th Street* exhibit with Macy's, who are donating one of the original Christmas windows. It just keeps evolving."[17] Elsewhere, O'Hara's awards will be on display, along with many costumes from her movies, with a special section devoted to (surprise, surprise) *The Quiet Man*.

O'Hara attended yet another showing of *The Quiet Man* at the Carnegie Arts Center in Kenmare, County Kerry, on February 25, 2011, prompting one to imagine that she could have recited the entire script by now. After the showing, a fan asked her how she occupied her time. Never short of a witty riposte, she said, "Trying to manage my walking stick." Pressed about her advancing years, she assured people she wouldn't be going gentle into the good night.

That night she appeared on TV on *The Late Late Show*, looking just as good as many women in their sixties and as mentally sharp as she'd ever been. She even sparred playfully with host Ryan Tubridy when the subject of Errol Flynn came up. Tubridy asked her if Flynn had "tried his charms" on her. When she said he hadn't, Tubridy asked, "I wonder why?" O'Hara responded, "What a nasty remark!" as if he were implying she had been "that kind of girl." She hadn't lost her ability to take on talk-show hosts, even at ninety.[18]

The only time she showed her age that night was when she forgot Herb Yates's name while telling the story of John Ford's exceeding his allotted two-hour running time for *The Quiet Man*. Messages of goodwill were beamed in to her from cinema legends Martin Scorsese, Steven Spielberg, and Robert Redford, but she seemed to get more excited while talking about all the *feiseanna* (Irish dancing competitions) she had won as a child. Toward the end of the interview she spoke of the legacy center, which was going to be a kind of extension of the Ena Mary Burke School. She felt indebted to the school because it had taught her how to speak properly, and now she wanted to do the same for a new generation.

In August of that year the first *Quiet Man* festival was held in Cong to celebrate her career. O'Hara was the guest of honor and stayed in Ashford Castle (where else?) for the duration (this time, she was given a better room than the one John Ford had arranged for her in 1951). Amazingly, it was the first time she'd ever attended a public event related to the movie.[19] She looked resplendent as she paraded around town. Two nights before, her father's old Shamrock Rovers soccer club had beaten Partizan Belgrade by a score of 2–1, thereby becoming the first Irish team to make the group stages of a European competition. "I should have been at the match," the effervescent nonagenarian told reporters, and few doubted her resolve. Time had marched on but her spirit stayed the same. "I used to be Dev's favorite pin-up girl," she bragged to Eamon O'Cuiv, Ireland's former minister for tourism and the grandson of "Dev"—the country's first president, Eamon de Valera.[20]

John Wayne's daughter Marisa also attended the festival, as did his granddaughter Laura Monoz Bottini. "Ireland held a special place in his heart," Marisa offered. "He always talked of bringing me here."[21] Everywhere she looked she saw photographs of him.

The festival was such a resounding success that some suggested it should become an annual event. Gerry Collins, who ran a museum dedicated to the movie, trilled: "People think when this generation is gone that *The Quiet Man* is gone [but] it's not because parents are bringing their children even to Cong." The seventy-eight-year-old Collins had worked in Ashford Castle while the film was being shot and brought O'Hara her breakfast every morning. He remembered her as being "a lovely lady. Very, very gracious in her manners."[22] Collins also ran a bed-and-breakfast, with every room named after a character in the film. "Every moment of every day," he reflected, "someone in the world is watching *The Quiet Man*."[23] Would it ever be remade? "Why would you ever re-make something that was that great?" asked O'Hara.[24] If anyone "dared" try, she vowed to "kill" them—a familiar threat.[25]

A new movie based on the making of *The Quiet Man* also began shooting at this time. Starring Roger Moore, Aidan Quinn, and Geraldine Chaplin, it details the arrival of John Ford (played by Stacy Keach) in Cong and the impact on the town (obtaining electricity and the like). The main plot centers around a romance between one of Ford's production assistants and an eighteen-year-old girl played by Heather O'Dea.

In May 2012 there were allegations that O'Hara had been the victim of "elder abuse."[26] Carolyn Murphy was accused of taking excessive control of O'Hara's life—a charge she vehemently denied. A rift between Murphy and the O'Hara family developed as Conor Beau and O'Hara's nephew

Charles became involved. Many people associated with O'Hara's foundation resigned amidst allegations that the monies collected had been misappropriated and misspent. The foundation was in debt, despite the many black-tie affairs held to raise money in preceding years. Murphy's power of attorney over O'Hara's affairs was revoked at this time. She employed a lawyer and threatened to sue for defamation if the allegations persisted. She felt she was a victim of "trial by media." "I never spent a penny without asking her," she insisted.[27]

By now, O'Hara had type 2 diabetes and was also suffering from short-term memory loss. She was reportedly "damned upset" over the rift with Murphy but stopped seeing her. Members of O'Hara's family were also concerned that Murphy was overworking O'Hara, scheduling too many engagements associated with the legacy center. Murphy replied, "I've always put Maureen first. She doesn't mind events. She always makes a big effort to look her best and that's often tiring."[28] As she once said, "I don't wake up as Maureen O'Hara, she has to be *created*." Though now in her tenth decade, and having been out of the movies for close to twenty years, she still didn't want to look like "the girl next door."

In May 2013 it was reported that O'Hara was leaving Ireland for good and returning to the States after forty years on her home soil. Interviewers were apparently lining up to ask her about the latest developments in her life: her health, her financial situation, the family squabbles. As she approached her ninety-third birthday there was talk of a new book and even another movie. Asked about the legal wrangle she found herself embroiled in, she replied that she was "damn angry."[29]

Whether at thirty-two or ninety-two, the aging "Mary Kate Danaher" figure was still stewing.

Acknowledgments

I would like to thank my editor Patrick McGilligan for all his help on this book, and also Anne Dean Watkins, who has been a continuous pleasure to work with.

Ned Comstock at USC unearthed a vast amount of material for me, and I thank him profusely for his supreme generosity with time and resources. Rebecca Grant of the Irish Film Institute was an invaluable help too. I much appreciate the assistance of Ian O'Sullivan at the British Film Institute Library, who provided me with newspaper and magazine articles from the BFI archives.

Thank you to Arthur Worboys and Adam Blackie at Picture Productions Ltd. in St. Albans for the promotional and background information they provided. Thanks to Laser Specialist DVD Libraries in South Andrew Street, Dublin, for all the films they ordered, and to Roberta Mitchell at Darker Image Video in Maine for being tremendously obliging in this regard.

The good people at North Staffordshire Press have been consistently accommodating. I wish to thank Jaris Ash in particular for her excellent secretarial skills and also Malcolm Henson and Chris Bailey. Thanks to Sandra Aguilera for articles and production files from the Warner Brothers archives, and to Mark Quigley from the UCLA Film and Television Archive.

David Frasier at the Lilly Library in Indiana provided me with much valuable material, including many letters from Michael Killanin to John Ford. I received assistance from various libraries throughout the British Isles—London, Edinburgh, and Manchester. In Dublin I am indebted particularly to the staff of Pearse Street, Raheny, Coolock and Donaghmede. Paul Wright helped me greatly with *The Quiet Man*, and I am grateful to the Heritage Center in Cong for pointing me toward productive avenues in this regard.

I would like to thank Kristine Krueger of the Margaret Herrick Library for her diligence in locating material for me, often on very short notice, and particularly for the interlibrary loan facility she set up for me. Thanks to Simon Elliott from the UCLA Library of Special Collections, to Andy Fairhurst, to Chris Smedley of Vicpine Films, to the staff of Rare Movies UK and Loving the Classics, and to Karen Wall for organizing a special showing of *Dreaming* The Quiet Man for me.

Much thanks to Keith for the books, films, and advice. Thanks to the researchers at the ILAC Center in Dublin for sourcing material for me overseas, and to Sean Carberry. Thank you to all the readers at the University Press of Kentucky who first surveyed my proposal and influenced its subsequent direction. Special thanks to Mary, who has been with me on this project from the beginning, and every step of the way.

I would like to thank the National Film Information Service, the UCLA Theater Archives, and the Library of Congress. Thanks also to Phil Murphy and Gerry Collins, and to Des Duggan, who worked tirelessly behind the scenes, as ever, and was always forthcoming with ideas. Apologies to anyone I've forgotten.

Filmography

1930s

My Irish Molly (1938, Alex Bryce)
Rocking the Moon Around (1938, Walter Forde)
The Hunchback of Notre Dame (1939, William Dieterle)
Jamaica Inn (1939, Alfred Hitchcock)

1940s

A Bill of Divorcement (1940, John Farrow)
Dance, Girl, Dance (1940, Dorothy Arzner)
How Green Was My Valley (1941, John Ford)
They Met in Argentina (1941, Leslie Goodwins)
The Black Swan (1942, Henry King)
Ten Gentlemen from West Point (1942, Henry Hathaway)
To the Shores of Tripoli (1942, H. Bruce Humberstone)
The Fallen Sparrow (1943, Richard Wallace)
The Immortal Sergeant (1943, John M. Stahl)
This Land Is Mine (1943, Jean Renoir)
Buffalo Bill (1944, William Wellman)
The Spanish Main (1945, Frank Borzage)
Do You Love Me? (1946, Gregory Ratoff)
Sentimental Journey (1946, Walter Lang)
The Homestretch (1947, Bruce Humberstone)
The Foxes of Harrow (1947, John M. Stahl)
Miracle on 34th Street (1947, George Seaton)
Sinbad the Sailor (1947, Richard Wallace)
Sitting Pretty (1948, Walter Lang)
Bagdad (1949, Charles Lamont)
Father Was a Fullback (1949, John M. Stahl)
The Forbidden Street (1949, Jean Negulesco)
A Woman's Secret (1949, Nicholas Ray)

1950s

Comanche Territory (1950, George Sherman)
Rio Grande (1950, John Ford)
Tripoli (1950, Will Price)
Flame of Araby (1951, Charles Lamont)
Against All Flags (1952, George Sherman)
At Sword's Point (1952, Lewis Allen)
Kangaroo (1952, Lewis Milestone)
The Quiet Man (1952, John Ford)
The Redhead from Wyoming (1952, Lee Sholem)
War Arrow (1953, George Sherman)
Fire over Africa (1954, Richard Sale)
Lady Godiva (1955, Arthur Lubin)
The Long Gray Line (1955, John Ford)
The Magnificent Matador (1955, Budd Boetticher)
Everything but the Truth (1956, Jerry Hopper)
Lisbon (1956, Ray Milland)
The Wings of Eagles (1957, John Ford)

1960s

Our Man in Havana (1960, Carol Reed)
The Deadly Companions (1961, Sam Peckinpah)
The Parent Trap (1961, David Swift)
Mr. Hobbs Takes a Vacation (1962, Henry Koster)
McLintock! (1963, Andrew V. McLaglen)
Spencer's Mountain (1963, Delmer Daves)
The Battle of the Villa Fiorita (1965, Delmer Daves)
The Rare Breed (1966, Andrew V. McLaglen)

1970s

How Do I Love Thee? (1970, Michael Gordon)
Big Jake (1971, George Sherman)
The Red Pony (1973, TV, Robert Totten)

1990s

Only the Lonely (1991, Christopher Columbus)
The Christmas Box (1995, TV, Marcus Cole)
Cab to Canada (1998, TV, Christopher Leitch)

2000s

The Last Dance (2000, TV, Kevin Dowling)

Notes

Introduction

1. *Los Angeles Times*, July 8, 1959.
2. Ibid.
3. Maureen O'Hara with John Nicoletti, *'Tis Herself: A Memoir* (Dublin: Town House and Country House, 2004), 177.
4. *Films in Review*, May 1990.
5. *Photoplay*, December 1952.
6. *Films in Review*, May 1990.
7. Ruth Barton, *Acting Irish in Hollywood* (Dublin: Irish Academic Press, 2006), 91.
8. *Screenland*, February 1943.
9. *Los Angeles Times*, March 3, 1966.
10. *Silver Screen*, March 1940.

1. Young Girl in a Hurry

1. O'Hara, *'Tis Herself*, 7–8.
2. *Nationwide*, RTE 1, August 16, 2004.
3. *Independent*, September 26, 2004.
4. *Silver Screen*, June 1945.
5. *Photoplay*, April 1943.
6. *Irish Independent*, June 12, 1991.
7. Ibid.
8. *Irish Tatler*, November 2010.
9. *Stardom*, April 1944.
10. *Modern Screen*, February 1948.
11. Ibid.
12. *Silver Screen*, March 1940.
13. Ibid.
14. *'Tis Herself*, 19. Her reminiscence in this regard contrasts sharply with an interview she gave to the *Sunday Press* on September 1, 1991. In that interview she recalled: "When I was at school in Milltown we would save pennies so we could go see Charles Laughton, Laurel and Hardy and Ginger Rogers and Fred Astaire. We used to go to 'The Prinner'—the Princess Theater in Rathmines—every Saturday. It was three pence admission and you sat on a

wooden bench. The other cinema was the Stella which was much swankier. The Prinner was more our style."

15. Eoghan Rice, *We Are Rovers: An Oral History of Shamrock Rovers Football Club* (Gloucestershire: Nonsuch Publishing, 2005), 21.

16. Ibid., 21–22.

17. Boyd Magers and Michael G. Fitzgerald, *Westerns Women: Interviews with 50 Leading Ladies of Movie and Television Westerns from the 1930s to the 1960s* (Jefferson, NC: McFarland, 2004), 171.

18. *Modern Screen*, February 1948.

19. James Robert Parish, *The RKO Gals* (London: Ian Allen, 1974), 645. O'Hara exhibited a theatrical element in many of her performances, particularly when she played Irish or Irish American parts for John Ford, as in *The Quiet Man* and *The Long Gray Line*. She met many Abbey alumni on the set of *The Quiet Man* and other Ford films. He had struck up an acquaintance with the Abbey players when they toured the United States in 1935, later recruiting many of them to his celluloid fold. For an in-depth treatment of this theme, see Adrian Frazier, *Hollywood Irish: John Ford, Abbey Actors and the Irish Revival in Hollywood* (Dublin: Lilliput Press, 2011).

20. She didn't mention this in her autobiography, perhaps feeling it would give the wrong message to her fans about how she came to be in the public eye. Like many beauties, she always believed her natural endowments prevented her from being taken seriously as an actress. In 1941 she told Ben Maddox, "It's so funny, my being pushed into the beauty category. I was never ranked that way until I reached California . . . the neighborhood gang cheered me up with announcements that I had skin like hide and hair like straw" (*Silver Screen*, November 1941).

21. *Silver Screen*, November 1941.

22. These skills came in handy when she took dictation years later for John Ford, who made her transcribe the script of *The Quiet Man* on his yacht. Her proficiency with shorthand was also useful on film sets, as she told Larry King when he asked her how she prepared for roles: "You start writing notes to yourself. You remember in scene so-and-so you're going to do so-and-so. Every page of your script is full of little notes. I used to do mine in shorthand so nobody would know what I was up to" (*Larry King*, October 29, 2000).

23. Parish, *RKO Gals*, 645, says that the venue for their meeting was a "civic reception." Although this is a fine account of O'Hara's life and career, Parish is inaccurate in some details, including calling Lennox Robinson "Lenox Roberts" (644).

24. Ibid., 645.

25. *Irish Independent*, June 12, 1991.

26. She would later exclaim extravagantly, "I owe my whole career to Mr. Pommer." See Ursula Hardt, *From Caligari to California* (Oxford: Berghahn Books, 1996), 1.

27. *Silver Screen*, March 1940.

28. *Irish Tatler*, November 2010.

29. *Screenland*, February 1942.

30. Nicola Depuis, *Mnánah Éireann: The Women Who Shaped Ireland* (Cork: Mercier Press, 2009), 219.

31. *Sunday Tribune*, August 15, 2010.

32. *Silver Screen*, March 1940. This was an attitude she expressed through-out her life, as if she were "slumming" by being in Hollywood.

33. *RTE Guide*, July 17, 1992.

34. *Silver Screen*, March 1940.

35. *What's on in London*, September 11, 1991.

36. *Nationwide*, RTE 1, August 16, 2010.

37. *Sunday Press*, September 1, 1991.

38. Sean Crossan and Rod Stoneman, eds., The Quiet Man *and Beyond: Reflections on a Classic Film, John Ford and Ireland* (Dublin: Liffey Press, 2009), 216.

39. Her brothers playfully mispronounced her new name as "Maureen O'Horror" whenever she annoyed them. When she started making desert dra-mas it became "Maureen Sahara."

40. Peter Conrad, *The Hitchcock Murders* (London: Faber and Faber, 2000), 60.

41. John Robert Colombo, ed., *Wit and Wisdom of the Moviemakers* (New York: Hamlyn, 1979), 32.

42. Leonard J. Leff, *Hitchcock and Selznick* (London: Weidenfeld and Nicolson, 1988), 245.

43. Donald Spoto, *The Dark Side of Genius: The Life of Alfred Hitchcock* (London: Plexus, 1973), 184.

44. Donald Spoto, *Spellbound by Beauty: Alfred Hitchcock and His Lead-ing Ladies* (London: Hutchinson, 2008), 56.

45. Paul Condon and Jim Sangster, *The Complete Hitchcock* (London: Virgin, 1999), 83.

46. Spoto, *Dark Side of Genius*, 184–85.

47. *Monthly Film Bulletin*, May 31, 1939.

48. Simon Callow, *Charles Laughton: A Difficult Actor* (London: Methuen, 1987), 130.

49. O'Hara, *'Tis Herself*, 29.

50. Ibid.

51. *Silver Screen*, March 1940.

52. *Daily Telegraph*, January 3, 2004.

53. *Classic Images*, December 1992.

54. *Screen*, May 1951.

55. *Irish Independent*, August 14, 2010.

56. *Sunday Independent*, March 12, 2006.

57. *Irish Independent*, June 12, 1991.
58. *Irish Times*, July 4, 1939.
59. *Irish Press*, July 24, 1939.

2. Maiden Voyage

1. *Parade*, June 2, 1991.
2. Charles Higham, *Charles Laughton: An Intimate Biography* (London: Coronet, 1976), 122.
3. *RTE Guide*, August 16, 2004.
4. *Photoplay*, July 1942.
5. Ronald L. Davis, *The Glamour Factory: Inside Hollywood's Star System* (Dallas: Southern Methodist University Press, 1993), 5.
6. *Classic Images*, January 1983.
7. Doug McClelland, ed., *Forties Film Talk* (Jefferson, NC: McFarland, 1992).
8. *Screenland*, February 1942.
9. *Empire Film Guide* (London: Virgin, 2006), 456.
10. Ibid.
11. Peter Underwood, *Death in Hollywood* (London: Piatkus, 1992).
12. Callow, *Charles Laughton*, 136.
13. Higham, *Charles Laughton*, 126.
14. *Film Dope*, June 1993.
15. Steve Brennan and Bernadette O'Neill, *Emeralds in Tinseltown: The Irish in Hollywood* (Belfast: Appletree Press, 2007), 138.
16. *Los Angeles Times*, May 4, 2004.
17. Parish, *RKO Gals*, 649.
18. O'Hara, *'Tis Herself*, 49.
19. Ibid., 49–50. The following year O'Hara warned her friend Anna Lee to steer clear of Farrow when he directed her in *Commandos Strike at Dawn*. "Lock your door, Anna," she advised. Lee took the advice, but Farrow still barged into her room one night. When she told him she wasn't interested in going to bed with him, he roared back at her, "Why you pious little puritan. You're probably no good in bed anyway, but I'm not going to waste my time tonight finding out. Just remember, if I want something badly I always get my way, no matter how long it takes" (Anna Lee with Barbara Roisman Cooper, *Memoir of a Career on* General Hospital *and in Film* [Jefferson, NC: McFarland, 2003], 142).
20. Paul Simpson, ed., *The Rough Guide to Cult Movies* (London: Haymarket, 2004), 70.
21. Judith Mayne, *Directed by Dorothy Arzner* (Bloomington: Indiana University Press, 1994), 2.
22. *Velvet Light Trap* 11 (Winter 1974).
23. Ann Lloyd, ed., *Movies of the Forties* (London: Orbis, 1982), 212.

24. Barton, *Acting Irish in Hollywood*, 94.

25. Brennan and O'Neill, *Emeralds in Tinseltown*, 137.

26. *Photoplay*, December 1948.

27. Molly Haskell, *From Reverence to Rape: The Treatment of Women in the Movies* (Chicago: University of Chicago Press, 1987), 147.

28. Pam Cook, ed., *The Movie Book* (London: Palgrave Macmillan, 2007), 470.

3. The Old Son of a Bitch

1. *Los Angeles Times*, March 3, 1966.

2. *Variety*, April 16, 1941.

3. *Motion Picture Herald*, May 24, 1941.

4. *Screenland*, February 1942.

5. *Screenland*, February 1942.

6. *Premiere*, July 1991.

7. *Silver Screen*, November 1991.

8. Leonard Mosley, *Zanuck: The Rise and Fall of Hollywood's Last Tycoon* (London: Panther, 1984), 266–67.

9. Philip Dunne, *Take Two: A Life in Movies and Politics* (San Francisco: McGraw-Hill, 1980), 99.

10. Allan Foster, *The Movie Traveler: A Film Fan's Guide to the UK and Ireland* (Edinburgh: Polygon, 2000), 249.

11. Lee, *Memoir of a Career on* General Hospital *and in Film*, 133–35.

12. McClelland, *Forties Film Talk*, 280–81.

13. Joseph McBride and Michael Wilmington, *Searching for John Ford: A Life* (London: Faber, 2003), 326.

14. Ibid., 332.

15. *The Quiet Man*, Collector's Edition (Artisan Home Entertainment, 2002).

16. *Films in Review*, April 1990.

17. *Newsweek*, June 28, 1999.

18. *Premiere*, July 1991, 64.

19. Ibid.

20. *Irish Tatler*, November 2010.

21. *Films in Review*, April 1990. The expression "in the barrel" apparently originated when a visibly hungover John Wayne turned up on the set one day, and Ford made him get into a barrel and stay there all morning. Afterward, it became a figurative way of conveying the fact that Ford could make one pay for minor impertinences.

22. McBride and Wilmington, *Searching for John Ford*, 327.

23. *New York Times*, October 29, 1941.

24. Robert Parrish, *Growing up in Hollywood* (London: Bodley Bead, 1976), 176.

25. O'Hara, *'Tis Herself*, 75.

26. *Motion Picture*, March 1945.

27. Ibid.

28. *Silver Screen*, August 1947.

29. *Modern Screen*, November 1947.

30. O'Hara, *'Tis Herself*, 78.

31. McClelland, *Forties Film Talk*, 415.

32. O'Hara, *'Tis Herself*, 83.

33. *Silver Screen*, October 1942.

34. Ibid.

35. O'Hara, *'Tis Herself*, 82.

36. Ibid., 83.

37. Brennan and O'Neill, *Emeralds in Tinseltown*, 139.

38. *Silver Screen*, October 1942.

39. *Movieland*, June 1943.

40. Ibid.

41. This observation is from Hector Arce in *The Secret Life of Tyrone Power* (New York: Bantam, 1980), 153. O'Hara sometimes considered this description an albatross, defining her career all the way from Mary Kate Danaher of *The Quiet Man* (1952) to the "revamped" Danaher of *Only the Lonely* (1991).

42. Brennan and O'Neill, *Emeralds in Tinseltown*, 139.

43. *Films in Review*, April 1990. This is probably a reference to Lana Turner—and another fairly typical example of O'Hara's artistic snobbery.

44. Brennan and O'Neill, *Emeralds in Tinseltown*, 136.

45. *Silver Screen*, October 1942.

46. Fred Lawrence Guiles, *Tyrone Power: The Last Idol* (London: Granada, 1980), 166.

47. *Screenland*, February 1943.

48. Ibid.

49. Ibid.

4. Saluting Uncle Sam

1. Peter Collier, *The Fondas: A Hollywood Dynasty* (London: HarperCollins, 1991), 60.

2. Callow, *Charles Laughton*, 166.

3. *Stardom*, April 1944.

4. Ibid.

5. Ibid.

6. *Motion Picture*, May 1945.

7. *Photoplay*, July 1945.

8. Ibid.

9. O'Hara, *'Tis Herself*, 91.

10. *Movieland*, August 1945.

11. O'Hara, '*Tis Herself*, 92.

12. *Photoplay*, June 1944.

13. Ibid.

14. O'Hara, '*Tis Herself*, 96–98.

15. *Wild Bill: Hollywood's Maverick*, vol. 3 of *Forbidden Hollywood* (Turner Entertainment Archives, 2002).

16. O'Hara, '*Tis Herself*, 93.

17. *Silver Screen*, June 1945.

18. Ibid.

19. This film was actually directed by Jean Renoir; Price was associate producer.

20. *Parade*, June 2, 1991. O'Hara related this story almost verbatim in nearly every interview she ever gave about *The Quiet Man*. In time, it came to be like a mantra for her.

21. *Irish Connections*, November 1, 2010.

22. *Daily Telegraph*, March 23, 2004. (One is tempted to inquire: wasn't there some other way to demonstrate this?)

23. Parish, *RKO Gals*, 658.

24. *Sunday Independent*, October 3, 2004.

25. *Picturegoer*, May 1946.

26. *New York Times*, March 7, 1946.

27. McClelland, *Forties Film Talk*, 312.

28. Ibid., 280.

29. O'Hara, '*Tis Herself*, 104.

30. Tom McGee, *Betty Grable: The Girl with the Million Dollar Legs* (New York: Vestal Press, 1995), 135.

31. Jeanine Basinger, *A Woman's View: How Hollywood Spoke to Women, 1930–1960* (New York: Knopf, 1993), 126–27.

32. *Premiere*, July 1991, 65.

33. Ibid.

34. *RTE Guide*, July 17, 1992.

35. *Daily Telegraph*, March 23, 2004.

36. Aubrey Malone, ed., *Talk Nation* (Dublin: Currach Books, 2004), 133.

37. *Films and Filming*, December 1972. O'Hara expressed similar sentiments in '*Tis Herself*, 106–7.

38. *Irish Press*, September 24, 1991.

39. Brennan and O'Neill, *Emeralds in Tinseltown*, 139.

40. Barton, *Acting Irish in Hollywood*, 97–98.

41. *Herald Express*, February 4, 1946.

42. Parish, *RKO Gals*, 660.

43. Ibid., 93.

44. *Los Angeles Times*, May 6, 1951.

45. *Photoplay*, June 1947.

46. Ibid.

47. Ibid.

48. Ibid.

49. Rudy Behlmer, ed., *Memo from Darryl F. Zanuck: The Golden Years at Twentieth Century–Fox* (New York: Grove Press, 1993), 147.

50. David Shipman, *The Great Movie Stars: The International Years* (London: Angus and Robertson, 1972), 401.

51. Rice, *We Are Rovers*, 22.

52. McClelland, *Forties Film Talk*, 312.

53. Suzanne Finstad, *Natasha: The Biography of Natalie Wood* (London: Century, 2001), 48.

54. *Irish Press*, November 11, 1946.

55. *Silver Screen*, April 1947.

56. McClelland, *Forties Film Talk*, 312.

57. Gavin Lambert, *Natalie Wood: A Life* (New York: Knopf, 2004), 45.

58. Finstad, *Natasha*, 54.

59. Tessa Clayton and Ian Fitzgerald, eds., *The Guinness Book of Film* (London: Guinness Publishing, 1998), 122.

60. John Eastman, *Retakes: Behind the Scenes of 500 Classic Movies* (New York: Ballantine Books, 1989), 213.

61. McClelland, *Forties Film Talk*, 309.

62. *Screen Stars*, April 1945.

63. Ibid.

64. O'Hara, *'Tis Herself*, 120.

65. Ibid., 119.

66. *Modern Screen*, January 1947.

5. Civvy Street

1. Jesse Lasky Jr., *Whatever Happened to Hollywood?* (New York: Funk and Wagnalls, 1975), 248.

2. *Larry King*, October 29, 2000.

3. *Silver Screen*, March 1940.

4. *Motion Picture*, December 1948.

5. *Premiere*, July 1991, 65.

6. *Films of the Golden Age*, Winter 1996/1997, 86.

7. *Screen Parade*, September 1951, 11.

8. O'Hara, *'Tis Herself*, 123. Her phrasing is unclear here. If the comment relates to Harrison's screen career, it's untrue; he had many critical and commercial successes after *The Foxes of Harrow*. She probably meant that, in his own mind, Landis's suicide cast a pall over everything he did.

9. Rex Harrison, *A Damned Serious Business: My Life in Comedy* (London: Bantam, 1990), 85.

10. *New York Times*, September 25, 1947.

11. *Silver Screen*, January 1948.
12. David L. Smith, *Sitting Pretty: The Life and Times of Clifton Webb* (Jackson: University Press of Mississippi, 2011), 188.
13. *Photoplay*, February 1948.
14. Ivy Crane Wilson, ed., *Hollywood in the 40s: The Stars' Own Stories* (New York: Ungar, 1980), 21.
15. Ibid.
16. Ibid.
17. Patrick McGilligan, *Nicholas Ray: The Glorious Failure of an American Director* (New York: itBooks, 2011), 144.
18. Bernard Eisenschitz, *Nicholas Ray: An American Journey* (London: Faber and Faber, 1993), 106.
19. Ibid., 107.
20. *Picturegoer*, May 20, 1950.
21. McClelland, *Forties Film Talk*, 166.
22. Finstad, *Natasha*, 69.
23. Ibid.
24. She was probably the only Arabian princess in the history of movies to have red hair, but this didn't affect box-office receipts. The film was such a big hit for Universal that it bought part of O'Hara's contract from Fox.
25. Magers and Fitzgerald, *Westerns Women*, 169.
26. Jeanine Basinger, *The Star Machine* (New York: Vintage, 2009), 503.
27. Ibid.
28. Basinger, *Woman's View*, 374.
29. *Irish Times*, December 6, 1952.
30. Basinger, *Woman's View*, 475–76.
31. *Irish Tatler*, November 2010.
32. *Evening Standard*, April 17, 1964.
33. Parish, *RKO Gals*, 664.
34. Otto Friedrich, *City of Nets* (London: Headline, 1986), 122.
35. O'Hara, *'Tis Herself*, 86. For O'Hara, this was probably career suicide as far as any future ventures with Hughes. Nor was she ever invited to the Farrow household again, although that was probably a blessing in disguise, as she always found herself engaged in a kind of competition with Farrow's wife, Maureen O'Sullivan.
36. Gene Tierney with Mickey Herskowitz, *Self-Portrait* (New York: Wyden Books, 1979), 38.
37. Ibid., 40.
38. *Film Dope*, June 1993, 10.
39. *Screen Parade*, September 1952.
40. Ibid.
41. O'Hara, *'Tis Herself*, 134–35.
42. Ibid., 145.

43. *Independent,* September 26, 2004.
44. *Irish Examiner,* August 14, 2010.
45. *Parade,* June 2, 1991.
46. *The Making of Rio Grande* (Jessiefilms, Universal Pictures, 2006).
47. Ibid.
48. Harry Carey Jr., *Company of Heroes: My Life as an Actor in the John Ford Stock Company* (Lanham, MD: Madison Books, 1996), 119.
49. Ibid.
50. Ian Cameron and Douglas Pye, eds., *The Movie Book of the Western* (London: Studio Vista, 1996), 81.
51. Lee Pfeiffer, *The John Wayne Scrapbook* (New York: Citadel, 1989), 55.
52. Lindsay Anderson, *About John Ford* (London: Plexus, 1981), 130.
53. Magers and Fitzgerald, *Westerns Women,* 1.
54. Anderson, *About John Ford,* 24.
55. *Premiere,* July 1991.
56. *Photoplay,* June 1953.

6. Sojourn in Cong

1. Anderson, *About John Ford,* 28–29.
2. McBride and Wilmington, *Searching for John Ford,* 27.
3. Chata was a nickname. Her full name didn't roll trippingly off the tongue: Esperanza Diaz Ceballos Morrison. Wayne's real name was also Morrison, but they weren't related.
4. *Irish Independent,* February 9, 1991.
5. James McKillop, ed., *Contemporary Irish Cinema: From* The Quiet Man *to* Dancing at Lughnasa (Syracuse, NY: Syracuse University Press, 1999), 177.
6. *The Quiet Man,* Collector's Edition. Maureen, of course, is also a version of Mary.
7. *Irish Times,* June 5, 1951.
8. *Connacht Tribune,* June 28, 1951.
9. *Connacht Tribune,* June 16, 1951.
10. Gerry McGuinness, *Movies Made in Ireland:* The Quiet Man (Dublin: GLI, 1996), 31.
11. *Connacht Tribune,* June 23, 1951.
12. Gerry McNee, *In the Footsteps of* The Quiet Man (Edinburgh: Mainstream, 2008), 182.
13. *Sunday Independent,* December 6, 1992.
14. McNee, *In the Footsteps of* The Quiet Man, 67.
15. *Irish Connections,* November 1, 2010.
16. Ibid.
17. *The Quiet Man,* Collector's Edition.
18. *Irish Connections,* November 1, 2010.

19. *The Quiet Man*, Collector's Edition.

20. *Sunday Telegraph*, November 29, 1992.

21. *Combustible Celluloid*, October 10, 2002.

22. *The Quiet Man*, Collector's Edition.

23. Martin McLoone, *Irish Film: The Emergence of a Contemporary Cinema* (London: British Film Institute, 2000), 55.

24. Anderson, *About John Ford*, 131.

25. Ibid., 196.

26. Des MacHale, *The Complete Guide to* The Quiet Man (Belfast: Appletree, 2000), 40.

27. Magers and Fitzgerald, *Westerns Women*, 173.

28. McNee, *In the Footsteps of* The Quiet Man, 104.

29. O'Hara, *'Tis Herself*, 167.

30. *Larry King*, October 29, 2000.

31. *Irish Connections*, November 1, 2010.

32. Barton, *Acting Irish in Hollywood*, 103.

33. Luke Gibbons, *Ireland into Film*, The Quiet Man (Cork: Cork University Press, 2002), 107.

34. Dan Ford, *Pappy: The Life of John Ford* (Englewood Cliffs, NJ: Prentice Hall, 1979), 244.

35. Kevin Rockett, *Irish Film Censorship: A Cultural Journey from Silent Cinema to the Internet* (Dublin: Four Courts Press, 2004), 13.

36. Des MacHale, *Picture* The Quiet Man: *An Illustrated Celebration* (Belfast: Appletree, 2004), 131.

37. *The Barbara Walters Show*, March 13, 1979.

38. McBride and Wilmington, *Searching for John Ford*, 515–16.

39. *Sunday Independent*, June 8, 1952.

40. Des MacHale, *A Quiet Man Miscellany* (Cork: Cork University Press, 2009), 96–97.

41. *Evening Standard*, April 14, 1964.

42. *Irish Times*, May 18, 1957.

43. *The Quiet Man*, Collector's Edition.

44. *Wall Street Journal*, September 26, 2002.

45. Anderson, *About John Ford*, 229.

46. MacHale, *Complete Guide to* The Quiet Man, 35.

47. Ibid.

48. Louisa Burns-Bisogno, *Censoring Irish Nationalism* (Jefferson, NC: McFarland, 2007), 115.

49. McNee, *In the Footsteps of* The Quiet Man, 176.

50. McGuinness, *Movies Made in Ireland:* The Quiet Man, 13.

51. Eastman, *Retakes*, 275.

52. McLoone, *Irish Film*, 50.

53. MacHale, *Complete Guide to* The Quiet Man, 243.

54. *Larry King*, January 2, 2003.
55. Gibbons, *Ireland into Film*, 87.
56. *The Quiet Man*, Collector's Edition.
57. Gibbons, *Ireland into Film*, 86.
58. *Irish Independent*, August 14, 2010.
59. McBride and Wilmington, *Searching for John Ford*, 519.
60. Ford, *Pappy*, 245–46.
61. Gibbons, *Ireland into Film*, 78.
62. Brennan and O'Neill, *Emeralds in Tinseltown*, 141.
63. *Irish Times*, August 21, 2010.
64. *Irish Independent*, August 14, 2010.
65. Brandon French, *On the Verge of Revolt* (New York: Frederich Unger, 1978), 16.
66. *Picture Show*, July 19, 1953.
67. Ibid.
68. Ibid.
69. MacHale, *Complete Guide to* The Quiet Man, 257.

7. Back to Bread and Butter

1. Geoff Tibballs, ed., *The Mammoth Book of Comic Quotes* (London: Constable and Robinson, 2004), 528.
2. O'Hara, *'Tis Herself*, 171–73.
3. *Los Angeles Times*, August 5, 1952.
4. O'Hara, *'Tis Herself*, 174.
5. Michael Munn, *Hollywood Rogues* (London: Robson, 1991), 22.
6. Michael Freedland, *Errol Flynn* (London: Arthur Barker, 1978), 211.
7. Ibid.
8. Danny Peary, *Closeups: Intimate Portraits of Movie Stars by Their Costars, Directors, Screenwriters and Friends* (New York: Simon and Schuster, 1978), 458.
9. *Sun*, June 9, 1973.
10. Peary, *Closeups*, 458.
11. Ibid.
12. *Larry King*, October 29, 2000.
13. O'Hara, *'Tis Herself*, 176.
14. *Photoplay*, December 1952.
15. Errol Flynn, *My Wicked, Wicked Ways* (London: Mandarin, 1992), 186–87.
16. Joseph Humphreys, ed., *James Dean on James Dean* (London: Plexus, 1990), 115.
17. *Photoplay*, December 1952.
18. *Screenland*, June 1953.
19. Ibid.

20. Magers and Fitzgerald, *Westerns Women*, 173.

21. *Irish Times*, October 17, 1953.

22. Shipman, *Great Movie Stars*, 401.

23. Guiles, *Tyrone Power*, 274.

24. Gordon Gow, *Hollywood in the Fifties* (New York: A. S. Barnes, 1971), 82.

25. Parish, *RKO Gals*, 669.

26. *Films in Review*, May 1990, 274.

27. *Irish Tatler*, November 2010.

28. O'Hara, *'Tis Herself*, 188.

29. Carey, *Company of Heroes*, 143.

30. McBride and Wilmington, *Searching for John Ford*, 541–42.

31. O'Hara, *'Tis Herself*, 190–91.

32. Ibid., 192.

33. Ibid.

34. *Irish Independent*, February 9, 1991.

35. Ibid.

36. O'Hara, *'Tis Herself*, 194.

37. Marlon Brando with Robert Lindsey, *Songs My Mother Taught Me* (London: Century, 1994), 199.

38. Ibid.

39. O'Hara, *'Tis Herself*, 195.

40. *Photoplay*, January 1954.

41. Parish, *RKO Gals*, 670.

42. *Budd Boetticher: An American Original*, Special Collector's Edition (Paramount Home Entertainment, 2007).

43. Ibid.

44. Anthony Quinn with Daniel Paisner, *One Man Tango* (London: Headline, 1995), 217.

45. Ibid.

46. Ibid.

47. *Larry King*, October 29, 2000.

48. *Larry King*, January 2, 2003.

49. Quinn, *One Man Tango*, 217–18.

50. *Irish Independent*, June 12, 1991.

51. Quinn, *One Man Tango*, 244–45.

52. Ibid., 245.

53. Ibid., 245–46.

54. Ibid., 246–47.

55. Ibid., 247–48.

56. Alvin H. Marrill, *The Films of Anthony Quinn* (Secaucus, NJ: Citadel, 1975), 150.

57. *Irish Times*, July 29, 1955.

58. O'Hara, *'Tis Herself*, 199. She seems to have forgotten that she was also the villain in *The Fallen Sparrow*.

59. Carey, *Company of Heroes*, 8.

60. Pilar Wayne with Alex Thorleifson, *John Wayne: My Life with the Duke* (New York: McGraw-Hill, 1987), 58.

61. Anderson, *About John Ford*, 160–61.

62. McBride and Wilmington, *Searching for John Ford*, 581.

63. Cameron and Pye, *Movie Book of the Western*, 78.

64. Peter Bogdanovich, *John Ford* (London: Studio Vista, 1967), 96. Ford actually wanted to call the movie *The Spig Wead Story*, but the studio deemed the name too weird.

65. Randy Roberts and James S. Olson, *John Wayne: American* (New York: Free Press, 1995), 433.

8. Keeping Things *Confidential*

1. *Esquire*, November 1956.

2. *Parade*, March 14, 1999.

3. Davis, *Glamour Factory*, 325.

4. *Irish Press*, September 24, 1991.

5. *Confidential*, March 1957.

6. Sam Kashner and Jennifer MacNair, *The Bad and the Beautiful: Hollywood in the Fifties* (London: Little Brown, 2002), 22.

7. *Confidential*, March 1957.

8. Val Holley, *Mike Connolly and the Manly Art of Hollywood Gossip* (Jefferson, NC: McFarland, 2003), 32.

9. Henry E. Scott, *Shocking True Story* (New York: Pantheon, 2010), 120.

10. John Marriott and Robin Cross, *The World's Greatest Hollywood Scandals* (London: Octopus Books, 1997), 89.

11. *Larry King*, January 2, 2003.

12. Marriott and Cross, *World's Greatest Hollywood Scandals*, 89.

13. *Los Angeles Times*, September 4, 1957.

14. O'Hara, *'Tis Herself*, 204.

15. Parish, *RKO Gals*, 672.

16. Marriott and Cross, *World's Greatest Hollywood Scandals*, 89. This begs the question: why was a lie detector test performed if O'Hara's passport rendered it superfluous?

17. *Irish Times*, August 20, 1957.

18. Scott, *Shocking True Story*, 170.

19. Ibid., 182–83.

20. Ibid., 183.

21. Tab Hunter with Eddie Muller, *Tab Hunter Confidential* (Chapel Hill, NC: Algonquin, 2005), 185.

22. *Irish Press*, July 2, 1958.
23. Parish, *RKO Gals*, 672.

9. Reality Bites

1. Brennan and O'Neill, *Emeralds in Tinseltown*, 141.
2. She didn't know what to answer because of her dual citizenship.
3. Alec Guinness, *Blessings in Disguise* (London: Hamish Hamilton, 1985), 203.
4. *Horizon*, November 1959.
5. Norman Sherry, *The Life of Graham Greene*, vol. 3, *1955–91* (London: Jonathan Cape, 2004), 106.
6. Piers Paul Read, *Alec Guinness: The Authorized Biography* (London: Simon and Schuster, 2003), 325.
7. Ibid.
8. O'Hara, *'Tis Herself*, 208–9.
9. Michael Troyan, *A Rose for Mrs. Miniver: The Life of Greer Garson* (Lexington: University Press of Kentucky, 1999), 282.
10. *The Parent Trap* (Buena Vista Home Entertainment, Disney Enterprises, 1961).
11. O'Hara's accent was also questionable, managing to be a cross between Dublin and Brooklyn. Such a hybrid was apparent in many of her performances. She was encouraged to play the "green card" even when portraying American women.
12. *The Parent Trap*.
13. Ibid.
14. Parish, *RKO Gals*, 674.
15. *Premiere*, July 1991.
16. McNee, *In the Footsteps of* The Quiet Man, 74.
17. O'Hara, *'Tis Herself*, 221.
18. Ibid., 222.
19. *Daily Telegraph*, March 23, 2004.
20. Marshall Fine, *Bloody Sam: The Life and Films of Sam Peckinpah* (New York: Hyperion, 2005), 54.
21. Ibid., 57.
22. Kevin J. Hayes, ed., *The Sam Peckinpah Interviews* (Jackson: University of Mississippi Press, 2008), 111.
23. Ibid., 55.
24. Magers and Fitzgerald, *Westerns Women*, 172–73.
25. O'Hara, *'Tis Herself*, 223–24.
26. Ibid., 224.
27. *Los Angeles Times*, March 3, 1966.

10. Love in the Air

1. O'Hara, *'Tis Herself*, 229.
2. James Lever, *Me Cheeta* (London: Fourth Estate, 2009), 229–30.
3. *Irish Times*, September 12, 1963.
4. O'Hara, *'Tis Herself*, 230.
5. Collier, *The Fondas*, 135.
6. Ibid.
7. *Premiere*, July 1991, 66.
8. Interview with Henry Fonda, *Spencer's Mountain* (Warner Bros. Entertainment, 2010).
9. Parish, *RKO Gals*, 674.
10. *McLintock!* Authentic Collector's Edition (Batjac Productions, Paramount Home Entertainment, 2007).
11. *Sun*, June 9, 1973.
12. *Time*, August 8, 1969.
13. *Sun*, June 9, 1973.
14. *McLintock!* Authentic Collector's Edition.
15. O'Hara, *'Tis Herself*, 236.
16. Magers and Fitzgerald, *Westerns Women*, 169–70.
17. *McLintock!* Authentic Collector's Edition.
18. McBride and Wilmington, *Searching for John Ford*, 639n.
19. *Evening Standard*, April 17, 1964.
20. Ibid.
21. *Los Angeles Times*, March 22, 1964.
22. Letter from Geoffrey Shurlock to Jack Warner, January 21, 1964, Warner Bros. Archives, USC.
23. McNee, *In the Footsteps of* The Quiet Man, 183.
24. *Los Angeles Examiner*, May 6, 1964.
25. O'Hara, *'Tis Herself*, 245.
26. *Parade*, June 2, 1991.
27. *Sunday Press*, September 1, 1991.
28. *News Times*, Television News, November 30, 1995.
29. *Sunday Independent*, October 3, 2004.
30. Depuis, *Mnánah Éireann*, 220.
31. *Films and Filming*, December 1972.
32. *Toronto Star*, April 2, 1955.
33. Herb Fagen, *Duke, We're Glad We Knew You* (New York: Citadel, 2009), 95.
34. Pat Stacy with Beverly Linet, *Duke: A Love Story* (London: Corgi, 1985), 11.
35. *Photoplay*, October 1973.
36. Carol Lea Mueller, ed., *The Quotable John Wayne* (Lanham, MD: Taylor Trade, 2007), 19.

37. Ibid., 37.

38. *Photoplay*, October 1973.

39. McNee, *In the Footsteps of* The Quiet Man, 171–72.

40. Stacy, *Duke: A Love Story*, 48.

41. O'Hara, *'Tis Herself*, 281.

42. *Photoplay*, October 1973.

43. Ibid.

44. Fagen, *Duke, We're Glad We Knew You*, 104.

45. *McLintock!* Authentic Collector's Edition.

46. *Sun*, June 9, 1973.

11. A Streetcar Named Retire

1. O'Hara, *'Tis Herself*, 258.

2. Ibid.

3. Ibid., 259.

4. Parish, *RKO Gals*, 678.

5. *Premiere*, July 1991.

6. *Evening Standard*, September 6, 1991.

7. *RTE Guide*, July 17, 1992.

8. *Toronto Star*, April 2, 1995.

9. Charlotte Chandler, *Not the Girl Next Door* (London: Simon and Schuster, 2008), 274.

10. *Premiere*, July 1991.

11. *Combustible Celluloid*, October 10, 2002.

12. *Movieland*, July 17, 1972.

13. Ibid.

14. Dunne, *Take Two*, 103.

15. O'Hara, *'Tis Herself*, 261.

16. *The Quiet Man*, Collector's Edition.

17. McBride and Wilmington, *Searching for John Ford*, 542.

18. Ibid.

19. O'Hara, *'Tis Herself*, 145.

20. *RTE Guide*, August 16, 2004.

21. *Directed by John Ford* (Turner Entertainment, Warner Home Video, 2009).

22. Donald Shepherd, Robert Slatzer, and Dave Grayson, *The Life and Times of John Wayne* (London: Warner, 1986), 363.

23. O'Hara, *'Tis Herself*, 282.

24. Mueller, *Quotable John Wayne*, 20.

25. *Larry King*, October 29, 2000.

26. *Irish Independent*, June 12, 1991.

27. *Nationwide*, August 16, 2004.

28. *People*, June 10, 1991.

29. *Larry King*, January 2, 2003.

30. O'Hara, *'Tis Herself*, 270.

31. Wayne, *John Wayne: My Life with the Duke*, 266.

32. *Saturday Evening Post*, August 15, 1965.

33. Mueller, *Quotable John Wayne*, 35.

34. Wayne, *John Wayne: My Life with the Duke*, 270.

35. Shepherd, Slatzer, and Grayson, *Life and Times of John Wayne*, 373.

36. Stacy, *Duke: A Love Story*, 17.

37. Ibid., 207.

38. O'Hara, *'Tis Herself*, 285.

39. Stacy, *Duke: A Love Story*, 208.

40. Ibid., 207.

41. *RTE Guide*, July 15, 1992.

42. O'Hara, *'Tis Herself*, 287.

43. Stacy, *Duke: A Love Story*, 209.

44. Fagen, *Duke, We're Glad We Knew You*, 231.

45. *The Quiet Man*, Collector's Edition.

12. Ready for Her Close-ups

1. *Ireland's Own*, October Monthly Special, 2004.

2. *Irish Independent*, July 27, 1982.

3. *Sunday Express*, January 26, 1986.

4. *Irish Independent*, June 29, 1988.

5. McNee, *In the Footsteps of* The Quiet Man, 173.

6. Lambert, *Natalie Wood*, 52.

7. *The Quiet Man*, Collector's Edition.

8. *People*, June 10, 1991.

9. Ibid.

10. *Los Angeles Times*, May 27, 1991.

11. *Los Angeles Times*, December 16, 1990.

12. *Los Angeles Times*, May 27, 1991.

13. *Evening Standard*, September 6, 1991.

14. *People*, June 10, 1991.

15. *Irish Independent*, June 12, 1991.

16. *Los Angeles Times*, May 27, 1991.

17. Ibid.

18. *Sunday Press*, September 1, 1991.

19. *Films in Review*, July/August 1991.

20. *Irish Stage and Screen*, Summer 1991.

21. *Premiere*, July 1991.

22. O'Hara, *'Tis Herself*, 303.

23. MacHale, *A Quiet Man Miscellany*, 32. He also toned down the profanity in the script, at her urging.

24. *People*, June 10, 1991.

25. *Evening Standard*, September 6, 1991.

26. *Sunday Press*, September 1, 1991.

27. *Irish Independent*, July 19, 1991.

28. *St. Louis Post*, May 3, 1994.

29. *News Times*, Television News, December 12, 1995.

30. Ibid.

31. Ibid.

32. *Past Issues*, Winter 1996.

33. *Larry King*, October 29, 2000.

34. *Daily Telegraph*, October 10, 1998.

35. McBride and Wilmington, *Searching for John Ford*, 542.

36. *Irish Independent*, August 22, 2000.

37. Ibid.

38. *Los Angeles Times*, October 28, 2000.

39. *Larry King*, October 29, 2000.

40. Ibid.

41. Ibid.

42. Judy Bachrach, *Tina and Harry Come to America: Tina Brown, Harry Evans and the Uses of Power* (New York: Free Press, 2001), 6–7.

43. Ibid., 21.

44. *Talk*, February 2002.

45. *The Irish in Hollywood*, TV3, December 25, 2010.

46. *RTE Guide*, August 6, 2004. "Herself" was John Ford's nickname for her.

47. O'Hara, *'Tis Herself*, 245.

48. *Sunday Independent*, June 19, 2011.

49. *Larry King*, January 2, 2003.

50. *Irish in Hollywood*.

51. *Ireland's Own*.

52. *Los Angeles Times*, May 2, 2004.

53. O'Hara, *'Tis Herself*, 233–34.

54. *Los Angeles Times*, March 22, 2004.

55. *RTE Guide*, August 16, 2004.

13. Grande Dame

1. *Irish Times*, September 15, 2009.

2. *Larry King*, January 2, 2003.

3. *Irish Independent*, January 24, 2010.

4. Ibid.

5. *Irish Independent*, August 14, 2010.

6. *Irish Examiner*, August 14, 2010.

7. *Irish Independent*, August 14, 2010.

8. *Daily Record*, August 16, 2010.
9. *Nationwide*, August 16, 2010.
10. *Irish Central*, September 27, 2010.
11. *Irish Independent*, November 12, 2010.
12. Ibid.
13. *Exposé*, TV3, November 15, 2010.
14. Ibid.
15. *Dreaming* The Quiet Man (Loopline, 2012).
16. *Irish Mail on Sunday*, November 7, 2010.
17. *Irish Tatler*, November 2010.
18. *The Late Late Show*, February 25, 2011.
19. *Irish Times*, August 27, 2011.
20. Ibid.
21. Ibid.
22. *Irish Independent*, August 27, 2011.
23. *Sunday Independent*, August 28, 2011.
24. *Irish Independent*, August 27, 2011.
25. *Sunday Independent*, August 28, 2011.
26. *Sunday World*, May 6, 2012.
27. *Sunday Independent*, July 22, 2012.
28. *Sunday Independent*, May 13, 2012.
29. *Evening Herald*, May 7, 2013.

Bibliography

Books

Anderson, Lindsay. *About John Ford*. London: Plexus, 1981.

Anger, Kenneth. *Hollywood Babylon*. London: Arrow, 1986.

Arce, Hector. *The Secret Life of Tyrone Power*. New York: Bantam, 1980.

Asbury, Darden. *Liberace: An American Boy*. Chicago: University of Chicago Press, 2000.

Bachrach, Judy. *Tina and Harry Come to America: Tina Brown, Harry Evans and the Uses of Power*. New York: Free Press, 2001.

Barson, Michael. *The Illustrated Who's Who of Hollywood Directors*. New York: Farrar, Straus and Giroux, 1995.

Barton, Ruth. *Acting Irish in Hollywood*. Dublin: Irish Academic Press, 2006.

——. *Irish National Cinema*. London: Routledge, 2004.

Basinger, Jeanine. *The Star Machine*. New York: Vintage, 2009.

——. *A Woman's View: How Hollywood Spoke to Women, 1930–1960*. New York: Knopf, 1993.

Behlmer, Rudy, ed. *Memo from Darryl F. Zanuck: The Golden Years at Twentieth Century–Fox*. New York: Grove Press, 1993.

Berg, Charles Ramirez. *The Margin as Center: The Multicultural Dynamics of John Ford's Westerns*. Bloomington: University of Indiana Press, 2001.

Bogdanovich, Peter. *John Ford*. London: Studio Vista, 1967.

——. *Who the Devil Made It?* New York: Knopf, 1997.

——. *Who the Hell's in It? Portraits and Conversations*. London: Faber, 2004.

Brando, Marlon, with Robert Lindsey. *Songs My Mother Taught Me*. London: Century, 1994.

Brennan, Steve, and Bernadette O'Neill. *Emeralds in Tinseltown: The Irish in Hollywood*. Belfast: Appletree Press, 2007.

Burns-Bisogno, Louisa. *Censoring Irish Nationalism*. Jefferson, NC: McFarland, 1997.

Callow, Simon. *Charles Laughton: A Difficult Actor*. London: Methuen, 1987.

Cameron, Ian, and Douglas Pye, eds. *The Movie Book of the Western*. London: Studio Vista, 1996.

Carey, Harry, Jr. *Company of Heroes: My Life as an Actor in the John Ford Stock Company.* Lanham, MD: Madison, 1996.

Chandler, Charlotte. *Not the Girl Next Door.* London: Simon and Schuster, 2008.

Christie, Ian, ed. *Scorsese on Scorsese.* London: Faber, 2003.

Clayton, Tessa, and Ian Fitzgerald, eds. *The Guinness Book of Film.* London: Guinness Publishing, 1998.

Collier, Peter. *The Fondas: A Hollywood Dynasty.* London: HarperCollins, 1991.

Colombo, John Robert, ed. *Wit and Wisdom of the Moviemakers.* New York: Hamlyn, 1979.

Condon, Paul, and Jim Sangster. *The Complete Hitchcock.* London: Virgin, 1999.

Connell, Brian. *Knight Errant: A Biography of Douglas Fairbanks Jr.* London: Hodder and Stoughton, 1955.

Conrad, Peter. *The Hitchcock Murders.* London: Faber and Faber, 2000.

Cook, Pam, ed. *The Movie Book.* London: Palgrave Macmillan, 2007.

Crossan, Sean, and Rod Stoneman, eds. The Quiet Man *and Beyond: Reflections on a Classic Film, John Ford and Ireland.* Dublin: Liffey Press, 2009.

Davis, Ronald L. *The Glamour Factory: Inside Hollywood's Star System.* Dallas: Southern Methodist University Press, 1993.

Depuis, Nicola. *Mnánah Éireann: The Women Who Shaped Ireland.* Cork: Mercier Press, 2009.

Dunne, Philip. *How Green Was My Valley: The Screenplay.* Santa Barbara, CA: Santa Teresa Press, 1990.

———. *Take Two: A Life in Movies and Politics.* San Francisco: McGraw-Hill, 1980.

Eastman, John. *Retakes: Behind the Scenes of 500 Classic Movies.* New York: Ballantine Books, 1989.

Eells, George. *Robert Mitchum: A Biography.* London: Robson, 1984.

Ehrenstein, David. *Open Secret.* New York: William Morrow, 1998.

Eisenschitz, Bernard. *Nicholas Ray: An American Journey.* London: Faber and Faber, 1993.

Empire Film Guide. London: Virgin, 2006.

Eyles, Allan. *This Was Hollywood: The 1930's.* London: B. T. Batsford, 1987.

Fagen, Herb. *Duke, We're Glad We Knew You.* New York: Citadel, 2009.

Feret, Bill. *Lure of the Tropix.* London: Proteus, 1984.

Fine, Marshall. *Bloody Sam: The Life and Times of Sam Peckinpah.* New York: Hyperion, 2005.

Finstad, Suzanne. *Natasha: A Biography of Natalie Wood.* London: Century, 2001.

Flynn, Arthur. *100 Years of Irish Film*. Dublin: Kestrel, 1996.

——. *The Story of Irish Film*. Dublin: Currach, 2006.

Flynn, Errol. *My Wicked, Wicked Ways*. London: Mandarin, 1992.

Ford, Dan. *Pappy: The Life of John Ford*. Englewood Cliffs, NJ: Prentice Hall, 1979.

Foster, Allan. *The Movie Traveler: A Film Fan's Guide to the UK and Ireland*. Edinburgh: Polygon, 2000.

Frazier, Adrian. *Hollywood Irish: John Ford, Abbey Actors and the Irish Revival in Hollywood*. Dublin: Lilliput Press, 2011.

Freedland, Michael. *Errol Flynn*. London: Arthur Barker, 1978.

French, Brandon. *On the Verge of Revolt*. New York: Frederich Unger, 1978.

Friedrich, Otto. *City of Nets*. London: Headline, 1986.

Gardner, Ava. *My Story*. London: Transworld, 1990.

Gibbons, Luke. *Ireland into Film: The Quiet Man*. Cork: Cork University Press, 2002.

Gledhill, Christine, ed. *Home Is Where the Heart Is: Studies in Melodrama and the Woman's Film*. London: British Film Institute, 1987.

Goldstein, Norm. *Henry Fonda: A Celebration of the Life and Works of One of America's Most Beloved Actors*. New York: Associated Press, 1982.

Gow, Gordon. *Hollywood in the Fifties*. New York: A. S. Barnes, 1971.

Grey, Michael. *Stills, Reels and Rushes: Ireland and the Irish in Twentieth Century Cinema*. Dublin: Blackhall, 1999.

Guiles, Fred Lawrence. *Tyrone Power: The Last Idol*. London: Granada, 1980.

Guinness, Alec. *Blessings in Disguise*. London: Hamish Hamilton, 1985.

Hadleigh, Boze, ed. *Hollywood Babbles On*. New York: Birch Lane Press, 1994.

Hardt, Ursula. *From Caligari to California*. Oxford: Berghahn Books, 1996.

Harrison, Rex. *A Damned Serious Business: My Life in Comedy*. London: Bantam, 1990.

Haskell, Molly. *From Reverence to Rape*. Chicago: University of Chicago Press, 1987.

Hayes, Kevin J., ed. *The Sam Peckinpah Interviews*. Jackson: University Press of Mississippi, 2008.

Higham, Charles. *Charles Laughton: An Intimate Biography*. London: Coronet, 1976.

Hirschhorn, Clive. *The Universal Story*. London: Octopus Books, 1985.

Holley, Van. *Mike Connolly and the Manly Art of Hollywood Gossip*. Jefferson, NC: McFarland, 2003.

Horsley, Edith. *The 1950s*. London: Bison Books, 1990.

Humphreys, Joseph, ed. *James Dean on James Dean*. London: Plexus, 1990.

Hunter, Tab, with Eddie Muller. *Tab Hunter Confidential*. Chapel Hill, NC: Algonquin, 2005.

Johns, Howard. *Hollywood Celebrity Playground*. Fort Lee, NJ: Barricade Books, 2006.

Karney, Robyn, ed. *The Movie Stars Story*. London: Octopus, 1984.

Kashner, Sam, and Jennifer MacNair. *The Bad and the Beautiful: Hollywood in the Fifties*. London: Little Brown, 2002.

Kent, Nicolas. *Naked Hollywood: Money, Power and the Movies*. London: BBC Books, 1991.

Kerbel, Michael. *Henry Fonda*. New York: Pyramid, 1975.

Lambert, Gavin. *Natalie Wood: A Life*. New York: Knopf, 2004.

Lanchester, Elsa. *Herself*. New York: St. Martin's Press, 1983.

Lasky, Betty. *RKO: The Biggest Little Major of Them All*. Santa Monica, CA: Roundtable, 1989.

Lasky, Jesse, Jr. *Whatever Happened to Hollywood?* New York: Funk and Wagnalls, 1975.

Leaming, Barbara. *Katharine Hepburn*. New York: Avon, 1996.

Lee, Anna, with Barbara Roisman Cooper. *Memoir of a Career on General Hospital and in Film*. Jefferson, NC: McFarland, 2003.

Leff, Leonard J. *Hitchcock and Selznick*. London: Weidenfeld and Nicolson, 1988.

Lever, James. *Me Cheeta*. London: Fourth Estate, 2009.

Lloyd, Ann, ed. *Movies of the Forties*. London: Orbis, 1982.

MacHale, Des. *The Complete Guide to* The Quiet Man. Belfast: Appletree, 2000.

———. *Picture* The Quiet Man: *An Illustrated Celebration*. Belfast: Appletree, 2004.

———. *A Quiet Man Miscellany*. Cork: Cork University Press, 2009.

Macpherson, Don. *Leading Ladies*. London: Conran Octopus, 1986.

Magers, Boyd, and Michael G. Fitzgerald. *Westerns Women: Interviews with 50 Leading Ladies of Movie and Television Westerns from the 1930s to the 1960s*. Jefferson, NC: McFarland, 2004.

Malden, Karl, with Carla Malden. *When Do I Start?* New York: Simon and Schuster, 1997.

Malone, Aubrey, ed. *Talk Nation*. Dublin: Currach Books, 2004.

Mann, William H. *Kate: The Woman Who Was Katharine Hepburn*. London: Faber, 2006.

Marrill, Alvin H. *The Films of Anthony Quinn*. Secaucus, NJ: Citadel, 1975.

Marriott, John, and Robin Cross. *The World's Greatest Hollywood Scandals*. (London: Octopus Books, 1997.

Mayne, Judith. *Directed by Dorothy Arzner.* Bloomington: Indiana University Press, 1994.

——. *The Woman at the Keyhole: Feminism and Women's Cinema.* Bloomington: Indiana University Press, 1990.

McBride, Joseph, and Michael Wilmington. *John Ford.* New York: Da Capo, 1980.

——. *Searching for John Ford: A Life.* London: Faber, 2003.

McClelland, Doug, ed. *Forties Film Talk.* Jefferson, NC: McFarland, 1992.

——. *Starspeak.* Boston: Faber, 1987.

McGee, Tom. *Betty Grable: The Girl with the Million Dollar Legs.* New York: Vestal Press, 1995.

McGilligan, Patrick. *Alfred Hitchcock: A Life in Darkness and Light.* West Sussex: Wiley, 2003.

——. *Film Crazy: Interviews with Hollywood Legends.* New York: St. Martin's Press, 2000.

——. *Nicholas Ray: The Glorious Failure of an American Director.* New York: itBooks, 2011.

McGuinness, Gerry. *Movies Made in Ireland:* The Quiet Man. Dublin: GLI, 1996.

McIlroy, Brian. *Irish Cinema: An Illustrated History.* Dublin: Anna Livia Press, 1988.

McKillop, James, ed. *Contemporary Irish Cinema: From* The Quiet Man *to* Dancing at Lughnasa. Syracuse, NY: Syracuse University Press, 1999.

McLoone, Martin. *Film, Media and Popular Culture in Ireland: Cityscapes/Landscapes/Soundscapes.* Dublin: Irish Academic Press, 2008.

——. *Irish Film: The Emergence of a Contemporary Cinema.* London: British Film Institute, 2000.

McNee, Gerry. *In the Footsteps of* The Quiet Man. Edinburgh: Mainstream, 2008.

McSharry, Ray, with Padraic White. *The Making of the Celtic Tiger.* Cork: Mercier Press, 2000.

Meyer, William R. *Warner Brothers Directors.* New York: Arlington House, 1978.

Miller, Frank. *Movies We Love: 100 Collectible Classics.* Atlanta: Turner Publishing, 1996.

Mordden, Ethan. *Movie Star: A Look at the Women Who Made Hollywood.* New York: St. Martin's Press, 1983.

Mosley, Leonard. *Zanuck: The Rise and Fall of Hollywood's Last Tycoon.* London: Panther, 1984.

Mueller, Carol Lea, ed. *The Quotable John Wayne.* Lanham, MD: Taylor Trade, 2007.

Munn, Michael. *Hollywood Rogues*. London: Robson, 1991.

———. *Jimmy Stewart: The Truth behind the Legend*. London: Robson, 2006.

Naremore, James. *Acting in the Cinema*. Berkeley: University of California Press, 1988.

Negra, Diane, ed. *The Irish in Us: Performativity and Popular Culture*. Durham, NC: Duke University Press, 2006.

Norman, Barry. *And Why Not?* London: Simon and Schuster, 2002.

———. *Talking Pictures*. London: BBC Books, 1987.

Nott, Robert. *He Ran All the Way: The Life of John Garfield*. New York: Limelight Editions, 2003.

O'Hara, Maureen, with John Nicoletti. *'Tis Herself: A Memoir*. Dublin: New Town House and Country House, 2004.

Parish, James Robert. *The Hollywood Book of Scandals*. New York: McGraw-Hill, 2004.

———. *The RKO Gals*. London: Ian Allen, 1974.

Parrish, Robert. *Growing up in Hollywood*. London: Bodley Bead, 1976.

Peary, Danny. *Closeups: Intimate Portraits of Movie Stars by Their Costars, Directors, Screenwriters and Friends*. New York: Simon and Schuster, 1978.

Pettit, Lance. *Screening Ireland*. Manchester: Manchester University Press, 2000.

Pfeiffer, Lee. *The John Wayne Scrapbook*. New York: Citadel, 1989.

Pickard, Roy. *James Stewart: The Hollywood Years*. London: Robert Hale, 1992.

Porter, Darwin. *Katharine the Great*. New York: Blood Moon Productions, 2004.

Powers, Stefanie. *One from the Hart: A Memoir*. London: JR Books, 2011.

Prigozy, Ruth. *The Life of Dick Haymes*. Jackson: University Press of Mississippi, 2006.

Quinn, Anthony, with Daniel Paisner. *One Man Tango*. London: Headline, 1995.

Rains, Stephanie. *The Irish-American in Popular Culture: 1945–2000*. Dublin: Irish Academic Press, 2007.

Randall, Stephen, ed. *The Playboy Interviews*. Portland, OR: M Press, 2006.

Read, Piers Paul. *Alec Guinness: The Authorized Biography*. London: Simon and Schuster, 2003.

Rice, Eoghan. *We Are Rovers: An Oral History of Shamrock Rovers Football Club*. Gloucestershire: Nonsuch Publishing, 2005.

Roberts, Jerry, ed. *Mitchum, in His Own Words*. New York: Limelight Editions, 2000.

Roberts, Randy, and James S. Olson. *John Wayne: American*. New York: Free Press, 1995.

Rockett, Kevin. *Irish Film Censorship: A Cultural Journey from Silent Cinema to the Internet*. Dublin: Four Courts Press, 2004.

Rockett, Kevin, Luke Gibbons, and John Hill. *Cinema and Ireland*. Syracuse, NY: Syracuse University Press, 1987.

Rosen, Marjorie. *Popcorn Venus*. New York: Avon, 1973.

Ruuth, Marianne. *Cruel City*. Santa Ana, CA: Roundtable, 1991.

Sanders, Coyne Steven, and Tom Gilbert. *Desilu: The Story of Lucille Ball and Desi Arnaz*. Manhattan Beach, CA: Harper Entertainment, 2001.

Sarvady, Andrea. *Leading Ladies*. San Francisco: Chronicle Books, 2006.

Schatz, Thomas. *Boom and Bust: American Cinema in the 1940s*. Berkeley: University of California Press, 1999.

Scott, Henry E. *Shocking True Story*. New York: Pantheon, 2010.

Server, Lee. *Ava Gardner: Love Is Nothing*. London: Bloomsbury, 2010.

Seydour, Paul. *Peckinpah: The Western Films, a Reconsideration*. Urbana: University of Illinois Press, 1997.

Shannon, Christopher. *Bowery to Broadway: The Classic Irish in Classic Hollywood Cinema*. Scranton, PA: University of Scranton Press, 2010.

Shepherd, Donald, Robert Slatzer, and Dave Grayson. *The Life and Times of John Wayne*. London: Warner, 1986.

Sherry, Norman. *The Life of Graham Greene*. Vol. 3, *1955–91*. London: Jonathan Cape, 2004.

Shipman, David. *The Great Movie Stars: The International Years*. London: Angus and Robertson, 1972.

———, ed. *Movie Talk: Who Said What about Whom*. London: Bloomsbury, 1988.

Sigillito, Gina. *Daughters of Maeve*. New York: Citadel, 2007.

Simmons, Garner. *Peckinpah: A Portrait in Montage*. Austin: University of Texas Press, 1982.

Simpson, Paul, ed. *The Rough Guide to Cult Movies*. London: Haymarket, 2004.

Smith, David L. *Sitting Pretty: The Life and Times of Clifton Webb*. Jackson: University Press of Mississippi, 2011.

Spoto, Donald. *The Dark Side of Genius: The Life of Alfred Hitchcock*. London: Plexus, 1973.

———. *Spellbound by Beauty: Alfred Hitchcock and His Leading Ladies*. London: Hutchinson, 2008.

Stacy, Pat, with Beverly Linet. *Duke: A Love Story*. London: Corgi, 1985.

Tibballs, Geoff, ed. *The Mammoth Book of Comic Quotes*. London: Constable and Robinson, 2004.

Tierney, Gene, with Mickey Herskowitz. *Self-Portrait*. New York: Wyden Books, 1979.

Troyan, Michael. *A Rose for Mrs. Miniver: The Life of Greer Garson*. Lexington: University Press of Kentucky, 1999.

Truffaut, Francois. *Hitchcock*. London: Paladin, 1986.

Underwood, Peter. *Death in Hollywood*. London: Piatkus, 1992.

Walsh, John. *Are You Talking to Me? A Life through the Movies*. London: Harper Perennial, 2004.

Wapshott, Nicholas. *Rex Harrison: A Biography*. London: Chatto and Windus, 1991.

Wayne, Pilar, with Alex Thorleifson. *John Wayne: My Life with the Duke*. New York: McGraw-Hill, 1987.

Weddle, David. *Peckinpah: The Western Films, a Reconsideration*. London: Faber and Faber, 1996.

Wilson, Ivy Crane, ed. *Hollywood in the 40s: The Stars' Own Stories*. New York: Ungar, 1980.

Articles

Abele, Robert. "Just One of the Guys." *Los Angeles Times*, May 2, 2004.

Andreeva, Tamara. "Every Woman Has Two Lives." *Stardom*, April 1944.

Armstrong, Maggie. "Magnificent Maureen." *Irish Independent*, August 14, 2010.

Barton, Dick. "Where Are They Now?" *Sunday Express*, January 26, 1986.

Beusse, Jacqueline Collins. "O'Hara Doesn't Need Oscar to Shine." *Irish Echo*, April 7, 2010.

Bramhill, Nick. "Hollywood Legend O'Hara's Legacy for Village." *Irish Mail on Sunday*, November 7, 2010.

Brock, Patrick. "These I Have Known." *Classic Images* 210 (December 1992).

Broeske, Pat H. "In Search of Maureen O'Hara." *Los Angeles Times*, December 16, 1990.

Caden, Sarah. "The Burden of Beauty." *Sunday Independent*, March 3, 2006.

Cameron-Wilson, James. "Cherishable Comeback." *What's on in London*, September 11, 1991.

Canfield, Alyce. "The Two Mrs. Prices." *Motion Picture*, May 1945.

Carberry, Sean. "Ireland's Gift to Hollywood." *Ireland of the Welcomes*, May/June 2009.

Cheatham, Maude. "Girls Don't Do That!" *Screenland*, February 1943.

Churchill, Reba, and Bonnie Churchill. "Irish Pixie." *Silver Screen*, June 1949.

Cleave, Maureen. "Miss O'Hara Misses the Twinkle." *Evening Standard*, April 17, 1964.

Coleman, James. "Hollywood Irish Stars Helped End Anti-Irish Racism." *Irish Central*, July 12, 2010.

Collins, Jessie. "The Grande Dame." *Irish Tatler*, November 2010.

Connolly, Mike. "Impertinent Interview." *Photoplay*, January 1954.

Cosby, Vivian. "The Little O'Hara Girl Grows Up." *Movie Show*, October 1945.

Coyle, Colin. "Moving On." *Sunday Times*, October 5, 2002.

Creedon, Conal. "Falling for Maureen O'Hara." *Irish Times*, April 6, 2001.

Crowther, Bosley. "A Beautiful and Affecting Film Achievement." *New York Times*, October 29, 1941.

Danker, Trevor. "Maureen O'Hara Keeps Charles' Memory Green." *Sunday Independent*, May 20, 1984.

Doherty, Michael. "The Quiet Woman." *RTE Guide*, August 16, 2010.

Dooley, Roger B. "The Irish on the Screen." *Films in Review*, June/July 1957.

Dudley, Fredda. "Three Little Girls in Green." *Modern Screen*, January 1947.

Duggan, Barry. "Quiet Woman Maureen Is Still a Star Attraction." *Irish Independent*, July 8, 2007.

Dwyer, Michael. "Still Scarlet after All These Years." *Irish Times*, August 21, 2010.

Edwards, Ralph. "Play Truth or Consequences." *Photoplay*, September 1948.

Edwards, Ruth Dudley. "Maureen O'Hara Might Seduce the Students, But It's Not Real History." *Sunday Independent*, September 5, 2000.

Egan, Barry. "The Not So Quiet Woman." *Sunday Independent*, October 3, 2004.

Fallon, John. "Museum to Display Man Chair." *Sun*, April 18, 2011.

Fanning, Aengus. "Hollywood Great Hails Birr Festival." *Sunday Independent*, July 25, 2004.

Farren, Ronan. "Ford's the Star of Hollywood Romp." *Sunday Independent*, June 19, 2011.

Fitzpatrick, Pat. "Irish Actors in Hollywood." *Sunday Independent*, May 15, 2011.

Flynn, Bob. "The Quiet Woman." *Independent*, September 26, 2004.

Fox, Julian. "Maureen O'Hara: Fighting Lady." *Films and Filming*, December 1972.

Garth, H. K. "I Was Kissed by a Movie Star." *Films of the Golden Age*, Winter 2009/2010.

Gebler-Davies, Stan. "Glowing Embers of a Flame-Haired Woman." *Sunday Independent*, December 6, 1992.

Gerard, Andrew. "Hollywood Legend Still Going Strong at 90." *Daily Record*, August 16, 2010.

Goodman, Mark. "The Eternal Colleen." *People*, June 10, 1991.

Graham, Sheilah. "Will and Me." *Photoplay*, June 1947.

Greene, Alice Craig. "How I Met My Husband." *Motion Picture*, March 1945.

Hall, Gladys. "All the World Will Be Talking about Her." *Silver Screen*, March 1940.

———. "Maureen O'Hara's Secret." *Movie Show*, August 1947.

———. "She Knows Where She's Going." *Photoplay*, December 1952.

Harnisch, Larry. "Maureen O'Hara Calls Story in Magazine Lie." *Los Angeles Times*, September 4, 1957.

Harrington, Suzanne. "How a Strong-Willed Dublin Girl Became 'Royalty' in Hollywood." *Irish Examiner*, August 14, 2010.

Hart, Henry. "The Quiet Man." *Films in Review*, August/September 1952.

Hayes, Kathryn. "Maureen O'Hara in Foynes for Opening of Museum." *Irish Times*, July 4, 2006.

Herbert, Susannah. "Eastwood's Double Take at BFI Awards." *Daily Telegraph*, September 27, 1993.

Holland, Jack. "Home Girl at Heart." *Silver Screen*, April 1947.

———. "Palsy-Walsy?" *Screenland*, May 1947.

Jacques, Steve. "The Queen Who Hit a Duke." *Sun*, June 9, 1973.

Kaufman, Wolfe. "My One-Day Marriage." *Modern Screen*, November 1941.

Kelleher, Olivia. "O'Hara's Dream Role to Develop Irish Talent." *Irish Examiner*, December 23, 2010.

Kelly, Antoinette. "Martin Scorsese Says He Was Inspired by Legendary Irish Movie." *Irish Central*, March 2, 2010.

King, Susan. "On a Sentimental Journey with Acting Legend." *Los Angeles Times*, October 28, 2000.

Leonard, Hugh. "The Curmudgeon." *Sunday Independent*, October 10, 2004.

Lewis, Kevin. "Maureen O'Hara." *Films in Review*, April 1990.

———. "Maureen O'Hara (Part 2)." *Films in Review*, May 1990.

Lister, David. "Film Fans Leave No Stone Unturned." *Times*, June 19, 2004.

Loper, Mary Lou. "It's the Rub o' the Red." *Los Angeles Times*, November 1, 1991.

Lowe, Herb. "Star-Spangled Colleen." *Photoplay*, February 1948.

Lucey, Anne. "Tearful Binoche Presented with O'Hara Award." *Irish Examiner*, November 11, 2010.

Lydon, Charlene. "Dreaming *The Quiet Man*." *Film Ireland*, Winter 2010.

Maddox, Ben. "I Want to Be Loved." *Photoplay*, April 1942.

———. "Oh, O'Hara!" *Photoplay*, August 1946.

———. "Redhead on Her Own." *Silver Screen*, November 1941.

McCreary, Alf. "The Quiet Man's Ireland." *British Heritage*, August/September 1997.

McDonough, David. "*The Quiet Man* Has Tiptoed into the Parade." *New York Times*, March 12, 1995.

McDowall, Roddy. "Sitting Pretty." *Premiere*, July 1991.

McGuane, Elizabeth. "The Quiet Woman." *Sunday Business Post*, August 5, 2004.

McGurn, William. "Quiet Maniacs Rejoice as a Film Turns 50." *Wall Street Journal*, September 26, 2002.

McLaughlin, Brian. "Foynes Recalls the Flying Boats Days." *Irish Times*, July 10, 1992.

Michael, Patricia. "You Can't Take It with You. . . ." *Screen Stars*, April 1945.

Molloy, Philip. "Queen of the Swashbucklers." *Irish Independent*, February 9, 1991.

Moore, Viola. "Pride of the Irish." *Modern Screen*, September 1949.

Myers, Denis. "I Like the Irish, But. . . ." *Picture Show*, July 19, 1952.

Noah, Timothy. "Wherein Tina Brown Ambushes Maureen O'Hara." *Slate*, January 3, 2002.

O'Cionnaith, Fiachra. "Screen Legend Plans Film School for Cork Village." *Irish Examiner*, November 11, 2010.

O'Dea, Tom. "An Irishman's Diary." *Irish Times*, August 8, 2000.

O'Hara, Maureen. "I'm Waiting for My Baby." *Photoplay*, June 1944.

——. "Temptations of a Girl Who Waits." *Photoplay*, July 1945.

——. "What Makes John Wayne Hollywood's Favorite Lover?" *Photoplay*, October 1973.

O'Leary, Dorothy. "Magnificent Marriage." *Silver Screen*, April 1946.

O'Neill, Ed. "Forty Years a-Growing." *Cara*, July/August 1991.

O'Neill, Nicholas. "Movie Queen Maureen Still in Love with the Silver Screen." *Sunday Press*, September 1, 1991.

O'Riordan, Alison. "Screen Icon to Be Honoured by Legacy Center." *Sunday Independent*, January 24, 2010.

O'Sullivan, Majella. "Maureen Won't Kiss and Tell at 'Quiet Man' Tribute." *Irish Independent*, February 26, 2011.

Pickard, Roy. "In the Picture." *Radio Times*, January 1984.

Pollock, Louis. "Moments of Maureen." *Modern Screen*, September 1947.

Power, Conor. "Shamrock Rovers Fan Who Became a Hollywood Queen." *Irish Examiner*, August 14, 2010.

Quinn, Tony. "Maureen O'Hara Tells *Irish Connections* a Few Stories." *Irish Connections*, November 1, 2010.

Richards, Jeffrey. "Queen of the Swashbucklers." *Daily Telegraph*, September 29, 1993.

Riegel, Ralph. "Week Long Party Planned for Maureen's 90th Birthday." *Irish Independent*, August 14, 2010.

Rieker, Jane. "After Her Flying Hero Husband Dies, Maureen O'Hara Fights to Keep His Dream Aloft." *People*, November 6, 1978.

Roberts, John. "The Queen of Technicolor." *Films of the Golden Age*, Winter 1996/1997.

Salisbury, Mark. "Return of Mary Kate Danaher." *Irish Press*, September 24, 1991.

Service, Faith. "Maureen's Letter to Her Daughter." *Silver Screen*, June 1945.

———. "The Stars Who Kiss Like Gentlemen." *Silver Screen*, October 1942.

Sessions, John. "No Star Too Far for a Compulsive Name-Dropper." *Daily Telegraph*, October 10, 1998.

Shane, Denny. "The Mystery of Maureen." *Screenland*, March 1953.

Shanley, Valerie. "Scarlet O'Hara." *Sunday Tribune*, October 31, 2010.

Shelden, Michael. "I Wasn't Going to Play the Whore." *Daily Telegraph*, March 23, 2004.

Skolsky, Sidney. "Close-up of Maureen O'Hara." *Motion Picture*, September 1945.

Stoddart, Sarah. "Flynn Flogs a Formula." *Picturegoer*, February 14, 1953.

Sweeney, Ken. "Culture Vultures Descend on Feast of the Arts." *Independent*, September 25, 2010.

Swet, Peter. "He Couldn't Forget Me." *Parade*, June 2, 1991.

Tanner, Louise. 1991. "Who's in Town." *Films in Review*, July/August 1991.

Troy, Catherine. "The Great Comeback." *Irish Independent*, February 9, 1991.

Vedrilla, Ronald. "*The Quiet Man* on Location." *Big Reel*, March 2004.

Walker, Helen Louise. "Danger—Popularity Ahead!" *Photoplay*, July 1942.

Weller, Helen. "What's Come over O'Hara?" *Motion Picture*, December 1948.

Wheeler, Lyle. "House with a Past." *Photoplay*, June 1944.

Willman, Chris. "Onscreen Adventure of Chris Columbus." *Los Angeles Times*, May 27, 1991.

Wilson, Elizabeth. "Maureen Makes Plans." *Screenland*, December 1944.

Wroe, Georgina. "Going Crazy over *Wayne's World*." *Times Weekend*, June 13, 1998.

Zeitlin, Ida. "Colleen in Clover." *Screenland*, February 1942.

———. "Peace on Earth." *Modern Screen*, January 1948.

Television, Radio, Film, and DVDs

The American West of John Ford. Delta Music, 2002.

Budd Boetticher: An American Original. Special Collector's Edition. Paramount Home Entertainment, 2007.

Directed by John Ford. Turner Entertainment, Warner Home Video, 2009.

Dreaming The Quiet Man. Loopline, 2012.

Hitchcock: The Early Years. Granada Ventures, Carlton Visual Entertainment, 1999.

The Irish in Hollywood. TV3, December 25, 2010.

Larry King. October 28, 2000; October 29, 2003.

The Late Late Show. February 25, 2011.

The Making of Rio Grande. Jessiefilms, Universal Pictures, 2006.

McLintock! Authentic Collector's Edition. Batjac Productions, Paramount Home Entertainment, 2007.

Nationwide. RTE 1, August 16, 2004.

The Parent Trap. Buena Vista Home Entertainment, Disney Enterprises, 1961.

The Quiet Man. Collector's Edition. Artisan Home Entertainment, 2002.

Quiet Maniacs. Dublin South FM, September 26, 2005.

Spencer's Mountain. Warner Bros. Entertainment, 2010.

Tubridy. RTE, December 29, 2009.

Wild Bill: Hollywood's Maverick. Vol. 3 of *Forbidden Hollywood.* Turner Entertainment Archives, 2002.

Index

Screen Classics

Screen Classics is a series of critical biographies, film histories, and analytical studies focusing on neglected filmmakers and important screen artists and subjects, from the era of silent cinema to the golden age of Hollywood to the international generation of today. Books in the Screen Classics series are intended for scholars and general readers alike. The contributing authors are established figures in their respective fields. This series also serves the purpose of advancing scholarship on film personalities and themes with ties to Kentucky.

Series Editor
Patrick McGilligan

Books in the Series

Mae Murray: The Girl with the Bee-Stung Lips
Michael G. Ankerich

Hedy Lamarr: The Most Beautiful Woman in Film
Ruth Barton

Von Sternberg
John Baxter

The Marxist and the Movies: A Biography of Paul Jarrico
Larry Ceplair

Warren Oates: A Wild Life
Susan Compo

Jack Nicholson: The Early Years
Robert Crane and Christopher Fryer

Being Hal Ashby: Life of a Hollywood Rebel
Nick Dawson

Intrepid Laughter: Preston Sturges and the Movies
Andrew Dickos

John Gilbert: The Last of the Silent Film Stars
Eve Golden

Mamoulian: Life on Stage and Screen
David Luhrssen